A **FALCON** GUIDE®

Hiking
COLORADO'S
SANGRE DE CRISTO
WILDERNESS

Jason Moore

FALCON®

GUILFORD, CONNECTICUT
HELENA, MONTANA
AN IMPRINT OF THE GLOBE PEQUOT PRESS

All photographs are by the author.
Maps: Topaz Maps Inc. © The Globe Pequot Press

Library of Congress Cataloging-in-Publication Data
Moore, Jason.
  Hiking Colorado's Sangre de Cristo Wilderness/Jason Moore. —1st ed.
      p. cm. — (A Falcon guide)
  Includes bibliographical references and index.
  ISBN 0-7627-1108-6
  1. Hiking—Sangre de Cristo Mountains (Colo. and N.M.)—Guidebooks. 2. Sangre de Cristo Mountains (Colo. and N.M.)—Guidebooks. I. Title. II. Series.
GV199.42.S28 M66 2002
978.8'49—dc21   2002035337

Manufactured in the United States of America
First Edition/First Printing

HIKING COLORADO'S
SANGRE DE CRISTO WILDERNESS

Contact

Help Us Keep This Guide Up to Date

Every effort has been made by the author and editors to make this guide as accurate and useful as possible. However, many things can change after a guide is published—trails are rerouted, regulations change, techniques evolve, facilities come under new management, etc.

We would love to hear from you concerning your experiences with this guide and how you feel it could be improved and kept up to date. While we may not be able to respond to all comments and suggestions, we'll take them to heart and we'll also make certain to share them with the author. Please send your comments and suggestions to the following address:

> The Globe Pequot Press
> Reader Response/Editorial Department
> P.O. Box 480
> Guilford, CT 06437

Or you may e-mail us at:

> editorial@globe-pequot.com

Thanks for your input, and happy travels!

Contents

Sangre de Cristo
Wilderness Area

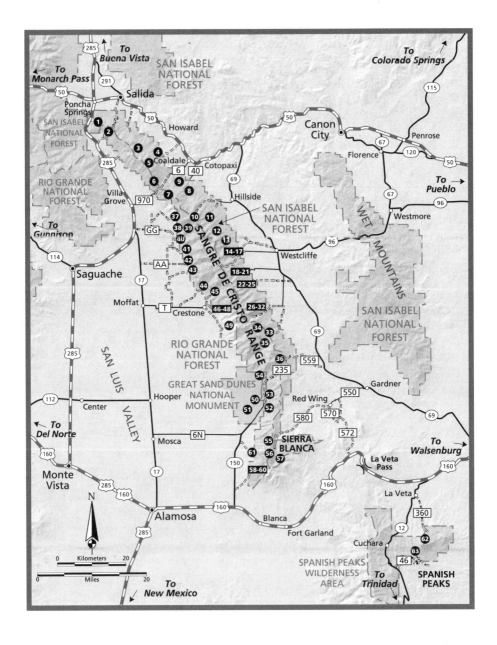

Central Sangre de Cristo, West Side

Great Sand Dunes National Monument and Preserve

Sierra Blanca

Spanish Peaks Wilderness Area

Acknowledgments

This project would never have been possible without the rock-solid support of my wife and best friend, Natalie. Having grown up together as teenagers, we have been best friends, partners, and supporters of each other's dreams for almost half of our lives. I feel truly fortunate to have been blessed by such a loving, friendly, tolerant, and open spirit.

I also have to thank my good friend and frequent hiking partner Jonathan Funk, who accompanied me on some of the hikes described here. I thank him sincerely for helping me create coherent and thorough descriptions. His long hours of review as deadlines pressed have not been forgotten. Nor have I forgotten our first trip together into the Sangre de Cristo, before this project even began. It was a three-day trip in snowpacked spring conditions up South Colony Creek, where we camped in solitude under clear skies, surrounded by the mighty Crestones. Our climb up windswept slopes to the summit of Humboldt Peak and our classic descent—a foot glissade 2,000 vertical feet down to camp, where we basked in a typical Sangre sunset—were highlights of a trip I will never forget. This was my first trip to the range, and never did I think at the time that I would be writing this guide.

It's fitting that Jon joined me for one of my last trips in the range. We started at North Crestone Trailhead, and spent the next four days backpacking up the North Fork, over the pass and across the San Isabel Valley. Our second pass brought us to camp at Rito Alto Lake, and we reached Cotton Lake for our last night before hiking out to the best Mexican food I have ever eaten. It was truly a great way to bracket my experiences in the Sangre de Cristo, with a good friend surrounded by incredible mountains.

My friends and family who have always encouraged me to take the trail of my own choosing, here's to you. My mother, Diane Sohn; my brother, Kevin Carr, who joined me for my second ascent of Humboldt Peak; Colleen Deffner; Russell Deffner; Mike and Pat Rines; Lee Deffner and Cindy Georger; my brother Bryan; my sister and brother-in-law, Melanie and Jon Acevedo; and Chris and Lance Brooks and their triplets Dillon, Tristen, and Cameron. All of you have been sources of energy for me when I was tired, blistered, cold, windburned, sunburned, dehydrated, and full of doubt. My grandfather Leonard Mattson and my late grandmother Pauline Mattson have also been in my thoughts while I have sat on high mountain summits and looked back at where I came from and where I wanted to go next.

Sincere thanks to all of you, for believing, inspiring, and supporting my lofty, high-altitude dreams.

USGS Topographic
Map Index

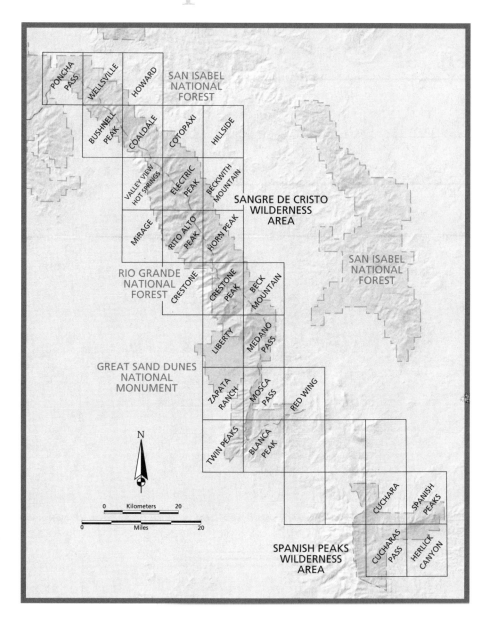

PONCHA PASS

WELLSVILLE

HOWARD

SAN ISABEL NATIONAL FOREST

BUSHNELL PEAK

COALDALE

COTOPAXI

HILLSIDE

VALLEY VIEW HOT SPRINGS

ELECTRIC PEAK

BECKWITH MOUNTAIN

SANGRE DE CRISTO WILDERNESS AREA

MIRAGE

RITO ALTO PEAK

HORN PEAK

RIO GRANDE NATIONAL FOREST

SAN ISABEL NATIONAL FOREST

CRESTONE

CRESTONE PEAK

BECK MOUNTAIN

LIBERTY

MEDANO PASS

GREAT SAND DUNES NATIONAL MONUMENT

ZAPATA RANCH

MOSCA PASS

RED WING

TWIN PEAKS

BLANCA PEAK

N

Kilometers 20
0

Miles 20
0

CUCHARA

SPANISH PEAKS

CUCHARAS PASS

HERLICK CANYON

SPANISH PEAKS WILDERNESS AREA

Map Legend

Map Legend

═══80═══ Interstate highway

═══36═══ US highway

───66─── State highway

─246─ County or Forest Service road

= = = = Unimproved road

– – – – – – Hiking trail

· · · · · · · · · Off-trail route

▬▬▬▬ Route

▲ Summit

⏝ Mountain pass

🚶 Trailhead

⛺ Campground

Ranger station, park entrance

🅟 Picnic area

🅟 Parking area

❓ Visitor center, information

Gate, road closure

〰 Stream

Waterfall

Lake

Introduction

When we hear the word *wilderness* we think of untracked valleys, remote mountains, solitude, wildlife, and wildness. We think of places where it is easy to lose our way, immerse ourselves in nature, and return to simpler living. Unquestionably, the Sangre de Cristo mountain range is wilderness, but it is wilderness redefined. It has all that we expect from wilderness but in ways that stretch the meaning and refine our view of wildlands. Although there are untracked valleys, most of them have good trails. Those paths have been well used over the years, first by wildlife, then by native people, followed by herds of cattle and goats, and more recently by outfitters, hunters, hikers, anglers, and climbers. The Sangre de Cristo has been hunted, grazed, trapped, mined, and harvested. Today, wildlife is diverse and plentiful and has recovered from the days of the trappers and hunters. There are abundant deer, mountain goats, and bighorn sheep. Hawks, eagles, and falcons are often seen patrolling the skies, while bears, mountain lions, and coyotes can wander from the eastern boundary to the western in a single day. Today's Sangre de Cristo remains a delicate string of alpine lakes with tundra-covered slopes and forests of spruce, pine, fir, and juniper, as well as a profusion of wildflowers and isolated wetlands. It is all split down the middle by a jagged crest of imposing, twisted, glacial carved stone.

The Sangre de Cristo Mountains have been described as an island. If you reward yourself and take the time to circumnavigate the entire range, you can see why. These mountains rise above the Wet Mountain and San Luis Valleys like islands above a sea. In places the wilderness is only 2 to 3 miles wide. Bound by rancher's fields, rural towns, and expansive valleys, you might expect any sense of remoteness to be fleeting. In such a narrow ribbon of mountains solitude is found, not from being just 3 or 4 miles from the trailhead, but from being a vertical mile above it.

Approaching the Sangre de Cristo by car is an enjoyable and scenic way to arrive in this mountainous region. Interstate 25 connects the Front Range cities of Denver and Colorado Springs to the southern Colorado town of Walsenburg. From Denver you can drive southwest on U.S. Highway 285 to South Park, the huge high-altitude mountain plain, through Fairplay, and finally south to Salida. From Colorado Springs, drive south on Colorado Highway 115 to Penrose and west on US 50 to Salida, or drive south on CO 67 through Wetmore and continue west on CO 96 to Westcliffe. From Walsenburg, drive west on US 160 over La Veta Pass to Alamosa, or drive west on CO 69 through Gardner and eventually north to Westcliffe.

Ranch near Westcliffe with Humboldt Peak and Colony Baldy beyond.

Approaching from the southwestern Colorado town of Durango, you can reach the wilderness area by driving east on US 160 through Pagosa Springs to Alamosa. From Montrose, drive east on US 50 through Gunnison over Monarch Pass to Salida.

No matter how you get there, the Sangre de Cristo Wilderness is a spectacular range of alpine valleys and mountain peaks. Most of the hikes in this area are difficult and steep, and some are even challenging scrambles. There are also technical climbs in the range, and a few of the routes described can be truly epic. During periods of low avalanche risk, these mountains are ideal for alpine snow climbing. All year round there are numerous possibilities allowing for long ridge crest hikes and many options to traverse over the crest of the range and connect the hikes on both sides.

The whole family can enjoy a few easy summer strolls, but most of these mountain trails are moderate to strenuous when done as day hikes. Many of these hikes are great overnight backpacking trips, and several trails can be linked to form long loops. With a car shuttle, the possibilities are almost endless; there are at least a dozen ways to connect trails over the crest of the range. And finally, no description of the range is complete without a mention of the continuous 90-mile-long Rainbow Trail and the possibility of trekking from Poncha Pass, around the northern end of the range and along the eastern side, continuing south all the way to Great Sand Dunes National Monument.

Being Prepared: Backcountry Safety and Hazards

A well-prepared hiker is usually a happy hiker. When unpredicted thunderstorms blow through or a midsummer snowstorm settles in for the weekend, the prepared hiker or backcountry traveler is able to enjoy the change. Being prepared is a matter of planning and experience. If you are new to visiting the wilderness, ask an experienced friend to join you, hire a responsible outfitter or guide, or study and practice with care. Falcon Guides *Wild Country Companion* and *Wilderness First Aid* are great resources for the beginner or for those returning to the backcountry. See Appendix B for more resources that can expand your knowledge of wilderness travel. Time spent in the mountains can be a richly rewarding experience; preparation can prevent you from being caught off guard.

Never hike without the ten essentials: map, compass, food, water, sunscreen and sunglasses, knife, fire kit, emergency blanket, mirror and whistle, and first-aid kit. It might sound like a lot to carry on an easy hike, but it can fit into a small stuff sack or resealable bag that you can put in your daypack. It is even a good idea to have these ten essentials in your car as well, especially during the winter season or when taking longer trips.

Dress Appropriately

Clothing can be a major contributor to your safety and enjoyment in the backcountry. It can also contribute directly to your discomfort, injury, and death. The phrase "cotton kills" is not a marketing ploy by outdoor gear companies to get you to buy expensive synthetics. It is sound advice from experienced hikers, professionals, and search-and-rescue experts. When cotton absorbs water and sweat, it stops insulating and begins conducting heat away from the body. Cotton will not dry out from body heat alone. Synthetics, on the other hand, are loath to absorb water, they continue to insulate even when wet, and they dry quickly from body heat. Wear layers made of synthetics, starting with a thin first layer. Add thicker and more insulating layers as required by the conditions, and finish with a water- and windproof shell. This provides a system of clothing that helps ensure maximum comfort and safety while allowing you to enjoy even the harshest conditions. See Appendix C for more specific clothing and gear recommendations.

Hiking at High Elevations

Altitude is an unseen adversary when climbing any high peaks. It might be invisible, but it can stop you in your tracks and end your enjoyment of the backcountry. It doesn't blow you down like a gale of wind or freeze your skin with its frigid chill, but it is important to consider when planning your trip to the mountains.

Common effects of hiking at high altitude include a headache, nausea, and a sense of fatigue. As your discomfort increases, you can be afflicted with acute mountain sickness (AMS). The warning signs are dizziness, weakness, shortness of breath, and a loss of coordination. If you remain at high altitude, your symptoms may subside after a day or two as your body adjusts to the lack of oxygen and lower barometric pressure. If you remain at one elevation and your sense of malaise persists or increases, it becomes critical to descend and recover at a lower altitude.

It is not uncommon for visitors to the high country to experience mild AMS. Occasionally, although it is infrequent, there are cases of the more severe high altitude pulmonary edema (HAPE) or even high altitude cerebral edema (HACE). These conditions are accompanied by a severe cough, disorientation, loss of coordination, and eventually a loss of consciousness. Rare though these conditions might be, if you suspect that you or a member of your party suffers from these more serious maladies, it is vitally important to descend and seek immediate medical attention.

If you are arriving in the mountains from elevations near sea level, it is essential to take it slow at first. There is a maxim used by experienced climbers: Climb high and sleep low. By gradually hiking higher into the mountains and returning to lower elevations to recover, you can train your body to respond more and more efficiently to high altitude. Avoid tobacco, alcohol, and any depressant drugs. Drink plenty of water, more than you think is necessary. Do not conserve water until you get thirsty. If you are thirsty, you are already dehydrated, which only increases the effects of altitude sickness. Your urine output should be copious and clear.

Everyone adjusts to the thin air of the high country at different rates. Pay attention to your body and don't let pride drive you beyond your limits. The mountains do not show mercy or bias. They cannot be conquered or dominated through willpower alone. If you are physically fit and properly acclimatized, these beautiful mountains may allow themselves to be climbed. If they do, your efforts will be richly rewarded.

Hypothermia

Be aware of hypothermia—the silent killer—a condition in which the body's internal temperature drops below normal. It can lead to mental and physical collapse and death. Hypothermia is caused by exposure to cold and is aggravated by wetness, wind, and exhaustion. The moment you begin to lose heat faster than your body produces it, you're suffering from exposure. Your body starts involuntary exercise, such as shivering, to stay warm and makes involuntary adjustments to preserve normal temperature in vital organs, restricting blood flow in the extremities. Both responses drain your energy reserves. The only way to stop the drain is to reduce the degree of exposure.

With full-blown hypothermia, as energy reserves are exhausted, cold blood reaches the brain, depriving you of good judgment and reasoning power. You won't be aware that this is happening. You lose control of your hands. Your internal temperature slides downward. Without treatment, this slide leads to stupor, collapse, and death.

To defend against hypothermia, stay dry. When clothes get wet, they lose about 90 percent of their insulating value. Wool loses relatively less heat; cotton, down, and some synthetics lose more. Choose rain clothes that cover the head, neck, body, and legs and provide good protection against wind-driven rain. Most hypothermia cases develop in air temperatures between 30 and 50 degrees, but hypothermia can develop in warmer temperatures.

If your party is exposed to wind, cold, and wet, watch yourself and others for uncontrollable fits of shivering; vague, slow, slurred speech; memory lapses; incoherence; immobile, fumbling hands; frequent stumbling or a lurching gait; drowsiness; apparent exhaustion; and inability to get up after a rest. When a member of your party has hypothermia, he or she might deny any problem. Believe the symptoms, not the victim. Even mild symptoms demand the following treatment:

- Get the victims out of the wind and rain.
- Strip off all wet clothes.
- If the victims are only mildly impaired, give them warm drinks, then put them in warm clothes and a warm sleeping bag. Warm victims further with well-wrapped water bottles filled with heated water.
- If the victims are badly impaired, attempt to keep them awake. Put each victim in a sleeping bag with another person—both naked. If you have double bags, put two warm people in with each victim.

Seasons and Weather

Weather in the Sangre de Cristo can be exceptionally unpredictable. Temperature and precipitation averages can be exceeded on a regular basis without any warning. Weather forecasts for this area are notoriously difficult to rely on because much of the range creates its own weather while the valleys may remain storm free. Being prepared for weather that can change dramatically, even over the course of one or two hours, can greatly increase your ability to enjoy this area safely. The elevation gains of most of the routes described make the variety of weather even more extreme, requiring respect and the flexibility to alter your plans and select other routes.

Typical summer months bring daytime temperatures in the 70s to the mountains, 60s in the high country, and 80s in the surrounding valleys. Nights are usually cool, often dropping into the 40s. July and August are the most popular time for hikers and backpackers; they are also the wettest months, with daily afternoon thunderstorm cycles and occasional severe electrical storms. When climbing the high peaks or even just hiking the valleys above the tree line, it is best to plan your day to be off exposed slopes and ridges and back below the tree line before noon. Lightning should never be taken lightly; it kills hikers every year in Colorado, especially on the high peaks.

Here are some basic safety tips in the event you encounter a lightning storm:

- Lightning can travel ahead of a storm, so take cover before the storm hits.
- Don't try to make it back to your vehicle. It isn't worth the risk. Instead, seek shelter even if it's only a short way back to the trailhead. Lightning storms usually don't last long, and from a safe vantage point, you might enjoy the sights and sounds.
- Be especially careful not to get caught on a mountaintop or exposed ridge; under large, solitary trees; in the open; or near standing water.
- Seek shelter in a low-lying area, ideally in a stand of small, uniformly sized trees.
- Avoid anything that attracts lightning, such as metal tent poles, graphite fishing rods, or pack frames.
- Crouch with both feet firmly on the ground.
- If you have a pack (without a metal frame) or a sleeping pad with you, put your feet on it for extra insulation against shock.
- Don't walk or huddle together. Instead, stay 50 feet apart, so if somebody gets hit by lightning, others in your party can give first aid.
- If you're in a tent, stay in your sleeping bag with your feet on your sleeping pad.

September and October can be exceptionally enjoyable months to explore the Sangre de Cristo Mountains. Most of the summer crowd has disappeared by then, along with the severe summer storms. Daytime temperatures usually remain warm; nighttime temperatures drop below freezing. The fall leaves begin to change to orange and gold, and a thin dusting of snow may blanket the higher slopes. From late September to mid-November, hunting is allowed in some areas and at different times during this season. Check with the Forest Service and the Division of Wildlife for more specific information, and wear a blaze orange vest and hat when hiking in those areas during hunting season. By November and December, deeper snow begins to cover the trails. Although it is common for much of the area to remain open to hikers equipped with good boots and gaiters well into December, an occasional storm or heavy snow year could leave the higher valleys filled with two to three feet of powder snow.

By January and February, much of the high country is ready to be explored on snowshoes or backcountry skis, but dry years do occur, leaving parts of the lower valleys and windswept slopes bare. March and April are often the snowiest months in the Sangre de Cristo, when daytime temperatures may reach the 40s and 50s in the valleys. The mountain temperatures remain below freezing and drop into the teens at night. Snowshoeing, backcountry skiing, and winter camping are often exceptional during these months, although there might not be enough deep snow for the straightforward construction of snow caves. April and May are often the most stable times of the year for snow climbing and alpine mountaineering.

By May and June the days begin to lengthen. The temperatures rise into the 40s in the high valleys, but the nights are still cold. The snow has usually melted off the

Winter tracks.

sunny slopes below the tree line, while the upper valleys and the north-facing slopes remain snow covered. Large portions of the high valleys can retain snow well into June and even July.

The winter season is a wonderful time to explore the mountains. It is a time of solitude and serene beauty. With the clean, untracked slopes of the Sangre de Cristo come the dangers of severe cold, biting wind, and avalanches. Instead of discouraging you from venturing into the mountains, winter can be a season to inspire you to learn and respect nature in a new way. The humility required to face the high peaks in winter only prompts you to enjoy the crispness of the air, the sparkle of fresh snow, or the tiny snow angel left by a bird's wings in ways more deeply than you thought possible. Take the time to learn the skills required and you will give yourself the keys you need to take advantage of this season of peace and renewal.

The Sangre de Cristo usually sees only a small amount of avalanche activity, so little that snow condition reports and avalanche forecasts for the area are hard to find. It is usually said that the range is too dry to see any significant slide action. This is misleading, however, as any slope at the proper angle with enough snow can slide, and any given slide can be the one that takes your life. Avalanches in the Sangre de Cristo are rare compared to the avalanche-prone San Juan and Central Mountains of Colorado, but you should never assume you are safe without carefully evaluating the snowpack and the terrain.

When traveling into the high country during winter, plan ahead to ensure a safer trip. Call the weather and avalanche hot lines or check the Web sites listed in Appendix A before you head out. Avalanche warnings might not apply directly to this area, but they can indicate the general trend for the region. When the avalanche danger is considered extreme or high in the San Juan or Central Mountains, it will also be high in the Sangre de Cristo. Plan a path most likely to cross safe terrain. Avoid slopes steeper than 25 degrees and stay off any steep terrain within twenty-four hours after heavy storms or periods of high wind. In general, south- and west-facing windward slopes tend to be more stable than east- and north-facing leeward slopes. Stay alert and reevaluate your route at every turn. Examine the surrounding slopes for signs of recent avalanche activity and avoid similar slopes during your trip. Telltale "whumping" sounds from the snow beneath your feet are warning flares, red flags, and danger signs all in one; when you get these signals always stay on gentle terrain and avoid the steeper slopes. If you must cross a suspect area, do so one person at a time and stay high and above the potential avalanche path. Never travel alone, and wear an avalanche beacon, know how to use it, and turn it on.

Beyond these basics, refer to the written resources listed in Appendix B. Take an avalanche class to learn more about how to identify dangerous terrain and how to evaluate snow conditions. Study the snowpack and expand your knowledge and judgment. When you do, the mountains cease being a distant white menace and become a beautiful and awesome landscape that commands the respect due a wild land.

Be Cougar Alert

Mountain lion encounters are extremely rare, and many veteran hikers never even see a mountain lion in the wild. However, the big cats, also called cougars or pumas, are potentially dangerous. It is wise to educate yourself before heading into mountain lion habitat.

To stay as safe as possible when hiking in mountain lion country, follow this advice:

1. Don't let small children wander away by themselves.
2. Don't let pets run unleashed.
3. Know how to behave if you encounter a mountain lion.

See Falcon's *Mountain Lion Alert* for more details and tips for safe outdoor recreation in mountain lion country.

Be Bear Aware

The first step of any hike in bear country is an attitude adjustment. Being prepared for bears doesn't only mean having the right equipment, it also means having the right information. Black bears do not as a rule attack humans, but they could pose a danger if you handle your food improperly. At the very least, letting a bear get human food can contribute directly to the eventual destruction of that bear. Think of proper bear etiquette as protecting the bear as much as yourself.

Camping in bear country. Staying overnight in bear country is not dangerous, but the presence of food, cooking, and garbage contributes an additional risk to your trip. Plus, you are in bear country at night when bears are usually most active. A few basic practices greatly minimize the chance of encounter.

To be as safe as possible, store everything that has any food smell. Resealable plastic bags are perfect for reducing food smell and help keep food from spilling on your pack, clothing, or other gear. If you spilled something on your clothes, change into other clothes for sleeping and hang the soiled clothes with the food and garbage. If you take them into the tent, you aren't separating your sleeping area from food smells. Try to keep food odors off your pack, but if you fail, put the food bag inside and hang the pack.

Be sure to finalize your food storage plans before it gets dark. It's not only difficult to store food after darkness falls, it's easier to forget some juicy morsel on the ground. Store food in airtight, sturdy, waterproof bags to prevent food odors from circulating throughout the forest. You can purchase dry bags at most outdoor specialty stores, but you can get by with a trash compactor bag. Don't use regular garbage bags, which can break too easily.

See the following diagrams for different ways to hang a bear bag. If you have two bags to hang, divide your food into two equal sacks. Use a stone to toss the end of a piece of nylon cord (parachute cord is fine, under most circumstances there is no need for the heavier stuff) over the limb well out from the trunk, then tie half your food to the end. Pull the food up to the limb, then tie your remaining food sack onto the cord as high as you can reach. Stuff the excess cord into the food sack,

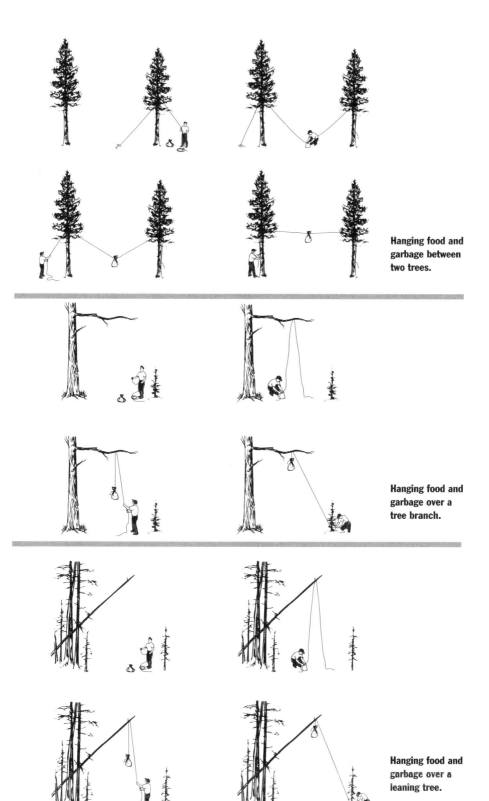

Hanging food and garbage between two trees.

Hanging food and garbage over a tree branch.

Hanging food and garbage over a leaning tree.

then use a stick to push the second sack several feet higher than your head. The first sack will act as a counterweight and descend a few feet, but it should remain at least as high as the second sack. In the morning, use a stick to pull down one of the sacks.

Don't get paranoid about the types of food you bring—all food has some smell. By consciously reducing the number of dishes (pack out all food scraps) and amount of packaging, consuming everything on your plate, and paying careful attention to storage, you not only make your backpacking culinary experience more enjoyable and hassle free but also more bear-proof.

Read Falcon's *Bear Aware* by Bill Schneider for complete information on camping in bear country.

Remember Rattlesnakes

Rattlesnakes are not common in the Sangre de Cristo Wilderness, but they are known to occur in the lower elevations. Rattlesnakes strike humans only in self-defense, when they're startled or otherwise afraid. The solution, of course, is to avoid scaring them. Look where you place your feet and hands when hiking in rattlesnake country. Fortunately, they almost always warn you of their presence with their telltale rattle.

If you encounter a rattlesnake, slowly back away and give it a chance to retreat. Almost invariably, it will seize the opportunity and slither away. If it doesn't, simply give the snake a wide berth and leave well enough alone. Do not throw rocks or sticks at it.

If bitten by a rattlesnake, don't panic. Rattlesnake bites can make you sick, but they are rarely fatal to healthy adults. Use a snakebite kit immediately to extract as much of the venom as possible. (It might actually be a "dry bite" in which no venom is delivered—intended only to frighten you.) Do not run or otherwise speed up your circulation, as that increases the spread of the venom in your bloodstream. Keep the bite site lower than your heart to decrease the spread of venom. Get medical attention as soon as possible, preferably within an hour.

Hiking with Children

Kids and trails are a natural combination. Including youngsters in this sport at the earliest age possible will increase the pleasure of both parents and children. Even if toddlers just ride on your back, they are becoming attuned to the experience of hiking. In time, they will graduate to more grown-up efforts, and be off on their own with self-confidence and awareness that can last a lifetime.

Just be certain not to discourage kids with overly ambitious plans. Take extra time for frequent stops, and fuel them up often with juice and snacks. Also remember that in their own small-sized way, children need to be as well prepared as adults. On extended hikes, make sure that they carry at a minimum rain gear, wool hats, mittens, and extra clothing comparable to yours.

On longer trails, kids more amiably accept the challenges of hiking if they share the companionship of other children. Team up with other parents, or check with your local YMCA, school, or various hiking clubs that sponsor group trips. Another alternative is to investigate trails associated with science centers, conservation groups, or the Audubon Society. Organizations like these frequently schedule family walks that cater to children's interests as part of their regular program of environmental education.

Zero Impact

Nowadays most wilderness users want to walk softly, but some aren't aware that they have poor manners. Often their actions are dictated by the outdated habits of a past generation of campers who cut green boughs for evening shelters, built campfires with fire rings, and dug trenches around tents. These practices might have been acceptable fifty years ago, but they leave long-lasting scars, and today such behavior is absolutely unacceptable.

Because wild places are becoming rare and the number of backcountry visitors is mushrooming, a new code of ethics is growing. Today, we all must leave no clues that we were there. Enjoy the wild, but leave no evidence of your visit.

THREE FALCON PRINCIPLES OF ZERO IMPACT
Leave with everything you brought in.
Leave no sign of your visit.
Leave the landscape as you found it.

Most of us know better than to litter—in or out of the backcountry. Be sure you leave nothing along the trail or at your campsite. Pack out all items, no matter now small, including orange peels, flip tops, cigarette butts, and gum wrappers, and do your best to pick up any trash others leave behind.

Follow the main trail. Avoid cutting switchbacks and walking on vegetation beside the trail. Don't pick up souvenirs, such as rocks or wildflowers. The next person wants to see them too, and collecting them violates many regulations.

Avoid making loud noises on the trail (unless you are in bear country) or in camp. Be courteous—remember, sound travels easily in the backcountry, especially across water.

Carry a lightweight trowel to bury human waste 6 to 8 inches deep at least 200 feet from any water source. Pack out used toilet paper.

Go without a campfire. Carry a stove for cooking and a flashlight, candle lantern, or headlamp for light. For emergencies, learn how to build a no-trace fire.

Camp in obviously used sites when they are available. Otherwise, camp and cook on durable surfaces such as bedrock, sand, gravel bars, or bare ground.

Details on these guidelines and recommendations of zero impact principles for specific outdoor activities can be found in the guidebook *Leave No Trace*. Visit your local bookstore or call (800) 243–0495 for a copy.

Geology

The Sangre de Cristo is one of the youngest mountain ranges in the continental United States. It stretches in an arc more than 150 miles long, from Salida, Colorado, in the north to Santa Fe, New Mexico, in the south. Although the range is geologically new, its foundation is ancient. The underlying stone is Precambrian igneous and metamorphic rock formed some 2 billion years ago below the earth's surface under high temperature and pressure. The Ancestral Rockies were uplifted during the Pennsylvanian period, about 300 million years ago. An inland sea on the west and an open ocean on the east bound the ancient mountains. The uplift accelerated the erosion of these highlands and generated enormous amounts of sediment. This debris was deposited into huge deltas along the coast, forming what is known as the Minturn Formation, which includes limestone composed of marine fossils. Later, from 290 to 245 million years ago, late in the Paleozoic period, the seas receded. By this time the Ancestral Rockies had been eroded into low hills. This erosion continued as streams deposited deep alluvial fans around the flanks of the highlands. This is known today as the Sangre de Cristo Formation and is marked by fine and coarse sandstones and conglomerates as well as oxidized iron, which creates the reddish color we see today.

Between 1.65 and 65 million years ago, compression of the continental plate caused fold-thrust faults to form on the east and west sides of the range. The compression faults were later reactivated when the Rio Grande rift began to extend and pull apart. This rift extends from the upper Arkansas Valley and continues south all the way into Mexico. The action of the rift initiated land movements that began to shake up the entire region. Earthquakes rocked the area as the San Luis Valley and Wet Mountain Valley subsided, while the Sangre de Cristo uplifted and profuse volcanic activity ignited the landscape. Lava flowed up onto the surface, and cinder cones sent ash plumes into the air. Magma intruded into the older rock above, depositing rich veins of minerals. The legacy left by this period drew modern prospectors and miners to the Cloverdale Basin and Orient Canyon of the Sangre de Cristo, as well as to the Upper Arkansas Valley, Wet Mountain Valley, and the Upper San Luis Valley during the late 1800s. The Rio Grande rift is still active today, albeit in less violent ways, drawing soakers to its many hot springs.

The Spanish Peaks were also produced during this volcanic period, about 35 million years ago. Magma swelled upward, splitting and cracking the rock above. This and later molten rock intrusions were forced up into the cracks that radiated out from the main magma body. The older rock layers overlying this bulge gradually eroded, eventually leaving the igneous formations exposed as the Great Dikes of the Spanish Peaks. These radial dikes, known around the world, are found nowhere else in such patterns and abundance. East and West Spanish Peaks are the

Sangre de Cristo conglomerate

obvious features from this time period, but the entire area is marked by this period of volcanism. Silver Mountain and Mount Maestas, northwest of La Veta, exhibit similar dike features. Cinder cones that mark the plain along U. S. Highway 69, and the solidified volcanic plug named Goemmer Butte are evidence of this violence, some of it occurring as recently as 10,000 years ago.

The Sangre de Cristo uplift continued to erode. Sediments filled the Wet Mountain Valley to a depth of up to 6,000 feet. Parts of the San Luis Valley were packed with as much as 19,000 feet of sediment and volcanic debris. During the past 2 million years, the Quaternary period, a series of glacial episodes began. As the glaciers formed and grew, they gouged the high mountain valleys into their current U-shape. Moraines were plowed up and the valleys furrowed with piles of rock and transported debris. The impressive vertical headwalls seen today near the crest of the range were carved at this time, and the high lake-filled basins were ground even wider. Glacial and stream erosion continued to fill the San Luis and Wet Mountain Valleys.

About 12,000 years ago, the Ice Age ended and the glaciers slowly retreated from the mountain slopes of the Sangre de Cristo and the San Juan to the west.

Remnants of this Ice Age remain on Blanca Peak's north face. Wind began to blow large amounts of fine sand that was freed from the ice, transporting it across the San Luis Valley. As the wind was forced over the low points of Sangre de Cristo at what is now Medano and Mosca Pass, the heavier sand was dropped off. An extensive sand sheet formed, and sand dunes began to take shape. Still continuing today, the prevailing west winds carry sand over the valley, across the dunes to their eastern edge, and beyond into the mountains to the east. Medano Creek flows all year, but the spring snowmelt boosts its flow as it retrieves the sand from the mountains and from the eastern edge of the dunes and returns it to the sand sheet to the west. This is part of a sustained cycle that helps maintain the dunes. Wind may continue to shape the dunes, but the major patterns we see today have changed very little since the first Europeans saw them. The high water table of the area, the rain, and the snowfall help maintain the dunes' high moisture content, which tends to stabilize the major dune features. Photographs taken from a century ago and surveys that produced more recent topographic maps suggest these features have a curious resolve to remain as they are.

The Sangre de Cristo Mountains we see today are a tangible legacy of the violent forces that continue to shape our planet. The torturous power required to heave an ocean floor miles above the surface of the sea is almost unimaginable. When you climb across a jagged ridge above 14,000 feet and find your hand grasping a rock containing a fossilized seashell, it can be both fascinating and humbling. Your first thought might be, "How did *this* get up here?" Then you realize that the bigger question is how did *here* get up here? The geologic story has a fascinating plot with twists and turns that we continue to unravel as we explore and probe the complex geology of the Sangre de Cristo.

History of Life in the Sangre de Cristo

et us paint the big picture of nature's history by reaching back into the past with broad strokes. Life on earth began during the Precambrian Age between 5 billion and 570 million years ago. Bacteria, algaelike plant life, and simple invertebrates like worms and jellyfish were the first to form. Our planet had one dominant ocean and a single continent with its landforms still in flux. During the Paleozoic era (570 to 240 million years ago), Pangea, the single supercontinent, split in two. As the southern continent and what was to become North America drifted, shallow seas encroached on the land. Almost all invertebrates exploded into existence at this time, followed by the amphibians and reptiles. From 225 to 65 million years ago, during the Mesozoic era, reptiles evolved into large land-dwelling dinosaurs. Flying reptiles and birds also appeared. Early mammalian ancestors existed, but they were dominated by the giant reptiles until they became extinct. Conifers were the most prevalent plant life during this time, and modern pines and sequoias first developed. Flowering plants, deciduous trees, and grasses also began to flourish.

Between 66 and 26 million years ago, during the Tertiary period, the picture becomes more familiar to us. The North American continent appeared similar to the way it does today. Mammals had replaced the reptiles as the dominant animals. Modern birds, reptiles, amphibians, and fish already existed or were soon to appear. The early mammals developed multiple forms, including rhinoceroses, camels, pigs, rodents, monkeys, whales, and the ancestral horse. Vegetation would have appeared familiar and the climate was warm. Carnivorous mammals, the early dogs and cats, made their appearance, along with beavers, mice, rabbits, and squirrels. The early apes also developed during this period in Europe, Asia, and Africa. From 5 to 2 million years ago, the climate became significantly cooler and drier, a presage to the glacial period to come.

During the Pleistocene, from 2 million to 10,000 years ago, North America was home to mastodons, mammoths, horses, musk ox, saber-toothed tigers, large wolves, giant armadillos, sloth, bison, camels, and wild pigs. Important excavations in southern and central Colorado have uncovered the remains of these animals, which roamed the region during this period. Many of these mammals, including the horse, were beginning the stampede toward their eventual extinction or extirpation from North America. About 100,000 years ago, and at first very quietly, a seemingly unimpressive animal had developed: The first modern humans walked the plains of Africa.

The migration of humans from East Asia to North America is thought to have taken place about 12,000 years ago as the last Ice Age came to an end. Evidence of Clovis and Folsom Man, identified by their stone tools and fluted spear points, has been found in several places in North America, especially in the Great Plains. Excavation sites in New Mexico and Colorado's San Luis Valley, near the Great Sand Dunes, reveal evidence of their presence and hunting prowess. The peoples of this time hunted big game, in particular the mammoth, which is now extinct. They appear to have practiced cooperative hunting techniques. Game was surrounded and systematically killed, trapped in constructed or naturally occurring corrals and stampeded off cliffs. Speculation links the hunting methods of these early people to the extinction of many large mammals, but skepticism about this theory still remains. Regardless of the cause, these extinctions forced native humans to adapt and change their survival strategy. People began to forage more, hunt smaller game, and likely became more nomadic due to the depletion of local resources.

In more recent times the Pueblo, Anasazi, Kiowa, Apache, and Comanche tribes frequented the Sangre de Cristo, although little evidence suggests more permanent occupation until the Ute Indians settled. The Ute dominated the area until the Spanish arrived. With the Spanish came the return of a North American original, the horse. As horses were traded, stolen, and lost to the Native Americans, the Comanche emerged as a dominant group in southern Colorado, forcing the less aggressive Utes out. Spaniards who first arrived in the area in the sixteenth century gave the range its name: the Sangre de Cristo or "Blood of Christ," named for the blazing red sunsets cast on the snowcapped peaks. As the Spanish attempted to secure their claims on this new land, they frequently battled with the Comanche. Juan Bautista de Anza commanded a troop of more than 500 men through the San Luis Valley and over Poncha Pass in 1779, in pursuit of Chief Cuerno Verde (Greenhorn) and his company of Comanche. The natives fled down the Arkansas River before being caught near the town of Rye. The Spanish also explored the Sangre de Cristo in search of gold and silver, and they made regular incursions as they attempted to defend their northern territory from Indians. The clash between the Indians and the Spaniards, followed by conflict with the Mexicans, would continue for more than two centuries.

In 1806 Lieutenant Zebulon Pike became the first American to explore the Wet Mountain Valley, the Sangre de Cristo Mountains, and the San Luis Valley. Pike and his men crossed the Wet Mountains and passed through the Westcliffe area. They skirted south along the mountains and climbed to the crest of the Sangre de Cristo. The expedition crossed the boundary of the Louisiana Territory at Medano Pass before descending west into the Spanish-held San Luis Valley. A replica of Pike's stockade has been built to mark the spot where the Spanish arrested Pike and his men and took them to Santa Fe for questioning. They were eventually taken to Chihuahua, Mexico, where they were detained before being released into American territory without any of their logs or maps. It is unknown whether Pike intended to be captured by the Spanish in order to spy on Mexican territory or whether his inept winter travels led him to an exhausted surrender.

In 1822, Mexico gained independence from Spain. The Sangre de Cristo area saw a continuation of the Indian conflict as well as a sharp increase in trade through the San Luis Valley on the Old Spanish Trail. This braided trail started in Santa Fe and ran along various routes for 1,200 miles to Los Angeles. From 1829 to 1850, the route served traders as they hauled Mexican goods to the west and Chinese goods back to the east. Emigrants also used the trail as they traveled west to California.

Large land grants were awarded to Hispanic settlers to help solidify Mexico's hold on its northern territory. These grants were later honored by the United States when the territory was ceded by Mexico in 1848, and they remain partially intact to this day. The Baca Grant's remaining 100,000 undeveloped acres could soon be linked with the Great Sand Dunes Monument as a part of an expanded national park. The Sangre de Cristo Grant, which includes the south face of 14,000-foot Blanca Peak and Little Bear Peak, originally extended into New Mexico and totaled more than a million acres. It exists today as the 175,000-acre Forbes-Trinchera Ranch.

By 1836, Mexico's tenuous hold over the region slipped as the Texas Rebellion drove the Mexicans out of the territory. Texans declared independence and claimed authority over the entire Sangre de Cristo area, including the Arkansas River Valley and the Wet Mountains.

During this same period of time, from about 1825 to 1840, the trappers and mountain men arrived. Kit Carson, Jim Baker, James Bridger, Thomas Fitzpatrick, "Uncle Dick" Wooten, and Jim Beckworth were some of the colorful characters who trekked through the area. They trapped, hunted, and traded beaver pelts, and probably explored every valley and stream of the Sangre de Cristo within a few short years. They were efficient at plying their trade, removing almost all of the beaver by the 1840s.

In 1842 the first of several surveys of the area was conducted. Lieutenant John C. Fremont led five expeditions over and around the Sangre de Cristo. The Gunnison expedition also explored the area. These expeditions were conducted both to map and document the area and to survey a route for the transcontinental railway. Their proposed route followed what is now Pass Creek Pass just west and north of Le Veta Pass. These surveys were a presage for the population boom that would eventually take place in the area.

In 1851, the United States annexed Texas and established control of the Sangre de Cristo for the first time. In the same year, the area's oldest town, San Luis, was founded. Communal irrigation ditches and common grazing lands were established near the settlement and are still intact today. Fort Massachusetts was built nearby to protect these new settlers from natives. By 1858 the garrison was moved to Fort Garland and housed more than a hundred men, including many buffalo soldiers. In 1866 Christopher "Kit" Carson, one of Fremont's guides and a local trapper and mountain man, was appointed commander of the fort, much of which is still intact today as a memorial to this era and the soldiers who served there.

The period from 1860 until the turn of the twentieth century saw a huge influx of settlers, as the discovery of gold drew prospectors and the Homestead Act prompted homesteaders to flow into the area. In 1876, this growth drove the Colorado territory toward statehood. Salida, Alamosa, and Westcliffe were established as the boom climaxed. Railroads were built through the Royal Gorge and eventually north up the Arkansas River to Leadville. Lines were also built in the south, over La Veta Pass and beyond, to serve the quickly growing region. Billions of dollars worth of silver, gold, and iron ore were eventually extracted from this region, most within a frantic 20-year period.

As the nineteenth century came to a close, the mountains of the Sangre de Cristo were more thoroughly mapped, surveyed, and catalogued. More mines and settlements were built, the demand for wood increased, and most of the original forests of the Sangre de Cristo fell to the woodcutter's ax and to the blades of the mill. The mining boom times were short lived, however, and as mines closed the rail lines fell out of use. Mining camps and towns were abandoned, the population throughout the region plummeted, and the local economy was forced to shift toward agriculture. The few remaining settlers scraped out a marginal living by ranching, farming, and grazing cattle in the surrounding mountains and alpine valleys.

Soon after the turn of the twentieth century, most of the Wet Mountains and Sangre de Cristo were given national forest designation in an attempt to better manage the area's resources. For almost a hundred years, these mountains had been trapped, hunted, fished, mined, logged, and grazed. It then became the unenviable task of the Forest Service to manage an overused mountain range and attempt to balance all of the competing interests. In 1932 the Great Sand Dunes were declared a national monument, and in 2000, legislation to expand and upgrade the area to national park status was passed.

The Sangre de Cristo Mountains did not receive wilderness designation until 1993, followed by the Spanish Peaks in 1999, bringing both areas the protections and the potential perils that come with it. More than ever, it is up to hikers, anglers, and climbers to enjoy this land with care and respect, to tread lightly, and to act as caretakers for the lands that truly belong to all of us and to those who follow.

Modern Wildlife of the Sangre de Cristo

The forests of the Sangre de Cristo have largely recovered from destruction caused by the railroad tie hacks and the sawmills. Today they are as diverse and varied as any forest in the Rocky Mountains. The exceptionally steep quality of these mountains creates valleys and peaks that include life zones from desert to alpine over the course of a few short miles. This variety makes these mountains even more interesting and provides a dramatic addition to the already spectacular landscape. In general, as we climb up from the valley floor to the crest of the range, we start at the foothill, or transition zone, then up through the montane, subalpine, and finally the alpine zone.

Prickly pear cactus.

The toes of the Sangre de Cristo lie in the foothill zone. This dry and warm transitional region extends from the valley floor up to about 8,000 feet. It is characterized by grassland, shrubs, yucca, cactus, and wild iris, with occasional stands of ponderosa pine and Douglas fir, and forests of pinyon and juniper. Deer, coyotes, foxes, skunks, porcupines, wild turkeys, red-tailed hawks, and golden eagles frequent the base of the mountains.

The montane zone above 8,000 feet is cooler and wetter than the valley and usually marks the lower limit of the dense forests of ponderosa pine and Douglas fir. Aspen, Engelmann spruce, bristlecone pine, and subalpine fir are found up to the upper limit of the zone around 10,000 feet. The montane is home to squirrels, chipmunks, black bears, deer, rabbits, hares, owls, hawks, hummingbirds, and woodpeckers.

The subalpine zone, from 10,000 to 11,500 feet, includes Engelmann spruce, subalpine fir, pine, aspen, and bristlecone pine, which grow slowly in this zone of colder temperatures and heavier rain and snow. Coyotes, black bears, and deer are seasonal visitors, while bighorn sheep, mountain goats, pikas, and marmots are common residents.

The alpine zone is my favorite. No trees grow above 11,500 feet, and the severe cold and gale-force winds limit the growing season to just six weeks on many slopes. Grasses, shrubs, mosses, and lichens grow in this forbidding environment. Pikas, ptarmigan, and yellow-bellied marmots eke out an existence in the alpine zone year-round, while bighorn sheep, mountain goats, and coyotes often migrate into this environment during the warmer months.

Threatened and Endangered Species

The Sangre de Cristo is a range long affected by human beings. From the original inhabitants to trappers, miners, hunters, and forest rangers, people have altered and shaped this landscape and its community of wildlife. Bison, long a major food source and cultural icon of the Native Americans, exist in Colorado today only in captive herds. Grizzlies were eradicated by the turn of the twentieth century, and wolves, which lingered in small numbers, were extirpated by the 1920s. Wolves have returned to the Sangre de Cristo region in a limited way, in the form of a captive breeding and rehabilitative refuge near Gardner. Lynx and wolverines are also thought to be absent from their original territories in the Sangre de Cristo. Lynx have recently been reintroduced in the San Juan Mountains to the west, and the possibility remains that a small number of the more adventurous cats could find their way to these mountains. The beaver population has largely recovered and returned to many of its original mountain valley ponds. Bald eagle and peregrine falcon populations are also recovering. The outlook for these animals and the hope of recovering and reintroducing other native species is largely up to us. Our support, and at times our demands, will ensure the future of these fragile populations.

Bighorn sheep on Kit Carson Mountain.

How to Use This Guide

election of hikes. The hikes chosen for this guide lead to significant natural features, such as a lake, a mountaintop, a free-flowing creek or river, or a waterfall. The hikes described here represent almost all of the hiking trails in the Sangre de Cristo mountain range. Most follow established trails that are recognized and periodically maintained by the National Forest Service. A small number of hikes were not included because they paralleled private land or because trailhead access was limited by private land. Some of the optional routes follow well-established paths that are neither recognized nor maintained by the Forest Service but are used regularly and are easy to follow. Many of the options are seldom used and require good route-finding skills and a zero impact ethic to follow responsibly.

To use this book effectively, please note the following items:

Highlights

This short description of each hike includes those special natural features for which it was chosen as well as any other aspects that make the trail outstanding.

Type of hike

Hikes fall into the following categories:

Day hike. Best for a short excursion only, usually less than 6 miles one way. These short trails could lack water or suitable camping sites.

Overnight/backpack. Best for backpacking with at least one night in the backcountry. Many overnight hikes can be done as day hikes if you have the time and stamina.

Loop. Starts and finishes at the same trailhead with no (or very little) retracing of your steps.

Out and back. Traveling the same route coming and going.

Shuttle. A point-to-point trip that requires two vehicles (one left at each end of the trial) or a prearranged pickup at a designated time and place. One effective way to manage the logistical difficulties of shuttles is to arrange for a second party to start at the other end of the trail. The two parties then rendezvous at a predetermined time and place along the trail and trade keys.

Total distance

This figure gives the total distance hiked. In an out-and-back hike, the number is twice the length of the trail. Measuring trail distances is an inexact science at best. In this guidebook, most distances have been taken from map measurements and from in-the-field estimates. Most wilderness trail signs do not include distance, and when they do you can bet they are just somebody else's best guess. Forest Service signs round the posted trail length to the nearest 0.5 mile. In a few instances, the text gives mileages that differ from the Forest Service's trail signs, based on the author's best calculations.

Keep in mind that distance is often less important than difficulty and that distances given only indicate map distances. Because maps reflect only the horizontal, a trail shown on the map as 1 mile but which climbs a steep slope is actually longer than a mile. Most hikers average about 2 miles per hour, although a steep 2-mile climb on rocky tread can take longer than a 4-mile stroll through a gentle river valley.

Difficulty. The average difficulty of each trail has been assessed given comparable conditions. Some "easy" trails, when snowpacked and choked with freshly downed timber, could be more difficult than "strenuous" trails in ideal conditions after recent maintenance. In general, I have divided trails into easy, moderate, and strenuous categories using the following criteria: Trails less than 6 miles in round-trip distance with a change in elevation of less than 2,000 vertical feet have been given an **easy** rating. Up to 8 or 9 miles of total round-trip distance and a vertical climb of as much as 3,000 vertical feet qualifies the trail as **moderate.** Trails with more than 8 miles of round-trip distance and a vertical climb of more than 3,000 vertical feet, or trails with exceptional route-finding difficulties, hand-and-foot scrambling, or long miles at high elevations, have been rated as **strenuous.**

These ratings are entirely subjective, but the intent is to apply a rating for routes relative to others within this mountain range. Specific trail or weather conditions always affect trail difficulty, and inquiries at the National Forest Service office about current conditions are usually met with helpful feedback (see Appendix A for contacts). Always consider the physical and mental condition of you and your party before committing to a difficult route. Be willing to turn back or have alternative routes and options available to you when conditions are worse than you anticipated. With proper preparation and planning, even an aborted attempt can be safe, relaxing, and enjoyable.

Best Months. Instead of attempting to indicate the months of the year a trail is "open" or snow free, this section indicates the months that allow the most reliable access to the trailhead. The best months for many hikers may be during early spring when snow blankets the trail and provides a rock-free route, or during fall when the crowds and thunderstorms have long passed. Most importantly, hikes are best when they are accessible. When winter snow or spring mud make the roads leading to the trailhead impassable, many of the hikes shown here become long backpacking trips instead of day hikes. Conditions vary from year to year so it is imperative to check with the Forest Service Office to get reliable road condition information, especially if you are hiking during the spring and fall seasons. See Seasons and Weather for more information about weather, snow, and trail conditions.

Maps. This section lists the applicable USGS 7.5-minute topo map or maps for each hike. They are the most detailed maps available, but they don't cover much area. For maps that cover a greater area use USDA Forest Service maps of the area. They are available at outdoors stores and at any Forest Service supervisor's office or ranger district.

Special considerations. Sometimes you should be aware of special circumstances before deciding on a hike or getting ready for one. You might want to know, for example, if you'll run into horse traffic, if the trailhead is accessible with a two-wheel-drive vehicle, or if the hike presents any unusual difficulties. This section tells you what to expect.

Finding the trailhead. Directions are given from the nearest town of a reasonable size. *Note:* The primary purpose of the "Finding the trailhead" section is to assist the reader in locating the route on a map prior to the trip. It is not advisable to use this section as your sole source of directions.

Key points. This heading includes trail junctions and major landmarks. Mileages are given within 0.1 mile but often reflect only a best estimate. The designations "right," "left," and "continue straight" indicate either a change of trails or the directions to go if the route is unclear.

Options. Optional routes are listed following the main hike description. These strenuous hikes and climbs are used to approach the many high summits and to connect with nearby trails in the adjacent valleys. Some of these optional hikes follow established trails, but most are off-trail and require a wide range of outdoor travel skills. You must know how to read a map and be able to use a compass in order to find and follow the trails that are often intermittent and sometimes altogether nonexistent. The ability to read the weather is vital, as many of these alternatives lead you to the highest reaches of the range and are exposed to potentially severe mountain weather. With the right skills, the options section will be a vital resource used to tailor your trip to your own particular abilities and ambitions.

Snow season. This entry describes access and trail conditions during typical late fall, winter, and early spring seasons. It is difficult to predict exactly when these snowy months may take place. Some trails may see a snow season from January to March while others will see a snow season from November to June with sections of trails that are dry and windblown year-round. It is best to research the weather resources and contacts listed in Appendix A to determine current conditions before setting out on a hike during these months. See **Seasons and Weather** for more information about weather and trail conditions.

Northern Sangre de Cristo

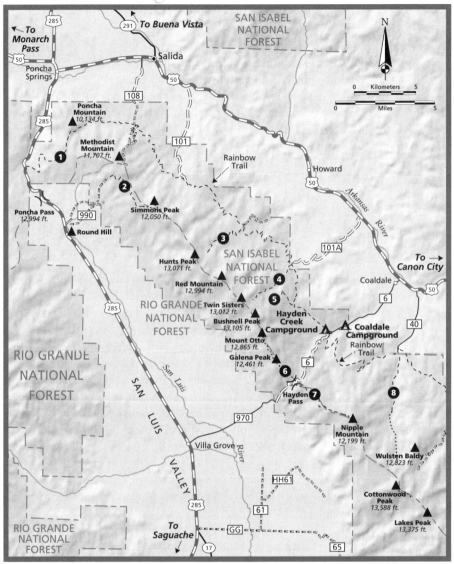

San Isabel National Forest

To Buena Vista

285
291
50
Salida
Poncha Springs
108
50
101

To Monarch Pass
50

Poncha Mountain
10,134 ft.
285

Methodist Mountain
11,707 ft.

❶

Rainbow Trail

Howard
50

Arkansas River

To → Canon City

Poncha Pass
12,994 ft.
990

❷

Simmons Peak
12,050 ft.

Round Hill

❸

SAN ISABEL NATIONAL FOREST

101A

Coaldale
50
6

Hunts Peak
13,071 ft.

RIO GRANDE NATIONAL FOREST

Red Mountain
12,994 ft.

Twin Sisters
13,012 ft.

❹

❺

Hayden Creek Campground

Coaldale Campground

40

Bushnell Peak
13,105 ft.

Rainbow Trail

285

Mount Otto
12,865 ft.

RIO GRANDE NATIONAL FOREST

San Luis River

SAN

LUIS

VALLEY

Galena Peak
12,461 ft.

❻

6

❼

Hayden Pass

❽

970

Nipple Mountain
12,199 ft.

Wulsten Baldy
12,823 ft.

Villa Grove

HH61

61

Cottonwood Peak
13,588 ft.

RIO GRANDE NATIONAL FOREST

285

To Saguache

GG

65

Lakes Peak
13,375 ft.

17

N

0   Kilometers   5
0   Miles   5

Northern
SANGRE DE CRISTO

Often overlooked and overshadowed by the 14,000-foot peaks of the Sawatch Range to the north and by the higher peaks of the central range to the south, the northern section of the Sangre de Cristo is nonetheless a stunningly steep and rugged land. Most of the range crest is above 12,000 feet and includes a half dozen lakes, fourteen major creeks, and twelve summits above 12,000 feet. This humble region is well worth the time spent climbing and exploring it, and it holds its own as a beautiful addition to the area.

The moderate-size town of Salida, at an elevation of 7,000 feet and with a population of about 5,000, provides the most convenient services for this area. It is an active town of artists, musicians, athletes, skiers, cyclers, ranchers, anglers, and hunters. There are major hotels and many affordable motels in addition to bed-and-breakfasts and inns that are open year-round. In summer there are art and music festivals, hot springs, and a kayaking rodeo on the Arkansas River, which flows through downtown. Camping gear and outdoor supplies can be found in a number of shops near the downtown area. Groceries and supplies are readily available at the major grocery store and superstore on U.S. Highway 50 and in downtown.

From Salida, US 50 follows the Arkansas River east through Howard and Coaldale, then past the Royal Gorge toward Canon City. The east side of the range is dominated by the Arkansas River; fishing, rafting, kayaking, picnic areas, and camping are available along the river. The east side of the range rises steeply above the river, up to several impressive high valleys below the jagged crest of the range. The west side of the range is accessed from the Salida area by driving south on US 285 over Poncha Pass to Villa Grove and then beyond toward Crestone, the Great Sand Dunes, and eventually Alamosa. The upper San Luis Valley, narrower and steeper than most of the lower valley, leads across flats of sage and rabbitbrush then abruptly up the west side of the range, passing through a narrow band of mixed forest and aspen stands before reaching the crest of the range. Most of the upper San Luis Valley is sparsely populated private and BLM ranchland up to the forest boundary before it climbs into the Wilderness Area. Several of the trailheads are accessible only with a high-clearance vehicle, and some require four-wheel drive. Your efforts will be rewarded, though, as you explore these unassuming but surprisingly stunning mountains.

Rainbow Trail

Poncha Pass to Hayden Creek

Highlights: *A long and fairly gentle trail with views of the Arkansas River valley and the Sawatch Range to the north.*

Type of hike: Out-and-back day hike, overnight backpack, or three- to five-day shuttle.
Total distance: 34 miles, with three intermediate points of access.
Difficulty: Easy to moderate, depending on length.

Best months: Spring and fall are best to avoid summer heat and afternoon thunderstorms; fall offers the possibility of good weather and turning leaves.
Maps: USGS Poncha Pass, Wellsville, Howard, and Coaldale quads.

Special considerations: The Rainbow Trail can be heavily used at times and is occasionally frequented by horse and llama trekkers as well as motorcycles, although I have never encountered any during my time in the area.

Finding the trailhead: From Poncha Springs, drive 6 miles south on U.S. Highway 285 from the intersection with US 50 to a small roadside parking area on the left (east) side of the road. This is the first trailhead access for the 90-mile-long Rainbow Trail (1336) and is also the access to the spur trail that leads west to the Continental Divide Trail and the Colorado Trail. Access to the Rainbow Trail can also be gained at the Methodist Mountain Trailhead (Forest Road 108), Bear Creek Trailhead (County Road 101), and Stout Creek Trailhead at the Kerr Gulch Road (101-A), as well as at Hayden Creek Campground (FR 6).

To reach the Methodist Mountain access, drive 4.2 miles east on US 50 from Poncha Springs and turn right (south) onto 107. Drive 6 miles (the road becomes 108), staying left as the road skirts private land and crosses the national forest boundary (CR 108 becomes FR 108 at the boundary). Follow this rough dirt road 1.2 miles to the intersection with the Rainbow Trail. This road could require a four-wheel-drive vehicle for the last mile to the trailhead.

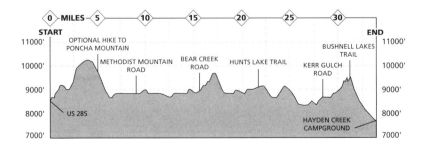

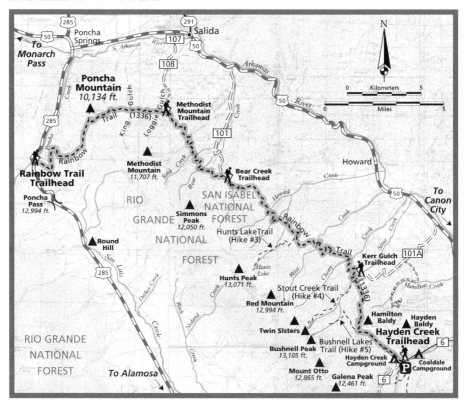

For access to the Bear Creek Trailhead from the intersection of US 50 and Colorado Highway 291 (Oak Street) at the east end of Salida, drive south 2.4 miles on US 50 and turn right (west) onto 101. After 0.9 mile, CR 101 becomes CR 49. Continue 2.3 miles to the national forest boundary, where CR 49 becomes 101. Continue 2.5 miles to the end of FR 101 at the Rainbow Trail. This road is rough and could require a four-wheel-drive vehicle, depending on the conditions.

See descriptions of Stout Creek (Hike 4) and Bushnell Lakes (Hike 5) for Kerr Gulch and Hayden Creek access points.

Parking and trailhead facilities: There is a small parking area at the US 185 trailhead. Parking and camping areas are available at the Kerr Gulch Road. A developed campground with water, rest rooms, and parking is available at the Hayden Creek Campground.

Key points:
- **0.0** US 285 Trailhead.
- **5.2** Poncha Mountain.
- **9.0** Methodist Mountain Road (FR 108).
- **16.0** Bear Creek Road (FR 101).

22.0 Hunts Lake Trail.

28.5 Kerr Gulch Road (CR 101-A) and Stout Creek Trail (1403).

31.0 Bushnell Lakes Trail (1402).

34.0 Hayden Creek Campground (FR 6).

The hike: From the US 285 access, hike east on the Rainbow Trail (1336) up steep switchbacks before climbing more gently past views to the north of the Arkansas Valley and the Sawatch Range. As the trail begins to drop toward the northeast, Poncha Mountain rises above and to the left (north) of the trail, where an easy climb through trees and up grassy slopes takes you to the summit. As you continue northeast along the trail, it becomes gentler and wraps itself around the northern end of the Sangre de Cristo above Poncha Springs and Salida, crossing seasonally dry creeks before reaching the Methodist Mountain Road.

The trail now offers views of the lower Arkansas River Valley and the mountains to the northwest. Hike up the Methodist Mountain road a short distance before turning left where the trail continues. Follow the trail as it dips and rises across several small seasonal creeks that may remain dry during much of the year. The trail is mostly level until reaching the Bear Creek Trailhead. Bear Creek provides the most reliable water source along the trail during this section of the trail.

Hike southeast and begin climbing steeply over the next mile before descending again to Howard Creek and across several smaller creeks. The trail passes through private land, and camping is not available through this short section. Follow the trail as it becomes gentler while still dipping into small creeks and hiking back out until reaching Hunts Lake Trail on the right. Continue south and descend again, crossing another creek before climbing steeply to high points overlooking the Arkansas River Valley. The trail descends to a low point crossing Cherry Creek before reaching the Kerr Gulch access, followed by the Stout Creek Trail (1403). This southern section of the trail has more creeks and streams available for water than the northern portion. Climb more steeply up to Hamilton Baldy's connecting ridge and pass the Bushnell Lakes Trail before the descent leading to Hayden Creek Campground.

Options: There are numerous backpacking and car shuttle options, including the hike of the entire 90-mile Rainbow Trail (see Hikes 9 and 17), or hiking the intersecting trails east up the valleys of Hunts Lake (Hike 3), Stout Creek (Hike 4), or Bushnell Lakes (Hike 5).

Snow season: This is a good hike during snow season. The access at US 285 and Hayden Creek Campground are the most reliable. The Methodist Mountain Road and Bear Creek Road might also be accessible, depending on the conditions. It is rare for the trail to be fully covered with snow; therefore, snowshoes or skis are not usually required.

Near the Rainbow Trail at Bear Creek.

Simmons Peak Trail

Highlights: *An infrequently used trail with an off-trail route to a high peak and multiple points of four-wheel-drive access.*

Type of hike: Out-and-back day hike or overnight backpack.
Total distance: 10.0 miles.

Difficulty: Moderate.
Best months: June to October.
Maps: USGS Poncha Pass and Wellsville quads.

Finding the trailhead: From Poncha Pass, drive 1.6 miles south on U.S. Highway 285 and turn left (east) onto Forest Road 990. It might be hard to see this road; if you pass Round Hill on the left as the road curves around it, you've gone too far. At the cattle guard, there might be a small sign for Dorsey Creek and the forest boundary. Continuing straight on FR 990 leads to a recent road closure; you can hike 1.0 miles along the creek up to the trail from this point. To drive the rerouted road all the way to the trailhead, turn right (south) 0.2 mile from US 285, cross the creek, and continue up the hill to the south. The road follows the ridge for 4 miles, passes a road, then drops down and off the ridge on the right before turning left and descending to the creek. Cross the creek and drive through a stockman's gate (close it behind you if you open it to pass through) before climbing along the left (north) side of the creek for another 1.7 miles to the wilderness boundary. The road is rough for the last mile and muddy during much of the season. Parking for one vehicle is available near the end of the road at the trailhead. Additional parking can be found about 0.5 mile and 1.0 mile from the end of the 4WD road.

It is also possible to access this trail farther south from the North Decker and Rock Creek Roads (948 and 980). For the North Decker Creek access, turn left (east) off of US 285 4.6 miles south of Poncha Pass. The rough road soon requires a high-clearance vehicle at a wide but shallow creek crossing. The road forks at this creek; staying left can be easier. The left fork dead-ends, so cross a shallow gully immediately after the creek crossing and return to the right fork for another 0.2 mile to a signed fork in the road. Turn left (north) for the road to North Decker Creek and drive about 3 miles (the road becomes 948) to the end at the wilderness boundary.

For access via Rock Creek, turn right (south) at the aforementioned signed fork and continue to another fork, this one signed for North and South Rock Creek. Turn left (east) on FR 980 to North Rock Creek. Continue on the North Rock Creek Road to the T intersection at North Rock Creek, then turn left (north) to drive a very rough road to North Decker Creek or right (south) and drive about 1.0 mile on FR 982 to South Rock Creek.

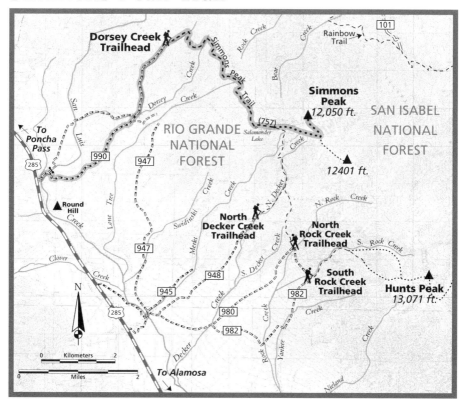

Parking and trailhead facilities: There is no parking at the Dorsey Creek Trailhead.

Key points:

- **0.0** Dorsey Creek Trailhead.
- **0.2** Simmons Peak Trail (757).
- **3.5** Salamander Lake.
- **5.0** Simmons Peak.

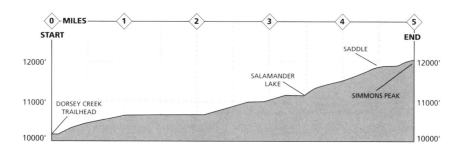

Hunts Peak from Unnamed 12,401.

The hike: From the Dorsey Creek Trailhead, the single-track trail (757) climbs for 0.2 mile along the left side of the creek before turning right (south). It continues parallel to the crest of the range for 3.5 miles until it descends at a spur trail southwest to the North Decker Creek road access. You may also continue south on the trail and descend to the four-wheel drive road just north of the North Rock Creek Road access.

For the approach to Simmons Peak, hike past the small Salamander Lake. Leave the Simmons Peak Trail and follow one of the thin trails on the left. Climb up the steep grassy slopes to the crest of the range for views of the upper San Luis and Arkansas River Valleys. Follow the ridge north to the top of Simmons Peak. You can also take the ridge to the north to the summit of Unnamed 12,401.

Options: From the trail leading up to the saddle below Simmons Peak it is possible to continue south descending steeply about 1.2 miles to the North Decker Trailhead. Continue on the trail past North Decker Creek and join a four-wheel-drive road before reaching the North Rock Creek Trailhead after another mile. From South Rock Creek it is possible to climb to the summit of Hunts Peak. To do so, hike northeast along the creek as it climbs into the valley and bushwhack south to the west ridge of Hunts Peak. Once on the ridge, continue east up to the summit.

Snow season: Access is somewhat difficult during snow season, but it can be reasonable during dry winters. The upper portions of these roads tend to be hard to drive, with drifts blocking the last couple of miles.

Hunts Lake

Highlights: *A long hike to a high scenic lake with access to Hunts Peak.*

Type of hike: Long out-and-back day hike or two- to three-day backpack.
Total distance: 18 miles.

Difficulty: Strenuous.
Best months: June to October.
Maps: USGS Wellsville quad.

Finding the trailhead: To access Hunts Lake Trail (1405) from the Bear Creek road, drive south on U.S. Highway 50 from its intersection with Colorado Highway 291 (Oak Street) at the east end of Salida. After 2.4 miles, turn right (south) onto Chaffee County Road 101/Fremont County Road 49, pass the forest boundary, and continue driving on Forest Road 101 to the Rainbow Trail access. The end of the road is rough and could require a four-wheel-drive vehicle.

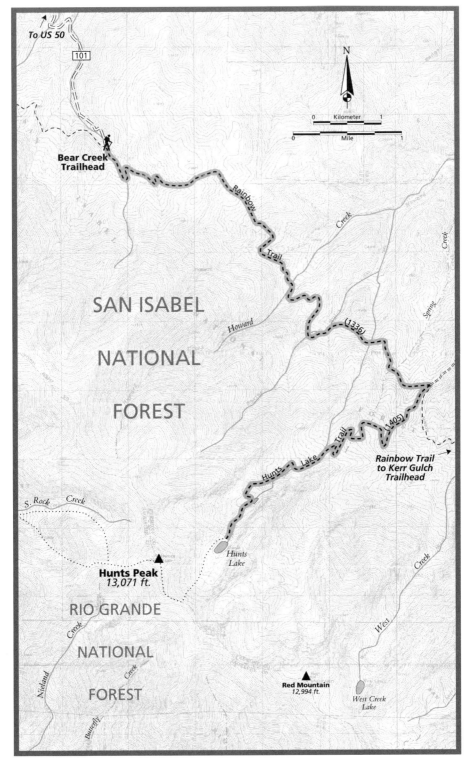

To US 50

101

N

0 Kilometer 1
0 Mile 1

Bear Creek
Trailhead

Rainbow

Creek

Trail

Creek

SAN ISABEL

Howard

(1336)

Spring

NATIONAL

FOREST

(1405)

Hunts Lake Trail

Rainbow Trail
to Kerr Gulch
Trailhead

S. Rock Creek

Hunts
Lake

Hunts Peak
13,071 ft.

Creek

RIO GRANDE

Creek

West

NATIONAL

Nieland

Creek

Red Mountain
12,994 ft.

West Creek
Lake

FOREST

Butterfly

Hunts Lake Trail (January).

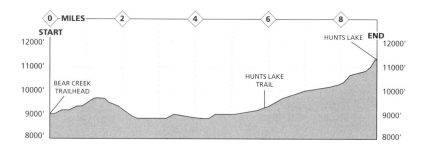

Key points:

0.0 Bear Creek Trailhead.

6.0 Hunts Lake Trail (1405); turn right.

8.0 Creek crossing.

9.0 Hunts Lake.

The hike: From the Bear Creek Trailhead hike southeast and begin climbing steeply over the next mile before descending again to Howard Creek and across several smaller creeks. The trail passes through private land and camping is not available through this short section. The trail becomes more gentle while still dipping to small creeks and climbing back out until it reaches Hunts Lake Trail on the right at about 6.0 miles. Just before you reach an obvious switchback in the Rainbow Trail look for an old road leading to private property on the left. Just opposite is the Hunts Lake Trail. A sign here indicates the continuation of the Rainbow Trail to Stout Creek to the south and Bear Creek to the north. The first two or three miles of the Hunts Lake Trail are gentle and follow a narrow jeep road often surrounded by aspens. At 8.0 miles, cross over to the north side of the creek and continue up the trail, which becomes steeper and rockier. Cross a flat meadow and hike up the final steep climb into the upper valley. Camping around the lake is limited, but there are some good sites below the lake.

Options: To climb to the summit of Hunts Peak, hike around the right (north) side of the lake and continue southwest up the valley toward the low point on the ridge just left (south) of Hunts Peak. Hike up grassy slopes to the ridge and climb up to the summit. The panoramic views from the top are well worth the effort.

Hunts Lake Trail can also be reached by hiking 7.0 miles north on the Rainbow Trail from the Kerr Gulch Trailhead (see Hike 4).

Snow season: This valley is a place of great solitude during snow season. The approach along the Rainbow Trail usually has only a light snow cover, but the trail to the lake will most likely require snowshoes.

4

Stout Creek

Highlights: *A steep trail to two large lakes above the tree line.*

Type of hike: Out-and-back day hike or overnight backpack.
Total distance: 7.6 miles.
Difficulty: Strenuous.

Best months: June to September.
Maps: USGS Bushnell Peak, Coaldale, and Howard quads.

Finding the trailhead: From Salida, drive southeast for 15.5 miles on U.S. Highway 50 and turn right (west) onto Kerr Gulch Road (County Road 101-A). From Canon City, drive 36 miles northwest on US 50, 12 miles past Cotopaxi, and turn left (west) on Kerr Gulch Road.

The dirt road winds past an old quarry, a mine site, and several smaller side roads. After 2.5 miles, pass through a gate, and continue to the top of a prominent ridge. At the top of the steep climb, a side road turns sharply to the left; stay right and continue straight for another 1.5 miles along the tree-lined road. Cross a small creek before climbing west up into a broad open meadow. In good conditions most cars can reach this point at the Forest Service bulletin board.

Parking and trailhead facilities: The trailhead has a large open area for parking.

Key points:

0.0	Kerr Gulch Trailhead.
0.5	Rainbow Trail (1336); turn left.
0.6	Stout Creek Trail (1403); turn right.
1.6	Creek crossing.
3.2	Falls.
3.8	Lower Stout Creek Lake.

The hike: From the parking area, hike up the road to the west until it joins the Rainbow Trail (1336). You might not find a sign at this first intersection, but turn left (south) and follow the four-wheel-drive road 0.1 mile to the Stout Creek Trail (1403). Turn right (west) and hike along a moderate climb through aspen and fir before a short descent to the creek crossing. Follow the trail as it climbs more steeply along the creek before turning up to the right above the creek.

Traverse to the left and back to the creek at a series of small falls that drop from a meadow containing a small pool at the tree line. Continue up to the right of the creek (north) as the trail runs high above the meadow then traverses back left (south)

41

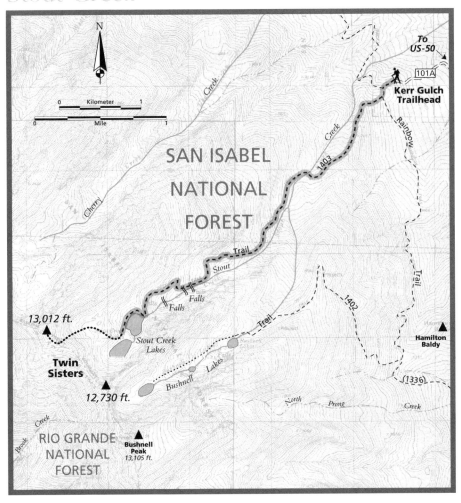

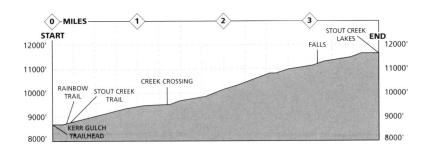

Stout Creek Lake (May).

toward the lake outlet above. The lake is impressive, surrounded by high peaks and a jagged ridgeline. Camping is limited and exposed above the upper meadow and is therefore not recommended. The best camping can be found in the meadows below the lake, while additional sites can be found near the lower creek crossing.

Options: Continue around the right (north) side of the lake to the upper bench and upper lake. Hiking right of the upper lake up gentle slopes to the west leads to the crest of the range and the northern summit of Twin Sisters at 13,012 feet.

Snow season: The last 2 miles of road access can be difficult with deeper snow cover, but it is possible to reach the trailhead with a four-wheel-drive vehicle. The trail is a very good but strenuous hike with snowshoes.

5

Bushnell Lakes

Highlights: *A steep trail to a series of high lakes in a narrow valley.*

Type of hike: Out-and-back day hike or overnight backpack.
Total distance: 10.4 miles.
Difficulty: Strenuous.

Best months: April to December.
Maps: USGS Bushnell Peak and Coaldale quads.

Finding the trailhead: From Salida, drive southeast on U.S. Highway 50 for 20 miles to Coaldale. Turn right (southwest) on County Road 6 and drive 5 miles, past Coaldale Campground, to the parking area on the left (south) about a quarter mile before Hayden Creek Campground.

Parking and trailhead facilities: Just past the small parking area is the Hayden Creek Campground, with a rest room, drinking water during the summer months, and a year-round self-service fee station.

Key points:
0.0 Hayden Creek Trailhead.
1.0 Creek crossings.
2.5 Bushnell Lakes Trail (1402); turn left.
3.6 Ridge crossing.
4.6 Lower Bushnell Lake.
5.2 Upper Bushnell Lake.

The hike: From the roadside parking area cross the road and hike north to find the Rainbow Trail where a small sign indicates the beginning of the trail. If starting at Hayden Creek Campground, start hiking north from the entrance of the campground on the Rainbow Trail (1336) as it climbs easily through willows and open forest. The forest grows dense as the trail crosses several small creeks. The ascent becomes steeper where the valley narrows as you approach the ridge above. At the top of the ridge, turn left (west) onto the Bushnell Lakes Trail (1402) and climb abruptly up steep switchbacks and across a long traverse north through aspens and fir. Just before a small open prospect pit, the trail turns sharply left and climbs up to a gentle trail along the top of the ridge, providing views of the upper valley and the peaks above. Hike the gentle traverse along the left (south) side of the valley on a good trail across talus slopes, before the last steep section below the lake. A limited number of small campsites is available along the upper valley.

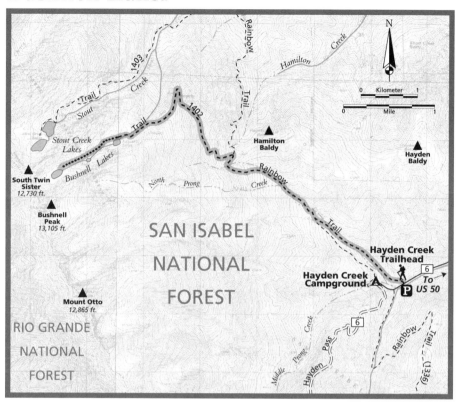

Options: Hike around the right (north) side of the lake and follow a thin trail to continue to the upper lakes. Pass near a couple well-used campsites and stay right of the creek through open meadows before reaching the middle lakes. Continue along the north side of the valley to reach the upper lake.

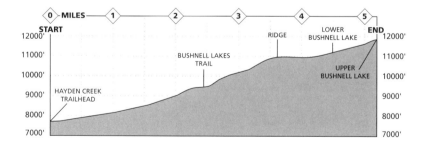

Lower Bushnell Lake.

Snow season: Access to the Rainbow Trail (1336) below the Hayden Creek Campground is usually good year-round, making this an attractive winter hike. The Rainbow Trail can be fairly easy to hike, although some of the more heavily treed areas could hold enough snow to require snowshoes or skis. The trail to the lakes can be strenuous but enjoyable with snowshoes up to the ridge and all the way to the lakes.

6

Galena Peak

Highlights: *An off-trail ridge-top climb to a high peak.*

Type of hike: Out-and-back day hike.
Total distance: 7.0 miles.
Difficulty: Moderate.

Best months: June to September.
Maps: USGS Coaldale and Bushnell Peak quads.

Special considerations: This is not a maintained trail and is not recognized by the Forest Service. The route is fairly short, but the ridge above the tree line is exposed to wind and weather. The hike all the way to Mount Otto should be done early in the day to avoid inclement weather.

Finding the trailhead: From Poncha Springs drive 22 miles south on U.S. Highway 285 to Villa Grove and turn left (east) on County Road LL57. From Alamosa, drive 54 miles north on US 17, past the intersection with US 285, and turn right (east) on CR LL57. Just north of the gas station in Villa Grove, CR LL57 turns east and curves left at a ranch entrance, then continues straight on a good dirt road. At the national forest boundary, the road becomes Forest Road 970; it is rougher and could be muddy and rutted. Most cars can continue to a point where the road turns sharply left (east) and becomes steep and rough. This last 2.5-mile steep section up to Hayden Pass usually requires high clearance and four-wheel drive.

The pass can also be reached on the east side through Coaldale, from Hayden Creek Campground (see Hike 5). From the campground entrance, turn left (south) onto the Hayden Pass Road (6.4) and drive 4.5 miles up to the pass. There are a couple of places to park along the road before reaching a section or two of rough road that requires four-wheel drive.

Parking and trailhead facilities: Only limited parking exists below Hayden Pass. The turnaround at the top of the pass provides a few spaces. Camping is possible here at a few well-used sites along the ridge.

Key points:
0.0 Hayden Pass.
0.8 Shoulder.
1.2 Point 11,870.
1.8 Galena Peak.
3.5 Mount Otto.

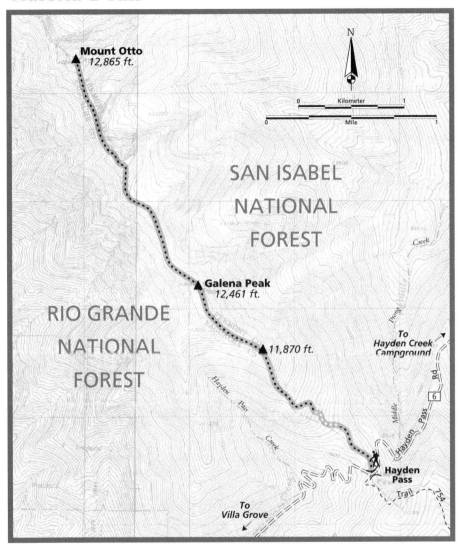

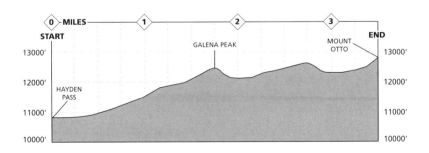

The hike: From Hayden Pass, hike north along a closed road that quickly becomes a trail through aspens and fir. The trail winds up to an open shoulder with views over the San Luis Valley and south along the crest of the range. Climb along the left of the rocky and exposed ridge up to Point 11,870. Continue north along the ridge on easier grassy slopes to the summit of Galena Peak. For a shorter hike (3.6 miles), turn around here and retrace the route to Hayden Pass. If the weather permits, continue to hike north along the crest of the tundra-covered ridge then over a false summit and on to Mount Otto.

Options: With a car shuttle, a longer ridge traverse is possible by backpacking two very long days or three moderate days to the access described in the Simmons Peak Trail (Hike 2) at the northern end of the range. Continue north from the summit of Mount Otto along the ridge crest as it stays above 12,000 feet. You will summit several prominent peaks including Bushnell Peak, Twin Sisters, Red Mountain, and Hunts Peak. This route is very exposed to severe weather and lacks water. You must be very well acclimatized and skilled in navigation, even though it follows the obvious ridge crest. From Hunts Peak descend west on the optional route described in

Galena Peak (January).

49

Hike 2 to reach South Rock Creek Trailhead. It is also possible to descend east from the range crest on the Stout Creek Trail (Hike 4).

Snow season: Galena Peak can be a worthy winter goal. The trail access is at the snow closures of the four-wheel-drive roads on either side of the range. From the lower winter access on the west side, the climb can be done in one day. From Hayden Creek Campground, the hike is usually done as a two- or three-day backpack trip.

7

Nipple Mountain

Highlights: *An easy ridge walk to a summit above the tree line, with access to Black Canyon Trail (Hike 37).*

Type of hike: Out-and-back day hike or overnight backpack.
Total distance: 9.0 miles.

Difficulty: Moderate.
Best months: June to September.
Maps: USGS Coaldale quad.

Finding the trailhead: From Poncha Springs, drive 22 miles south on U.S. Highway 285 to Villa Grove and turn left (east) on County Road LL57. From Alamosa, drive 54 miles north on US 17, past the intersection with US 285, and turn right (east) on CR LL57.

Just north of the gas station in Villa Grove, CR LL57 turns east and curves left at a ranch entrance, then continues straight on a good dirt road. At the national forest boundary, the road becomes Forest Road 970; it is rougher and could be muddy and rutted. Most cars can continue to a point where the road turns sharply left (east) and becomes steep and rough. This last 2.5-mile steep section up to Hayden Pass usually requires high clearance and four-wheel drive.

The pass can also be reached on the east side through Coaldale, from Hayden Creek Campground (see Hike 5). From the campground entrance, turn left (south) onto the Hayden Pass Road (6.4) and drive 4.5 miles up to the pass. There are a couple of places to park along the road before reaching a section or two of rough roach that requires four-wheel drive.

Parking and trailhead facilities: Only limited parking exists below Hayden Pass. The turnaround at the top of the pass provides a few spaces. Camping is possible here at a few well-used sites along the ridge.

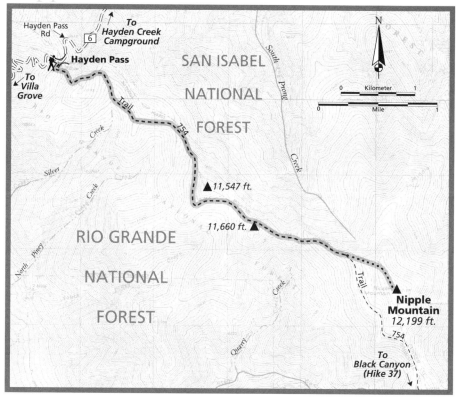

Key points:

0.0   Hayden Pass.
2.5   Point 11,547.
3.0   Point 11,660.
4.5   Nipple Mountain.

The hike: From the top of Hayden Pass, hike south through the trees and up to the base of the steep switchbacks and the hardest part of the trail (754). Once on the ridge, hike the trail as it descends through the trees to the right of the broad ridgeline and along a gentle climb back up to the crest of the range. Hike up the grassy slopes around the right (west) side of Point 11,547, an obvious high point along the ridge. Briefly descend again, then climb to Point 11,660. Hike down along the tundra then up again into trees where the trail becomes harder to find.

Stay to the right of the ridge and find the trail as it traverses around Nipple Mountain, or stay on the ridge to climb to the summit. Downed timber could block portions of the trail before tundra leads you up the slopes to the false summit and then on to the true summit of Nipple Mountain. Views from the top are dominated to the south by Cottonwood Peak, out west over the upper San Luis Valley, and

Nipple Mountain Trail.

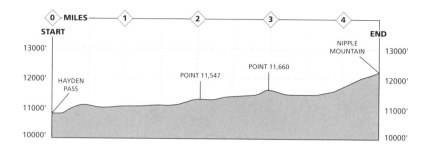

north over the northern section of the range, the Arkansas Valley, and the peaks of the Sawatch Mountains.

There are several good places to camp along the ridge, but you must carry all your water if backpacking during the spring and summer months, after the snowmelt.

Options: With a car shuttle, you can continue south another 2 miles to Point 12,503, and then down to the Black Canyon Trail (Hike 37) for a moderate two-day backpack trip or a strenuous 12-mile day hike.

Snow season: Snow season access is from either Hayden Creek Campground on the east or the Hayden Road snow closure on the west. Skis or snowshoes are required to go up the road and the lower trail. Parts of the ridge and treeless slopes remain windswept all season.

8

Big Cottonwood Creek

Highlights: *A rarely visited high basin with access to Nipple Mountain and Cottonwood Peak.*

Type of hike: Out-and-back day hike or overnight backpack.
Total distance: 10.0 miles.

Difficulty: Strenuous.
Best months: June to October.
Maps: Coaldale.

Special considerations: This unmaintained trail is not recognized by the Forest Service. It requires route-finding skills and some difficult bushwhacking along its upper reaches.

Finding the trailhead: From Salida, drive southeast 19 miles on U.S. Highway 50 past Coaldale. Turn right (south) onto County Road 40 (Big Cottonwood Road). From Canon City, drive 39 miles west on US 50, past Cotapaxi, to CR 40; turn left (south). Follow this road for approximately 3 miles to the Wolf Creek Trailhead.

Parking and trailhead facilities: A small parking area and turnaround are at the trailhead.

Key points:
- **0.0** Wolf Creek Trailhead.
- **3.0** Bushwhacking.
- **5.0** Upper Basin.

The hike: Stay to the right of the creek as the closed road runs up the valley and eventually becomes a thinner and harder-to-follow trail. Cross the creek as required at several locations, hiking along the forested trail as it becomes steeper

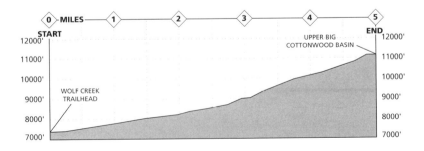

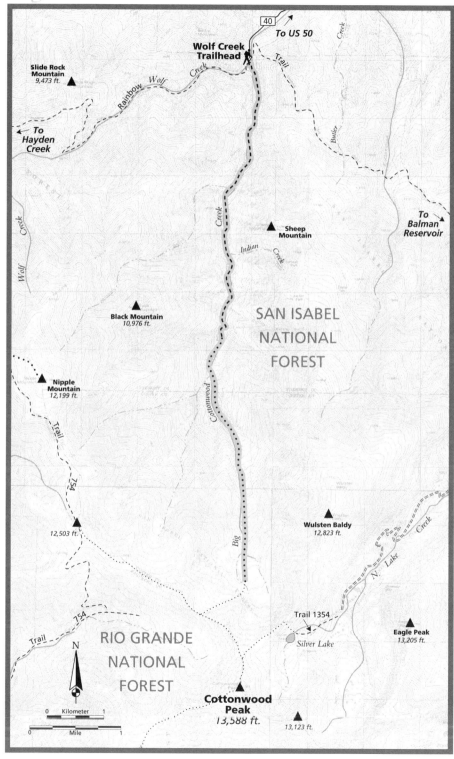

To US 50

40

Wolf Creek
Trailhead

Trail

Slide Rock
Mountain
9,473 ft.

Rainbow   Wolf   Creek

To
Hayden
Creek

Butler

Creek

Creek

To
Balman
Reservoir

Wolf   Creek

Sheep
Mountain

Indian   Creek

SAN ISABEL

NATIONAL

FOREST

Black Mountain
10,976 ft.

Nipple
Mountain
12,199 ft.

Cottonwood

Trail

754

12,503 ft.

Big

Wulsten Baldy
12,823 ft.

N. Lake   Creek

Trail 1354

754

Trail

N

RIO GRANDE

NATIONAL

FOREST

Silver Lake

Eagle Peak
13,205 ft.

Cottonwood
Peak
13,588 ft.

13,123 ft.

0   Kilometer   1

0   Mile   1

Near Big Cottonwood Creek.

and rougher after 3 miles. Some bushwhacking is necessary up to the upper reaches of the basin at around 10,000 feet, where you will find some good camping.

Options: From the upper basin, it is possible to ascend to the crest of the range and hike north to the summit of Nipple Mountain. Hike grassy slopes to the west of the upper Big Cottonwood basin along a climbing traverse toward the low point on the ridge south of Nipple Mountain. Turn right and hike north over tundra-covered slopes to the summit. From the summit of Nipple Mountain, you can continue hiking north on the Nipple Mountain Trail (Hike 7) or south to the Black Canyon Trail (Hike 37).

Turning left (south) from the top of the ridge above Big Cottonwood, you can follow the crest of the range toward Cottonwood Peak. The ridge becomes rocky, and a bit of scrambling is required before the final push to the summit. From Cottonwood Peak, it is possible to continue along its east ridge to connect with the Cloverdale Basin (Hike 10), along the west ridge to Hot Springs Canyon (Hike 38), or south to Garner Creek (Hike 39).

These are all long car shuttles that cover long distances over steep terrain, with longer exposures to potential severe weather.

Snow Season: The trailhead is usually accessible throughout the year, and the hike up the valley can be a good snowshoe.

Central
SANGRE DE CRISTO,
EAST SIDE

Few sights are more impressive than the view from the Wet Mountain Valley of this 30-mile stretch of mountains. The crest of the range, from Cottonwood Peak in the north to Marble Mountain in the south, forms a continuous ridgeline that never drops below 12,500 feet. With twenty-five summits over 13,000 feet and at least eighteen steep stream-filled valleys, this is as complex a mountainous area as anywhere in the Rocky Mountain region.

At 7,800 feet, the coupled towns of Westcliffe and Silver Cliff form a fortunate community of fewer than 1,000 people. The modest town of ranchers and farmers provides several affordable motels as well as a selection of bed-and-breakfasts, inns, lodges, and guest ranches in the area. Camping and outdoor gear is hard to come by, and nightlife even harder, but the town is pleasant and the setting inspiring. Nearby Lake Deweese makes a good rest day or alternate destination when the weather in the high country is nasty.

Mission: Wolf, a wolf sanctuary in Gardner, is also an interesting feature of the valley, with almost fifty captive bred wolves and wolf-dog hybrids. The experience of seeing these natives in their home territory inspires hope for their reintroduction into the wild. With the added attractions of fishing, hunting, horse and llama packing, and some of the best alpine mountaineering opportunities in Colorado, the Wet Mountain Valley is a uniquely valuable part of the region.

From Westcliffe, Colorado Highway 69 travels south to South Colony Creek, Medano Pass, and the Huerfano Valley, and on to Walsenberg and Interstate 25. Driving north from Westcliffe, CO 69 leads to Texas Creek and US Highway 50, then west to Salida or east to Canon City. Exploring the county roads in the Wet Mountain Valley is an enjoyable way to learn about the area, both past and present. If you are fortunate enough to spend time in the valley, I hope you find it as beautiful and friendly as I have.

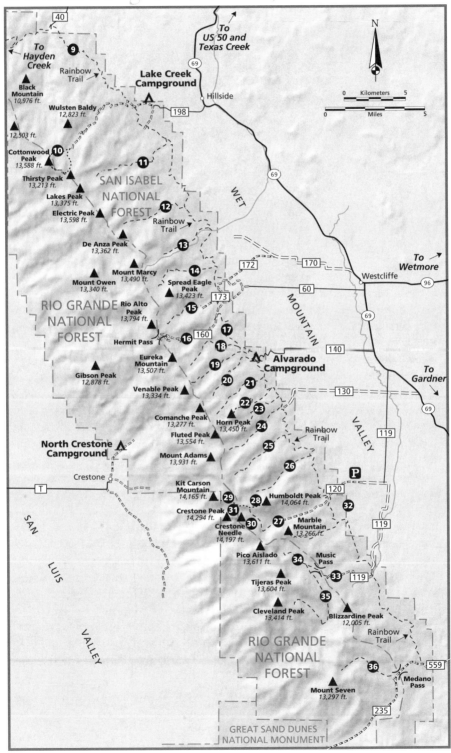

N

To
US 50 and
Texas Creek

To
Hayden
Creek

Rainbow
Trail

⑨

69

**Lake Creek
Campground**

Hillside

198

Kilometers 5

Miles 5

Black
Mountain
10,976 ft.

Wulsten Baldy
12,823 ft.

12,503 ft.

Cottonwood
Peak
13,588 ft.

⑩

⑪

Thirsty Peak
13,213 ft.

Lakes Peak
13,375 ft.

Electric Peak
13,598 ft.

**SAN ISABEL
NATIONAL
FOREST**

⑫

Rainbow
Trail

WET

69

De Anza Peak
13,362 ft.

⑬

Mount Marcy
13,490 ft.

⑭

172

170

**To
Wetmore**

Mount Owen
13,340 ft.

Spread Eagle
Peak
13,423 ft.

173

60

Westcliffe

96

**RIO GRANDE
NATIONAL
FOREST**

Rio Alto
Peak
13,794 ft.

⑮

⑯

160

⑰

69

Hermit Pass

⑱

140

Eureka
Mountain
13,507 ft.

⑲

**Alvarado
Campground**

MOUNTAIN

**To
Gardner**

Gibson Peak
12,878 ft.

Venable Peak
13,334 ft.

⑳

㉑

130

㉒

㉓

VALLEY

Comanche Peak
13,277 ft.

Horn Peak
13,450 ft.

㉔

119

Fluted Peak
13,554 ft.

㉕

Rainbow
Trail

**North Crestone
Campground**

Mount Adams
13,931 ft.

㉖

Crestone

T

P

Kit Carson
Mountain
14,165 ft.

㉙

㉘

Humboldt Peak
14,064 ft.

120

㉜

SAN

㉛

Crestone Peak
14,294 ft.

㉚

㉗

Marble
Mountain
13,266 ft.

119

Crestone
Needle
14,197 ft.

LUIS

Pico Aislado
13,611 ft.

㉞

Music
Pass

Tijeras Peak
13,604 ft.

㉝

119

VALLEY

㉟

Cleveland Peak
13,414 ft.

Blizzardine Peak
12,005 ft.

Rainbow
Trail

**RIO GRANDE
NATIONAL
FOREST**

559

㊱

Medano
Pass

Mount Seven
13,297 ft.

235

**GREAT SAND DUNES
NATIONAL MONUMENT**

9

Rainbow Trail
Hayden Creek to Hermit Pass Road

Highlights: *A long but gentle trail with views of the Wet Mountain Valley.*

Type of hike: Out-and-back day hike, overnight backpack, or three- to five-day shuttle.
Total distance: 34 miles, with three intermediate points of access.
Difficulty: Easy to moderate, depending on length.

Best months: Spring and fall are both good to avoid summer heat and afternoon thunderstorms; fall offers the possibility of good weather and turning leaves.
Maps: USGS Coaldale, Cotapaxi, Electric Peak, and Beckwith Mountain quads.

Special considerations: The Rainbow Trail can be heavily used at times and is occasionally frequented by horse and llama trekkers as well as motorcycles, although I have never encountered any during my time in the area.

Finding the trailhead: To reach the Hayden Creek Trailhead, drive southeast from Salida on U.S. Highway 50 for 20 miles to Coaldale. Turn right (southwest) on County Road 6 and drive 5 miles, past Coaldale Campground, to the parking area on the left (south) about a quarter mile before Hayden Creek Campground.

To reach the trailhead at Hermit Pass Road from the intersection of Colorado Highways 69 and 96 in Westcliffe, drive south 0.3 mile on CO 69 and turn right (west) onto Hermit Road (160). After approximately 6 miles, the road turns sharply to the right then back to the left. At this point the road gets rougher as it climbs for another 2.0 miles to the intersection with the Rainbow Trail (1336) on the right (north).

See the descriptions of Big Cottonwood Creek (Hike 8), North Brush Creek (Hike 11), and Lakes of the Clouds (Hike 14) for directions to the other access points.

Parking and trailhead facilities: The Hayden Creek Campground is about a quarter mile past the small parking area at the northern trailhead. It has a rest room, drinking water during the summer months, and a year-round self-service fee station. There are small parking areas provided at the Duckett Creek Trail, Gibson Creek Trailhead, and parking and roadside camping available at the Hermit Pass Road.

Key points:
0.0 Hayden Creek Trailhead.
9.0 Big Cottonwood Trailhead access (CR 40).
16.5 Balman Reservoir Road.
18.0 Duckett Creek Trailhead access (Forest Road 337).

Rainbow Trail

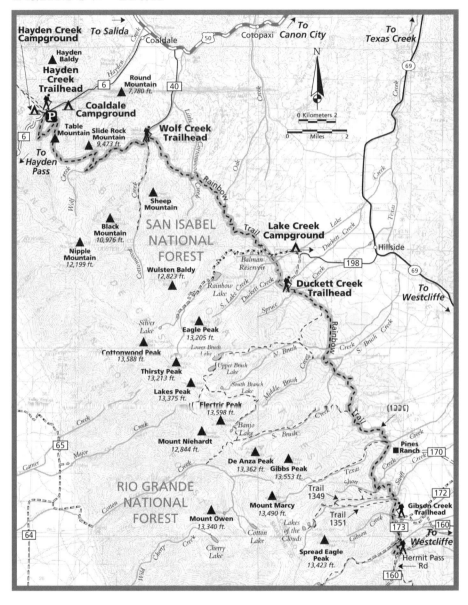

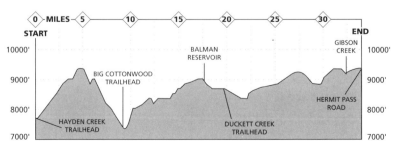

19.0	North Brush Creek Trail (1356).
24.0	South Brush Creek Trail (1355).
27.0	Texas Creek Trail.
30.0	Lakes of the Clouds Trail (1349).
31.0	Gibson Creek Trailhead access (CR 172).
32.0	North Taylor Creek access (FR 173).
34.0	Hermit Pass Road (FR 160).

The hike: From Hayden Creek Campground, hike south up this infrequently used section of the Rainbow Trail (1336) over the high point near Slide Rock Mountain. Descend past Big Cottonwood Creek and continue south before climbing up again to the intersection with the Balman Reservoir four-wheel-drive road. Hike southeast down the road for almost 0.5 mile and turn right to continue south on the Rainbow Trail.

Hike down the trail for 1.2 miles to the Duckett Creek Trailhead. Continue hiking south for 1.0 mile before reaching the North Brush Creek Trail on the right (west).

From here it is 6.0 miles to the South Brush Creek Trail, then another 3.0 miles south to the Texas Creek Trail. The trail climbs up steadily to the Lakes of the Clouds Trail before dropping down to and passing the Gibson Creek Trailhead access. The North Taylor Creek Road access is reached at mile 32 and finally the Hermit Pass Road. If continuing south hike right (west) up the road to the intersection of the Rainbow Trail (Hike 17) where it heads left (south).

Camping is available along the trail and water is usually plentiful over its entire length. The National Forest Lake Creek Campground is located just east down the Balman Reservoir Road at mile 16.5. There are some local outfitters out of Westcliffe that will provide support along the trail from the points of road access for a fee.

Options: Any portion of the Rainbow Trail can be combined with day hikes along any of the intersecting trails. The South Brush Creek Trail (Hike 12) may be the most rarely visited of those along this section. See Hikes 1 and 17 for the northern and southern portions of the 90-mile Rainbow Trail.

Snow season: This can be an enjoyable hike during snow season. Access at Hayden Creek Campground, Big Cottonwood Creek, and Gibson Creek are the most reliable; Duckett Creek and Cloverdale Basin could also be accessible depending on snow conditions. The trail is rarely entirely covered with snow, and only portions of it may require skis or snowshoes.

10

Cloverdale Basin

Highlights: *A four-wheel-drive road to two high basins and access to Cottonwood Peak, Thirsty Peak, and Garner Creek Trail (Hike 39).*

Type of hike: Loop day hike.
Total distance: 6.0 miles.
Difficulty: Moderate.

Best months: July to September.
Maps: USGS Electric Peak quad.

Finding the trailhead: From the town of Texas Creek on U.S. Highway 50, drive south 11 miles on Colorado Highway 69 to the small town of Hillside. Continue 0.2 mile south and turn right (west) onto Custer County Road 198, which is usually signed for the Lake Creek Campground. From Westcliffe, drive north on CO 69 for 13 miles and turn left (west) onto CR 198.

Follow the dirt road 3 miles, passing the Lake Creek Campground and the Rainbow Trail Lutheran Camp. A small parking area is located below the camp entrance at the national forest boundary where Balman Reservoir road (Forest Road 198) becomes much more rocky and rough, requiring four-wheel drive and high clearance. Continue past the Balman Reservoir, 2.5 miles from the forest boundary, and on to Rainbow Lake (reservoir) at 5 miles. The road becomes rougher below the Cloverdale Mine property, and ends approximately 7 miles from the Lutheran Camp.

Parking and trailhead facilities: There are several places to camp and park along the Balman Reservoir four-wheel-drive road up to the Cloverdale Basin. Do not camp or park on the private property near the Cloverdale Mine.

Key points:
0.0 Silver Lake Trailhead.
2.0 Garner Pass.
2.2 Unnamed 13,123.
3.0 Cottonwood Peak.
5.5 Silver Lake.
6.0 Silver Lake Trailhead.

The hike: From the end of the four-wheel drive road there are two trails. The easier, more obvious trail (1354) follows an old road on the north side of the basin for 0.5 mile to Silver Lake northwest of Cottonwood Peak. The other trail (752) leads first southwest then south up into the valley north of Thirsty Peak and beyond to Garner Pass. The loop continues via the ridge crest over the summits of Unnamed

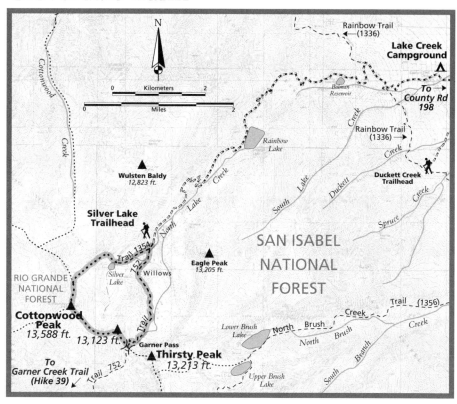

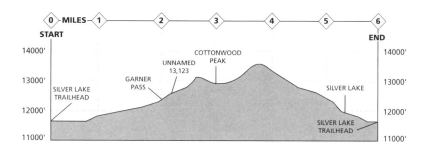

13,123 and Cottonwood Peak, then descends to Silver Lake and returns to the trailhead on Trail 1354.

To hike the entire loop in a clockwise direction, start by taking Trail 752 to the left of the old road that leads to Silver Lake. Follow the northern edge of the willows to the right of the creek and marshes. Skirt these wetlands on the higher ground to the north, where you might find evidence of the trail. Continue southwest until you reach the talus slopes on the lower edge of Unnamed 13,123's northeast face.

Thirsty Peak from Cloverdale Basin Trail.

Turn left (southeast), skirt to the right past the willows and the creek, then climb up the slopes leading into the upper valley. Eagle Peak can now be seen behind you and to the left (northeast), Thirsty Peak remains directly ahead (south), and Unnamed 13,123 is above you to the right (northwest). Hike south across the expansive valley floor, where an intermittent trail stays to the right (north) of the lower marshes and begins to switchback up the slopes. The trail leads southwest to Garner Pass, which can be seen as the low point on the crest of the range between Thirsty Peak and Unnamed 13,123.

From Garner Pass, a trail goes left (southeast) and climbs 0.5 mile to the summit of Thirsty Peak. Turn right (northwest) and climb to the summit of 13,123. Descend along the ridge over rocky ground to the saddle, then climb steeply to the summit of Cottonwood Peak. The views from the summit lead north along the crest of the range to the Arkansas River Valley, the Wet Mountain Valley to the east, San Luis Valley to the west, and extend south 20 miles to Kit Carson Mountain.

To continue the loop, descend north from Cottonwood Peak to the broad connecting ridge between Cottonwood Peak and Wulsten Baldy. Follow this broad ridge northeast to the saddle above Silver Lake and then descend south over steep grassy slopes to the lake. On the southeast side of the lake, rejoin the trail, which follows the old road and descends 0.5 mile to the trailhead.

Options: The climb of Wulsten Baldy can be added to the loop or hiked as a separate climb. It is also possible to descend from Garner Pass west to Garner Creek (Hike 39). A very ambitious hike continues from Garner Pass south over Thirsty Peak and Lakes Peak to either North Brush Creek (Hike 11) or Major Creek (Hike 40).

Snow season: After snow closes off access, the four-wheel-drive road becomes a much more attractive hike, snowshoe, and/or ski, although you may occasionally share it with snow machines. Take care to avoid private mine property near the upper basin and avoid possible avalanche terrain on the slopes above the upper basins during periods of high danger. With a four-wheel-drive vehicle, it may be possible to drive far up the road even into October and November.

11

North Brush Creek

Highlights: *A popular trail to two large lakes, with access to Thirsty Peak, Lakes Peak, and Eagle Peak.*

Type of hike: Two- to three-day out-and-back backpack.
Total distance: 13.0 miles.

Difficulty: Strenuous.
Best months: June to September.
Maps: USGS Electric Peak quad.

Finding the trailhead: From the town of Texas Creek on U.S. Highway 50, drive south 11 miles on Colorado Highway 69 to the small town of Hillside. Continue 0.2 mile south and turn right (west) onto County Road 198, which is usually signed for the Lake Creek Campground. From Westcliffe, drive north on CO 69 for 13 miles and turn left (west) onto CR 198.

Follow the dirt road 3 miles, passing the Lake Creek Campground and turning left on Forest Road 337 at the fork in the road. Continue up the road for 1.5 miles to access the Rainbow Trail at the Duckett Creek Trailhead.

With a high-clearance vehicle (sometimes a four-wheel-drive vehicle is required) you can follow the rough road to the North Brush Creek Lakes Trailhead. To do so, continue southwest past the Duckett Creek Trailhead and follow the road as it turns left (southeast) and winds about 2.0 miles through forest and scrub on 337. Stay on FR 337 as it turns sharply left (northeast) past several smaller side roads then across an unsigned intersection with the Rainbow Trail before turning right (southeast) then right again (southwest) to the corral-like North Brush Creek Trailhead.

Parking and trailhead facilities: Limited parking and camping are available near the Duckett Creek Trailhead and at Lake Creek Campground, which is open during the summer season.

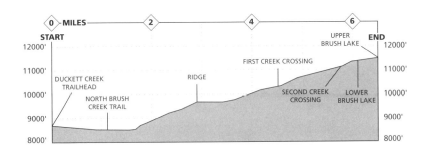

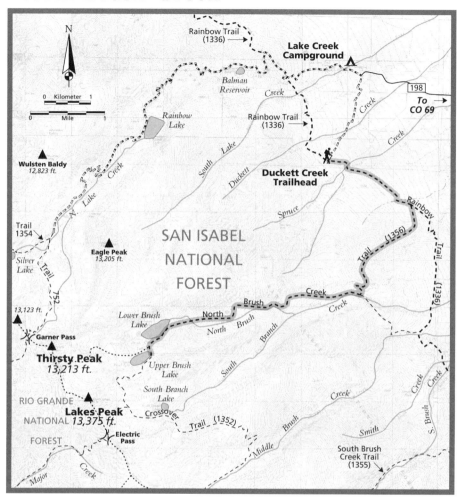

Key points:

0.0 Duckett Creek Trailhead.
1.0 North Brush Creek Trail (1356); turn right.
2.5 Ridge.
4.2 Spur trail.
5.5 Second creek crossing.
6.0 Lower Brush Lake.
6.5 Upper Brush Lake.

The hike: From the Duckett Creek Trailhead hike south for 1.0 mile on the Rainbow Trail (1336) to the North Brush Creek Trail (1356) and turn right (west). Climb south following the steep trail up forested slopes to a prominent ridge north of the North Brush Creek valley. Hike west down the trail into the valley and continue up to the first creek crossings. Across to the left (south) side of the creek is a thin spur trail that heads left (south) and leads up to South Branch Creek, stay on the trail to the right. Follow the main trail west into the upper valley. At 5.5 miles cross to the left (south) side of the creek and hike up several switchbacks before you reach the lower lake. Continue around the left side of the lake west then south up to the upper lake. There are heavily used camping sites around the lower lake; the upper lake remains more pristine.

Options: From the south side of the upper lake, continue up Lakes Peak's east ridge and down a very thin trail south to South Branch Lake and beyond to Middle Brush Creek and Banjo Lake via the Crossover Trail (1352). From here you can hike to Electric Peak, the Cotton Creek Trail (Hike 41), or over a very thin crossover trail south to South Brush Creek (Hike 12).

To climb Thirsty Peak from the Brush Creek Lakes, continue up the valley to the north side of the upper lake, and then right (north) into the upper basin along a seasonal creek. From the crest of the range, turn right (north) along the ridge to the summit of Thirsty Peak. Turn left (south) from the crest of the range to hike to the summit of Lakes Peak.

Hiking directly north of the lakes to the ridge east of Thirsty Peak accesses the ridge leading north to Eagle Peak.

Snow season: Access to the Duckett Creek Trailhead could be difficult for the last mile due to deep snow. The longer distance involved with this hike makes it more difficult during snow season.

South Brush Creek

Highlights: *An infrequently used trail with access to Electric Peak, De Anza Peak, and the Cotton Creek Trail (Hike 41).*

Type of hike: Two- to three-day out-and-back backpack.
Total distance: 20.0 miles.

Difficulty: Strenuous.
Best months: July to September.
Maps: USGS Electric Peak quad.

Finding the trailhead: From the town of Texas Creek on U.S. Highway 50, drive south 11 miles on Colorado Highway 69 to the small town of hillside. Continue 0.2 mile south and turn right (west) onto county Road 198, which is usually signed for the Lake Creek Campground. From Westcliffe, drive north on CO 69 for 13 miles and turn left (west) onto CR 198.

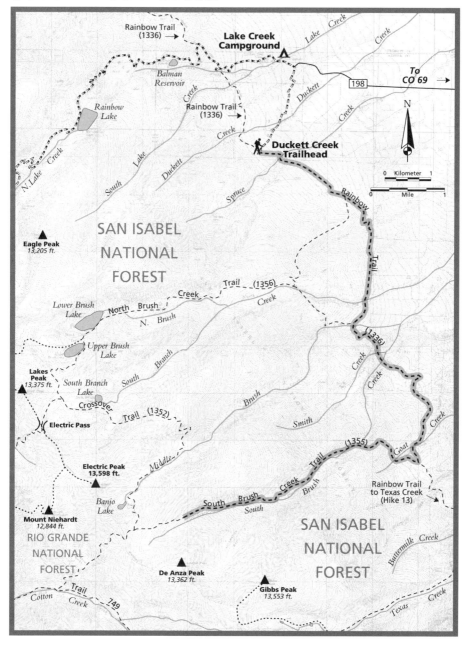

Follow dirt road 3 miles, passing the Lake Creek Campground and turning left on Forest Road 337 at the fork in the road. Continue up the road for 5 miles to access the Rainbow Trail a the Duckett Creek Trailhead. See Hike 11 for access to the North Brush Lakes trailhead.

As an alternate route, hike 8 miles north on the Rainbow Trail from the Gibson Creek Trailhead; see Lakes of the Clouds (Hike 14) for directions. Gibson Creek tends to be an easier approach for passenger cars.

Parking and trailhead facilities: Limited parking and camping are available near the Duckett Creek Trailhead and at Lake Creek Campground, which is open during the summer season.

Key points:
0.0 Duckett Creek Trailhead.
1.0 North Brush Creek Trail (1356).
4.0 South Brush Creek.
6.0 South Brush Creek Trail (1355); turn right.
7.0 Creek crossing.
10.0 Upper basin.

The hike: From the northern approach start at the Duckett Creek Trailhead and hike south on this gentle section of the Rainbow Trail as it descends past the North Brush Creek Trail at 1.0 mile. Continue hiking south, crossing several small creeks before reaching South Brush Creek at 4.0 miles. Hike another 2.0 miles south to the South Brush Creek Trail (1355) and turn right (west). From the southern access, climb steadily up the Rainbow Trail past the Lakes of the Clouds Trail. Follow the Rainbow Trail, dropping down past the Texas Creek Trail before climbing back up to the intersection with the South Brush Creek Trail; turn left.

Hike southwest on the South Brush Creek Trail, steadily climbing for 0.6 mile to the top of a low ridge before dropping into the South Brush Creek valley. Cross over to the right (north) side of the creek and follow the trail as it climbs up the valley and into the upper basin. There is good camping in the upper portion of the valley.

Options: From the upper basin, descend steeply to the northeast on a good trail to Banjo Lake and north over the intermittent Crossover Trail (1352) to South Branch Lake. From here you can continue over the ridge to the north before descending to the North Brush Lakes (Hike 11).

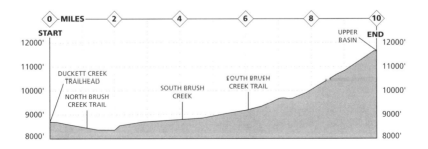

With a car shuttle, you can continue up the valley west to the crest of the range, then descend west on Trail 856 to Horsethief Basin and Cotton Creek (Hike 41). By hiking north along the crest of the range, you can climb to the summit of Electric Peak, and Mount Niedhardt.

Hiking south along the crest of the range brings you to the summit of De Anza Peak and on to Gibbs Peak. An ambitious loop would be to descend south from point 13,227 down Texas Creek (Hike 13) to the Rainbow Trail and the Gibson Creek Trailhead.

Snow season: This valley is very rarely visited during snow season because of its remote access relative to most trails in the area. It is therefore a good option for an ambitious trip away from any crowds.

13

Texas Creek

Highlights: *A lesser-traveled trail to a scenic upper basin and access to Mount Marcy and the Lakes of the Clouds (Hike 14).*

Type of hike: Long day hike or two-day out-and-back backpack.
Total distance: 13.0 miles.
Difficulty: Strenuous.

Best months: July to September.
Maps: USGS Electric Peak and Beckwith Mountain quads.

Special considerations: Outfitters and horse and llama trekkers use this trail in the summer and fall months. When wet, portions of the trail could be muddy and rutted.

Finding the trailhead: From the intersection of Colorado Highways 96 and 69 in Westcliffe, drive south on CO 69 for 0.3 mile and turn right (west) onto Hermit Road (County Road 160). After another 5.9 miles, the road curves to the north past ranches and residential drives to intersect with 172. At CR 172, turn left (west) and drive another 1.5 miles to the national forest boundary. The road becomes rougher and heavily rutted; most cars will have difficulty driving the last 0.2 mile to the trailhead.

Parking and trailhead facilities: There is a small parking area and turnaround at the Gibson Creek Trailhead. If it is necessary to park along the road before reaching the trailhead, please respect the adjacent private property.

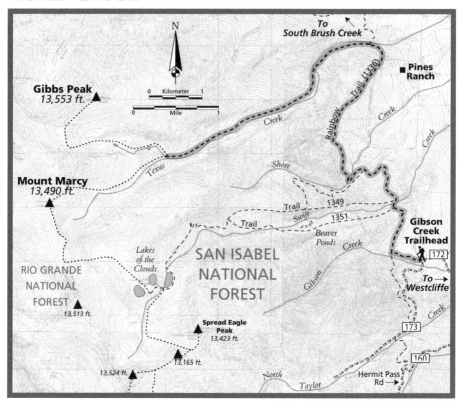

Key points:

- **0.0** Gibson Creek Trailhead.
- **0.6** Lakes of the Clouds Trail southern branch (1351).
- **1.5** Lakes of the Clouds Trail northern branch (1349).
- **3.5** Texas Creek Trail; turn left.
- **6.0** Creek fork.
- **6.5** Upper basins.

The hike: From the Gibson Creek Trailhead, hike north 3.5 miles along the Rainbow Trail (1336), climbing moderately past the Lakes of the Clouds Trail (1349) before descending to the Texas Creek Trail on the left. The turnoff might be unmarked but can be found climbing west from the Rainbow Trail near the Pines Ranch. Follow the trail as it climbs up the valley past some heavily used horse camps, after which the trail thins and continues up the valley. This trail stays right of the creek and winds up the right (north) side of the valley to a group of small lakes in a beautiful alpine basin and massive boulder fields near the tree line. Camping is best found here near the tree line.

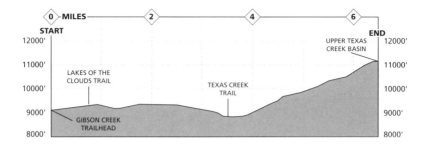

Options: To continue up the valley along the south fork of the creek stay left where the thin trail forks to the north and continue hiking west up into a seldom visited alpine meadow filled basin. Climbing west from the end of either fork, the crest of the range is reached. From the crest, turn left (south) to hike to the summit of Mount Marcy, or turn right (north) to hike, with the occasional scramble, over Point 13,335 and Point 13,227 to the summit of Gibbs Peak.

Snow season: The longer approach along the Rainbow Trail makes this a rarely visited hike compared to most in the area, and a more ambitious destination. The valley up to the tree line can be a very good snowshoe hike or ski and makes an enjoyable two- to three-day backpack trip.

Lakes of the Clouds

Highlights: *High lakes in a broad valley with access to Spread Eagle Peak and Mount Marcy.*

Type of hike: Out-and-back day hike or overnight backpack.
Total distance: 9.0 miles.
Difficulty: Moderate.

Best months: April to December.
Maps: USGS Electric Peak and Beckwith Mountain quads.

Finding the trailhead: From the intersection of Colorado Highways 96 and 69 in Westcliffe, drive south on CO 69 for 0.3 mile and turn right (west) onto Hermit Road (County Road 160). After another 5.9 miles, the road curves to the north past ranches and residential drives to intersect with 172. At CR 172, turn left (west) and drive another 1.5 miles to the national forest boundary. The road becomes rougher and heavily rutted; most cars will have difficulty driving the last 0.2 mile to the trailhead.

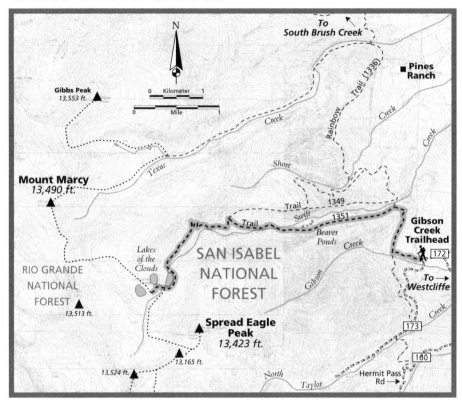

Parking and trailhead facilities: There is a small parking area and turn-around at the Gibson Creek Trailhead. If it is necessary to park along the road before reaching the trailhead, please respect the adjacent private property.

Key points:
- **0.0** Gibson Creek Trailhead.
- **0.1** Rainbow Trail (1336); turn right.
- **0.6** Lakes of the Clouds Trail (1351); turn left.
- **1.6** Beaver ponds.
- **2.0** Creek crossing.
- **4.0** Lower lake.
- **4.5** Upper lake.

The hike: From the parking area, hike to the right of the private cabin, then along the fence line, west to the intersection with the Rainbow Trail (1336). Turn right (north) and follow the gentle trail through open meadows overlooking the Wet Mountain Valley and up a gradual climb to the Lakes of the Clouds Trail (1351).

Lakes of the Clouds (March).

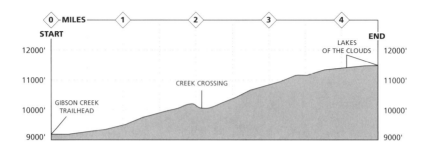

Be aware that this trailhead is not the trail shown on older USGS maps. The trail (1349) shown climbing up the north side of the valley from the Rainbow Trail is 0.4 mile farther north. Turn left on this first trail (1351), which runs up the left (south) side of the Swift Creek valley through open meadows and past small beaver ponds with views of Spread Eagle Peak on the left.

At 2.0 miles the trail crosses the creek and continues up the right (north) side of the valley, traversing higher onto the south-facing slopes. As you approach an open snowslide path containing a seasonal waterfall, switchback to the right, then immediately back to the left following the long traverse, climbing higher above the valley floor. The trail stays high and well above the creek before curving back south to the outlet of the lower lake. Skirt to the left of the lake and climb up to the middle and upper lakes above. There is good camping north of the lakes.

Options: From the lower lake, you can climb south then east to Spread Eagle Peak, which is now visible to the southeast. Follow a seasonal stream up to the upper bench at approximately 12,250 feet. Curve to the left (south) on grassy slopes, and then east on to the saddle between Point 13,165 and Spread Eagle's summit. From the saddle, turn left (north) to hike to the summit, or turn right and climb up to Unnamed 13,524.

To climb Mount Marcy, hike across the outlet of the upper lake by picking your way along an intermittent stream that turns left (west) up grassy slopes before breaking off to the right to the crest of the range. Proceed north along the ridge over one false summit and on to the top of Mount Marcy. This climb is harder than Spread Eagle due to its length and time exposed to the wind and weather.

An ambitious shuttle hike is possible by descending west from the ridge south of Mount Marcy, or from its summit, to Cotton Lake and the Cotton Creek Trail (Hike 41).

Snow season: Access is usually good up to the national forest boundary just before the Gibson Creek Trailhead. The road is not maintained the last 0.2 mile to the trailhead. The steeper south-facing sections of the trail before the lake can make this a difficult approach on skis, but it can be a good snowshoe day hike or overnight backpack.

15

North Taylor Creek

Highlights: *A trail to a small lake with access to Rito Alto Peak, Unnamed 13,524, and Spread Eagle Peak.*

Type of hike: Out-and-back day hike or overnight backpack.
Total distance: 10.0 miles.
Difficulty: Moderate.

Best months: June to November, with superb fall foliage along the lower valley.
Maps: Rito Alto Peak, Horn Peak, Beckwith Mountain.

Finding the trailhead: From the intersection of Colorado Highways 96 and 69 in Westcliffe, drive south on CO 69 for 0.3 mile and turn right (west) onto Hermit Road (County Road 160). After another 5.9 miles, the road curves to the north past ranches and residential drives to intersect with 172. At CR 172, turn left (west) and drive another 1.5 miles to the national forest boundary. The road becomes rougher and heavily rutted; most cars will have difficulty driving the last 0.2 mile to the trailhead.

For easier access with a high-clearance vehicle, drive the North Taylor Road (Forest Road 173) beyond the Rainbow Trail and into the lower valley. The road turns left (south) from Hermit Road (CR 172) just before the national forest boundary. This is a rough road near the Rainbow Trail; it could require four-wheel drive to reach the lower valley, approximately 0.5 mile past the Rainbow Trailhead on the south side of the road. There are limited opportunities to park or turn around beyond the Rainbow Trail.

Parking and trailhead facilities: There is a small parking area and turnaround at the Gibson Creek Trailhead. If it is necessary to park along the road before reaching the trailhead, please respect the adjacent private property.

Key points:
0.0 Gibson Creek Trailhead.
0.1 Rainbow Trail (1336); turn left.
1.6 North Taylor Road (FR 173).
2.5 North Taylor Creek Trail (1348)
2.8 First creek crossing.
3.2 Second creek crossing.
4.5 Meadow.
5.0 Megan Lake.

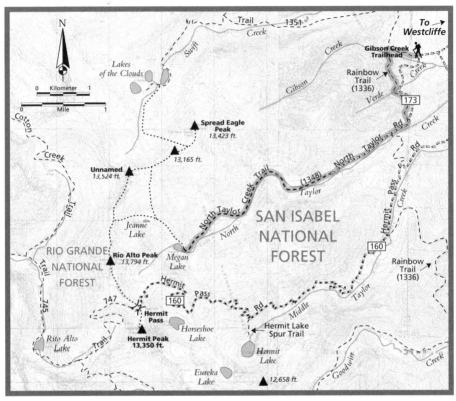

The hike: From the Gibson Creek Trailhead, hike 0.1 mile to the Rainbow Trail (1336) and turn left (south). Hike to the North Taylor Road (FR 173) and follow it west into the broad valley up to where the North Taylor Creek Trail (1348) begins. Cross the creek for the first time over a log bridge, and continue up the left (south) side of the creek as the valley rises and narrows. Continue up the valley to the second creek crossing. From here, the trail steepens to a moderate grade and climbs to about 10,700 feet before tapering off. The trail begins to thin, becoming hard to follow at the head of a broad meadow. Continue across the meadow in the direc-

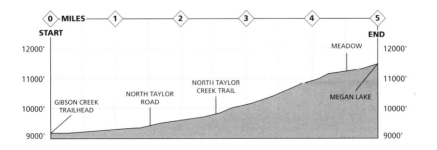

View south from Rito Alto Peak (October).

tion of the original trail (southwest) and pick up the continuation of the trail directly below the lowest point on the low ridge ahead, where the outlet of Megan Lake cascades down and forms the North Taylor Creek. Hike up to Megan Lake for views of Rito Alto to the west, Unnamed 13,524 to the northwest, and Spread Eagle Peak peering over the ridge to the northeast.

Options: From Megan Lake, both Rito Alto Peak and Spread Eagle Peak can be climbed in half a day. To climb Rito Alto Peak from Megan Lake, hike around the east shore, then begin climbing through willows and grassy slopes north of the lake, then left (northwest) to Jeanne Lake. Stay to the north of the lake and begin to hike west then southwest up to the saddle between Rito Alto Peak and Unnamed 13,524. Once on the saddle, climb the north slopes up solid talus, the most stable of which is to the right side of the face, where you might actually find a faint trail. Continue on the ridge crest to the summit.

Descend by retracing your route to the saddle and continue north along the ridge to the summit of Unnamed 13,524. This small summit provides excellent views across the valleys containing Rito Alto Creek, Lakes of the Clouds, and North Taylor Creek.

Descend east and hike along the crest of the ridge toward the summit of Spread Eagle Peak. Descend back along the ridge to the low point between Spread Eagle

Peak and Unnamed 13,524, and begin a traverse down grassy slopes to Megan Lake. One or two camping sites are available at Megan Lake, while more sites can be found in the upper meadow below the lake and in the valley near the trailhead before the first creek crossing.

It is also possible to descend south from the summit of Rito Alto to Hermit Pass Road (see Hike 16).

Snow season: The lower portions of the trail provide enjoyable skiing. Access along North Taylor Road will usually be closed by snow below the point where it intersects the Rainbow Trail. The Gibson Creek Trailhead usually allows good access, with regular snow removal up to the nearby housing developments. If it is necessary to park along the road, please respect the adjacent private property. When hiking into the upper valley, care must be taken to avoid possible avalanche conditions above the second creek crossing on the steep slide path before the upper basin.

16

Hermit Pass Road

Highlights: *A rough road past a high lake to 13,000-foot Hermit Pass, with access to Hermit Peak, Rito Alto Peak, and Rito Alto Lake (Hike 43).*

Type of hike: Out-and-back day hike or overnight backpack.
Total distance: 14.4 miles.
Difficulty: Strenuous.

Best months: July to September.
Maps: USGS Rito Alto Peak, Horn Peak, and Beckwith Mountain quads.

Special considerations: This is a popular road that gets heavy use up to Hermit Lake during the summer months. Avoid weekends and holidays to escape most of the crowds.

Finding the trailhead: From the intersection of Colorado Highways 69 and 96 in Westcliffe, drive south on CO 69 for 0.3 mile and turn right (west) onto Hermit Road (County Road 160). After approximately 6 miles, the road turns sharply to the right then back to the left. At this point the road gets rougher as it climbs for another 2.0 miles to the intersection with the Rainbow Trail (1336) on the right (north). After another 1.0 mile, the Rainbow Trail continues south of the Hermit Pass Road, which switchbacks up the valley about 3.0 miles to a sharp right-hand turn. Here the Hermit Lake spur trail goes left (south), and a wide section of road allows for some parking. Most higher-clearance vehicles can reach this point, but

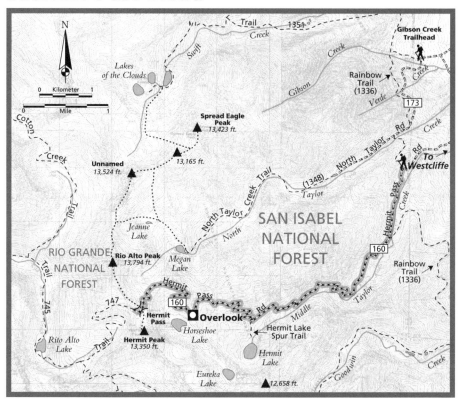

the road above becomes dramatically rougher as it climbs into the upper valley above the tree line. Snow and slide paths could block the road above Horseshoe Lake as late as July. Access all the way to the pass by four-wheel drive is best in late August and September. There is no vehicle access down from the west side of Hermit Pass.

Parking and trailhead facilities: At the point where the road becomes impassible for your vehicle, there are several places along the road to park and camp. Limited parking is available at the Rainbow Trail where it continues north, additional roadside parking and camping sites can be found near the Rainbow Trail where it heads south.

Key points:

- **0.0** Hermit Pass Road at Rainbow Trail.
- **1.0** Beaver ponds. Rainbow Trail goes left (south); continue straight.
- **4.0** Hermit Lake spur trail.
- **6.2** Horseshoe Lake overlook.
- **7.2** Hermit Pass

Eureka Mountain and Horseshoe Lake from Hermit Pass Road.

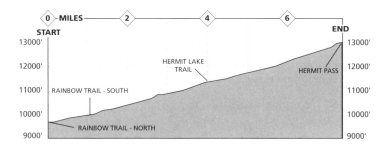

The hike: Hike south on the Hermit Pass Road (Forest Road 160) as the Rainbow Trail (1336) goes to the right (north). After 1.0 mile, the Rainbow Trail continues south. Follow the Hermit Pass Road, which switchbacks up the valley about 3.0 miles to a sharp right-hand turn. Here the Hermit Lake spur trail goes left (south). Continue on FR 160 as it becomes rougher and climbs 2.2 miles to the ridge above Horseshoe Lake. From here you can see east down the Middle Taylor Creek valley, northeast across North Taylor Creek to Spread Eagle Peak, and west to Hermit Peak and Rito Alto Peak. Hike another 1.0 miles up a rough and rocky road well above the tree line, surrounded by alpine tundra and views over the Hermit Lake valley. Continue to views west over ito Alto Creek at the road closure at Hermit Pass.

Options: FR 160 is drivable past the beginning of the hike at the Rainbow Trail. At the Hermit Lake spur trail, a wide section of road allows for some parking. Most high-clearance vehicles can reach this point, but the road above becomes dramatically rougher as it climbs into the upper valley above the tree line. Snow and slide paths could block the road above Horseshoe Lake as late as July. Access all the way to the pass by four-wheel drive is best in late August and September. There is no vehicle access down from the west side of Hermit Pass. You can continue hiking past the road closure at Hermit Pass and down the trail (747) leading to Rito Alto Lake.

From the pass, it is also possible to climb several high peaks along the crest of the range. Turn right and hike north up the ridge over solid talus and grassy slopes to the summit of Rito Alto Peak. From here you can continue north to Unnamed 13,524 and Spread Eagle Peak, then down into North Taylor Creek (Hike 15).

Turn left (south) from Hermit Pass to climb up easy ground to Hermit Peak and beyond along the ridge to Eureka Mountain. From here, you can continue south and connect to Goodwin Creek (Hike 18), Venable Creek (Hike 19), Comanche Creek (Hike 20), or the North Fork of North Crestone Creek (Hike 45). Take care to watch the weather closely; the exposure to storms along the ridge is severe.

Snow season: With a four-wheel-drive vehicle, it could be possible to drive well up the road even into October and November. After the snow begins to close off access, the road becomes a much more attractive hike, snowshoe, or ski, although you may occasionally share it with snow machines.

Rainbow Trail

Hermit Pass Road to Medano Pass

17

Highlights: *A long and fairly gentle trail with views of the Wet Mountain Valley.*

Type of hike: Out-and-back day hike, overnight backpack, three- to five-day shuttle.
Total distance: 32 miles, with four intermediate points of access.
Difficulty: Easy to moderate, depending on length.

Best months: Spring and fall are both good to avoid summer heat and afternoon thunderstorms. Fall offers the possibility of good weather and changing foliage color.
Maps: USGS Horn Peak, Crestone Peak, and Beck Mountain quads.

Special considerations: The Rainbow Trail can be heavily used at times and is occasionally frequented by horse and llama trekkers as well as motorcycles, although I have never encountered any during my time in the area.

Finding the trailhead: To reach the trailhead at Hermit Pass Road from the intersection of Colorado Highway 69 and 96 in Westcliffe, drive south 0.3 mile on CO 69 and turn right (west) onto Hermit Road (County Road 160). After approximately 6 miles, the road turns sharply to the right then back to the left. At this point the road gets rougher as it climbs for another 2.0 miles to the intersection with the Rainbow Trail (1336) on the right (north).

To reach the Medano Pass Trailhead from the intersection of CO 69 and 96 in Westcliffe, drive south for 24 miles on 69 and turn right (west) onto 559, which usually has signs for Medano Pass. Drive west past private ranch land on a good dirt road for 7.0 miles to the national forest boundary. The road begins to climb more steeply and usually requires four-wheel drive for the last 2.0 miles to Medano Pass. Continue over the pass and down 0.5 mile to an open meadow and the spur road leading right (north) for another 0.2 mile to the Medano Lake Trailhead.

See the descriptions of Goodwin Lake (Hike 18), Horn Peak Trail (Hike 22),

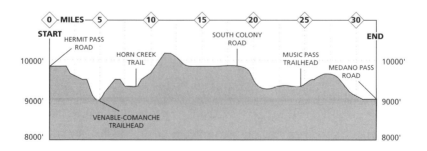

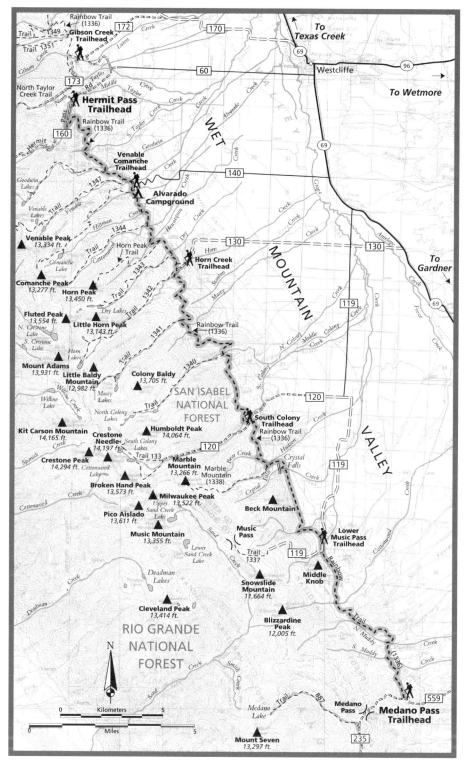

Rainbow Trail

Rainbow Trail (1336)
Trail 1349
Trail 1351
172
170
To Texas Creek
69
96
Gibson Creek Trailhead
Luton
Creek
60
Westcliffe
173
North Rd Taylor Creek
North Taylor Creek Trail
Middle Taylor Creek
S. Taylor
To Wetmore
69
Hermit Pass Trailhead
Rainbow Trail (1336)
160
Hermit Pass
Goodwin
140
WET
69
Venable Comanche Trailhead
Alvarado Campground
Creek
Creek
Creek
Creek
Creek
Goodwin Lakes
1347
Venable Trail
Hillman
Creek
Dry Creek
Honeymoon Creek
130
130
To Gardner
Venable Lakes
Venable Peak 13,334 ft.
Comanche Lake
1344
Horn Peak Trail
Horn Creek Trailhead
Horn
Stanton
Creek
119
69
Comanche Peak 13,277 ft.
Horn Peak 13,450 ft.
1343
1342
Macey
Creek
Creek
MOUNTAIN
Fluted Peak 13,554 ft.
N. Crestone Lake
S. Crestone Lake
Dry Lakes
Little Horn Peak 13,143 ft.
1341
Rainbow Trail (1336)
N. Colony Creek
Middle Colony Creek
Horn Lakes
S. Colony
Mount Adams 13,931 ft.
Little Baldy Mountain 12,982 ft.
Colony Baldy 13,705 ft.
1340
120
119
Willow Lake
Macey Lakes
SAN ISABEL NATIONAL FOREST
VALLEY
Kit Carson Mountain 14,165 ft.
North Colony Lakes
Trail
Creek
Spanish Creek
Crestone Needle 14,197 ft.
South Colony Lakes
Humboldt Peak 14,064 ft.
South Colony Trailhead
Rainbow Trail (1336)
119
Crestone Peak 14,294 ft.
Cottonwood Lake
Trail 133
120
Marble Mountain 13,266 ft.
Marble Mountain (1338)
Spear Creek
Crystal Falls
Broken Hand Peak 13,573 ft.
Cottonwood Creek
Crystal Creek
Pico Aislado 13,611 ft.
Upper Sand Creek Lake
Milwaukee Peak 13,522 ft.
Beck Mountain
Lower Music Pass Trailhead
Music Mountain 13,355 ft.
Sand Creek
Music Pass
119
Rainbow Trail
Lower Sand Creek Lake
Trail 1337
Middle Knob
Deadman Lakes
Snowslide Mountain 11,664 ft.
Deadman Creek
Cleveland Peak 13,414 ft.
Blizzardine Peak 12,005 ft.
N. Muddy Creek
RIO GRANDE NATIONAL FOREST
Creek
S. Muddy Creek
N
Sand Creek
Smith Creek
Trail (1336)
Creek
Kilometers
0
5
Medano Trail
887
Medano Pass
Medano Pass Trailhead
559
Miles
0
5
Medano Lake
235
Mount Seven 13,297 ft.

South Colony Lakes (Hike 27), and Music Pass (Hike 33) for directions to the other access points.

Parking and trailhead facilities: Limited parking is available at the Hermit Pass Road where the Rainbow Trail continues north, additional roadside parking and camping sites can be found near the Rainbow Trail where it heads south. A small turnaround is provided at the Medano Pass Trailhead. The National Forest Alvarado Campground is located just south of the Venable-Comanche Trailhead. There are some local outfitters out of Westcliffe that will provide support along the trail from the points of road access for a fee.

Key points:

0.0 Hermit Pass Road.
1.0 Turn left to remain on Rainbow Trail (1336).
3.5 Goodwin Trail.
4.5 Venable-Comanche (1347 and 1345) Trailhead at Forest Road 140.
7.0 Cottonwood Trail (1344).
8.5 Horn Peak Trail.
9.0 Dry Creek Trail (1343).
9.5 Horn Creek Trailhead at Custer County Road 130.
12.0 Macey Lakes Trail (1341).
15.5 North Colony Creek Trail (1340).
18.5 South Colony Road access (120).
25.0 Music Pass Trailhead at 119.
32.0 Medano Pass Road (559 on the east side of the pass, FR 235 on the west side).

The hike: This section of the Rainbow Trail is the most heavily used portion of its entire 90-mile length. It is used primarily as a connector trail to gain access to the many side trails leading into the high valleys on the west side. From the intersection of the Rainbow Trail (1336) and the Hermit Pass Road, hike west up the road for 1.0 mile, then follow the Rainbow Trail as it heads south. The trail establishes a repetitive pattern of dropping down to the bottom of a valley and across a creek, climbing up over a ridge, and then descending to the next creek. Overall, the trail descends to the Venable-Comanche Trailhead at 4.5 miles, then climbs steadily to its high point near Macey Creek before dropping again near the lower Music Pass Trailhead at 25 miles. Views of the Wet Mountain Valley and the rolling Wet Mountains to the east are numerous and awesome as the trails wind in and out of aspen and timber stands and cross many creeks along the way.

From the lower Music Pass Trailhead, the trail continues south and is steep in sections as it crosses through extensive aspen stands. After 32 miles, the trail reaches Muddy Creek Road (FR 412); follow the road for about 2.0 miles before reaching the Medano Pass Road, which leads 1.5 miles west to Medano Pass.

Camping is readily available along the trail, and water is usually plentiful over its entire length.

Options: Any section of this hike can be combined with day hikes of any of the intersecting trails, of which Cottonwood and North Colony are the least visited. See Hikes 1 and 9 for the northern sections of the 90-mile Rainbow Trail.

Snow season: This is a good hike during snow season, with access at the Venable-Comanche, Horn Creek, and Music Pass Trailheads being the most reliable. South Colony Creek may also be accessible, depending on conditions. The trail is not often fully covered with snow and usually does not require snowshoes or skis.

18

Goodwin Lakes

Highlights: *A lesser-used trail to three small lakes.*

Type of hike: Out-and-back day hike or overnight backpack.
Total distance: 10.0 miles.

Difficulty: Moderate.
Best months: May to November.
Maps: USGS Horn Peak quad.

Finding the trailhead: From the intersection of Colorado Highways 69 and 96 in Westcliffe, drive south 3.4 miles on CO 69. Turn right (west) on Schoolfield Road (County Road 140) and drive 4.5 miles west to a **T** intersection. Turn left and drive the winding road about 2 miles, following signs to the Venable-Comanche Trailhead on the right just before reaching the Alvarado Campground. Follow the trail to the right (north) of the parking area.

Parking and trailhead facilities: There is a parking area at the trailhead with rest rooms but no water. The Alvarado Campground just south of the trailhead is open only for the summer season.

Key points:
- **0.0** Venable-Comanche Trailhead.
- **0.2** Rainbow Trail (1336); turn right.
- **1.5** Goodwin Creek Trail; turn left.
- **2.5** Beaver ponds.
- **4.0** Creek crossing.
- **4.5** Lower Goodwin Lake.
- **5.0** Upper Goodwin Lake.

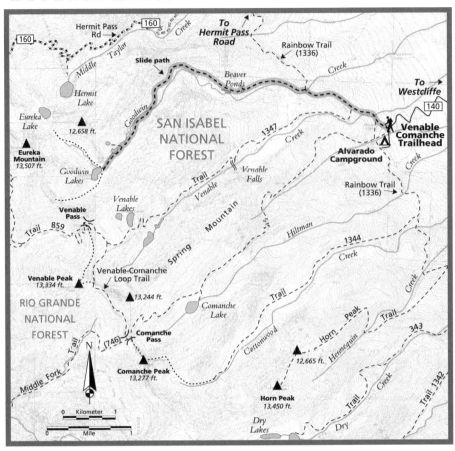

The hike: From the Venable Trail sign, hike steeply west to the intersection with the Rainbow Trail, then turn right (north) and continue along the gentler trail to the Goodwin Creek trail at 1.5 miles. Turn left (west) and hike up the trail above and to the right (north) of the creek, through aspen groves and past several small beaver ponds. Continue hiking past open meadows, then reenter the evergreen forest as the trail climbs into the upper Goodwin Creek valley. Cross a slide path filled

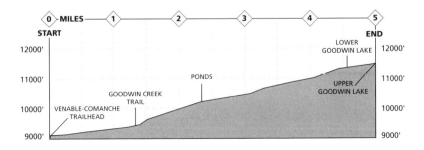

Upper Goodwin Lake.

with downed timber and cross over to the left (south) side of the creek at 4.0 miles. Continue up the occasionally steep and winding trail to the lower Goodwin Lake. Across the outlet, a short but thin trail leads to the small lake to the north. To continue to the upper Goodwin Lake, stay to the left (south) of the lower lake and hike through the willows on a short jaunt with excellent views of the crest of the range.

Options: Continue climbing up the narrow valley directly southwest of the upper lake by hiking northwest to the crest of the range. From the crest, you can go north to Eureka Mountain or south to Venable Pass and descend west to the North Fork of North Crestone Creek (Hike 45) or east to Venable Creek (Hike 19). These are strenuous options that could involve some scrambling. An ice ax is recommended when climbing the seasonal steep snow slopes below the crest.

From the upper lake, you can also continue up Goodwin Creek to the north into a small alpine basin and to the ridge between Eureka Mountain and Unnamed 12,658 overlooking Hermit Lake.

Snow season: This is a good snow-season hike, rarely visited, with deeper snows above the beaver ponds. The optional climbs should only be attempted during safe spring snow conditions due to high avalanche danger.

19

Venable Creek

Highlights: *A scenic trail to high lakes with access to Venable Pass, Venable Peak, and the Venable-Comanche loop trail.*

Type of hike: Out-and-back day hike.
Total distance: 10.0 miles.
Difficulty: Moderate to lower Venable Lake, more strenuous beyond.

Best months: May to December.
Maps: USGS Horn Peak and Rito Alto Peak quads.

Finding the trailhead: From the intersection of Colorado Highways 69 and 96 in Westcliffe, drive south 3.4 miles on CO 69. Turn right (west) on Schoolfield Road (County Road 140) and drive 4.5 miles west to a T intersection. Turn left and drive the winding road about 2 miles, following signs to the Venable-Comanche Trailhead on the right just before reaching the Alvarado Campground. Follow the trail to the right (north) of the parking area.

Parking and trailhead facilities: There is a parking area at the trailhead with rest rooms but no water. The Alvarado Campground just south of the trailhead is open only for the summer season.

Key points:
0.0 Venable-Comanche Trailhead.
0.2 Rainbow Trail (1336); turn right.
0.4 Venable Trail (1347); turn left.
2.5 Venable Falls.
3.5 Lower lakes.
4.2 Venable Lakes.
5.0 Venable Pass.

The hike: From the right (north) side of the parking area, hike up the spur trail to the intersection with the Rainbow Trail (1336). Continue to the right for a short distance before turning left (west) onto the Venable Trail (1347). Hike along the right (north) side of the valley past willow and aspen groves. The forest becomes denser and the trail gets steeper as you approach the falls. A small sign indicates the steep spur trail on the left (south) that descends to the Venable Falls overlook area. The main trail stays to the right and continues to climb until it reaches the open valley and the lower lakes at the tree line. Pass an old cabin on the right and continue up into the upper valley. The trail stays to the right and begins to switchback up to a high bench containing the Venable Lakes. The hike becomes more strenu-

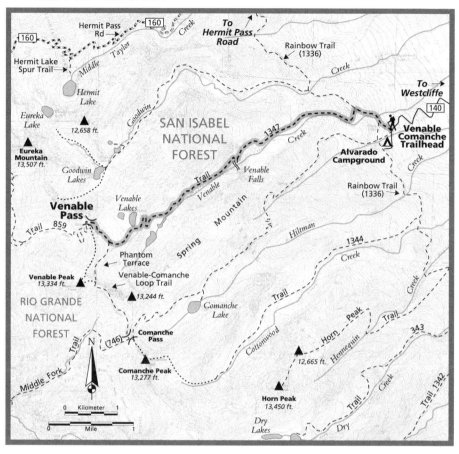

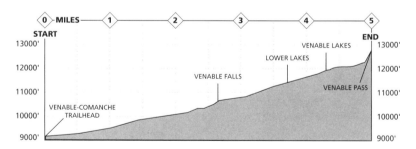

ous as the trail climbs toward Venable Peak's east ridge. Where the trail splits, stay right to go to Venable Pass. A left leads across Phantom Terrace to the unnamed pass east of Venable Peak.

Options: From Venable Pass you can continue hiking west to the North Fork of North Crestone Creek (Hike 45). From the unnamed pass east of Venable Peak,

Venable Falls.

you continue along the Venable-Comanche Loop Trail as it traverses to another pass and descends east to Comanche Creek (Hike 20) or west to the Middle Fork of North Crestone Creek (Hike 45).

Venable Peak can be climbed either from Venable Pass, by proceeding south along the ridge to the summit, or from the unnamed pass south of Phantom Terrace, by ascending up grassy slopes to the summit.

Snow season: The steeper sections of this trail make it a difficult snow-season hike or snowshoe. Phantom Terrace should be traversed carefully, and only when free of unstable snow.

Comanche Lake

Highlights: *A scenic trail to a high lake, with access to Comanche Peak, Middle Fork of North Crestone Creek (Hike 45), and Venable-Comanche Loop.*

Type of hike: Out-and-back day hike.
Total distance: 9.0 miles.
Difficulty: Moderate.

Best months: May to November.
Maps: USGS Horn Peak quads.

Finding the trailhead: From the intersection of Colorado Highways 69 and 96 in Westcliffe, drive south 3.4 miles on CO 69. Turn right (west) on Schoolfield Road (County Road 140) and drive 4.5 miles west to a T intersection. Turn left and drive the winding road about 2 miles, following signs to the Venable-Comanche Trailhead on the right just before reaching the Alvarado Campground. Follow the trail to the left (south) of the parking area.

Parking and trailhead facilities: There is a parking area at the trailhead with rest rooms but no water. The National Forest Alvarado Campground just south of the trailhead is open for the summer season only.

Key points:
- **0.0** Venable-Comanche Trailhead.
- **2.2** Slide path.
- **3.2** Ridge.
- **4.5** Comanche Lake.

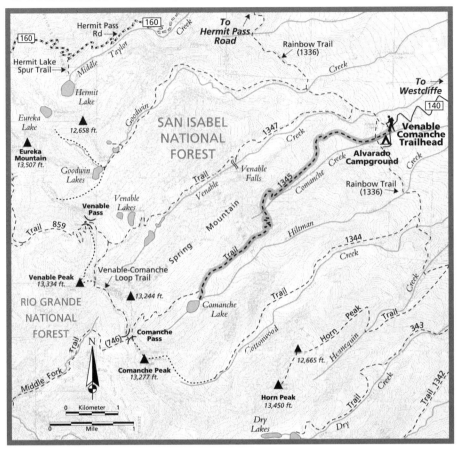

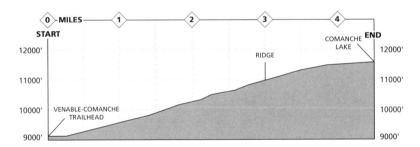

The hike: Hike to the left (south) of the parking area and follow the signed Comanche Trail (1345). Climb steadily west up through aspens and willows, then start curving left across a willow-filled slide path. Hike up and switchback for about a mile through thick forest to the ridge above. Here you enter the Hiltman Creek drainage that leads to Comanche Lake, with views of Horn Peak to the south and Comanche Peak farther up the valley (west). Past the ridge, the trail hugs the

Comanche Peak.

south-facing slopes, well above the wide valley floor. Hike up the gentle trail to the spur trail that leads down to the lake. The main trail continues 1.5 miles up to the unnamed pass north of Comanche Peak.

Options: From the lake spur trail, continue on the main trail (1345) that climbs up to the right, with occasional switchbacks as it approaches the crest of the range. A snowfield may remain just below the ridge well into summer. From the pass, turn left (south) and continue a half mile up just to the right (west) of the ridge to the summit of Comanche Peak. Turn right (north) at the pass to continue the Venable-Comanche Loop Trail, a good trail across the west-facing slope of Unnamed 13,244 toward Venable Peak. Proceed over to Phantom Terrace and down Venable Creek (Hike 19) to complete the loop, or continue on to Venable Pass and down the North Fork of North Crestone Creek (Hike 45)

It is also possible to descend from the pass north of Comanche Peak to the Middle Fork of North Crestone Creek (Hike 45).

Snow season: The lower steep sections of the trail make this a more difficult hike during snow season. Care must be taken when crossing the slide-prone willow slopes before the steep climb to the ridge and the Hiltman Creek drainage. Once in the drainage, the upper valley is much easier and is sure to be secluded.

Cottonwood Creek

Highlights: *A lesser-used trail to a high basin with access to Comanche Peak.*

Type of hike: Out-and-back day hike or overnight backpack.
Total distance: 8.0 miles.

Difficulty: Moderate.
Best months: June to September.
Maps: USGS Horn Peak quad.

Finding the trailhead: From the intersection of Colorado Highways 69 and 96 in Westcliffe, drive south 3.4 miles on CO 69. Turn right (west) on Schoolfield Road (County Road 140) and drive 4.5 miles west to a **T** intersection. Turn left and drive the winding road about 2 miles, following signs to the Venable-Comanche Trailhead on the right just before reaching the Alvarado Campground. Follow the trail to the left (south) of the parking area. During the summer, it is possible to drive to the south end of the Alvarado Campground to the Rainbow Trail access.

Parking and trailhead facilities: There is a parking area at the trailhead with rest rooms but no water. The National Forest Alvarado Campground just south of the trailhead is open for the summer season only.

Key points:
- **0.0** Venable-Comanche Trailhead.
- **0.2** Rainbow Trail (1336); turn left.
- **1.2** Cottonwood Creek Trail (1344); turn right.
- **3.0** Lower meadows.
- **4.0** Upper meadows.

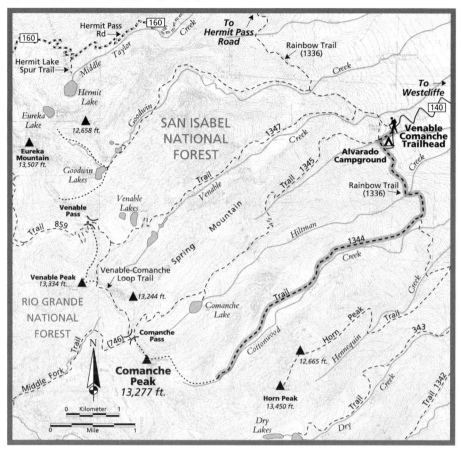

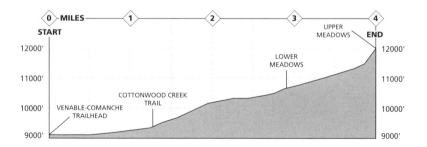

The hike: Hike west up to the Rainbow Trail (1336) and turn left (south) for 1.0 mile along the gentle trail to the Cottonwood Trail (1344). Turn right (west) and hike up the trail as it climbs steeply along the right (north) side of the creek before becoming gentler below the lower meadows. With Horn Peak dominating the view on the left (south), continue up the trail through evergreen forest until reaching the

Horn Peak and Cottonwood Creek viewed from Comanche Peak.

small upper meadows. From here, there are views of Unnamed 13,419 above to the west and Comanche Peak to the northwest. Limited camping is available throughout the lower valley with the best sites found in the upper valley near the tree line.

Options: Climb northwest of the upper basin to Comanche Peak's east ridge and then west up to the summit. The ridge might require some hand and foot scrambling and could be difficult with snow around the summit.

Snow season: This is a rarely used snow-season hike, but attempting the route up to Comanche Peak may be worth the effort.

22 Horn Peak Trail

Highlights: *A good trail to a high peak with impressive views of the range to the north and south.*

Type of hike: Out-and-back day hike.
Total distance: 9.0 miles.
Difficulty: Strenuous.

Best months: Year-round.
Maps: USGS Horn Peak quad.

Special considerations: Above timberline, this route follows Horn Peak's east ridge, exposing hikers to wind and weather; be prepared. From the summit, avoid the temptation to descend directly south to the Dry Lakes. The slopes of scree are steep and loose.

Finding the trailhead: From the intersection of Colorado Highways 69 and 96 in Westcliffe, drive south on CO 69 for 3.4 miles and turn right (west) on Schoolfield Road (County Road 140). After 0.9 mile, turn left (south) on Colfax Road (CR 129), then continue 2.0 miles and turn right (west) at Horn Creek Road (CR 130). Drive 2.2 miles and veer left, following the signs to Horn Creek Ranch. At the ranch entrance, stay right and continue 0.2 mile to Horn Creek Trailhead.

Parking and trailhead facilities: A parking area and toilet are at the trailhead. Please respect the private property that lies south and east of the trailhead.

Key points:
- **0.0** Horn Creek Trailhead.
- **0.5** Rainbow Trail (1336); turn right.
- **1.8** Horn Peak Trail; turn left.
- **2.8** Creek crossing.
- **3.0** Ridge.
- **4.2** False summit.
- **4.5** Horn Peak summit.

The hike: From the Horn Creek Trailhead, hike up the spur trail to the right (west) of the four-wheel-drive road to the Rainbow Trail (1336). Turn right (north) onto the Rainbow Trail, pass the Dry Creek Trailhead, and continue 0.5 mile over gentle terrain to the Horn Peak Trail; turn left (west). The lower portion of the trail climbs steeply before leveling off as it crosses Hennequin Creek. The trail switches back to the right (north) 150 feet past the creek crossing, and begins a traversing climb to Horn Peak's east ridge. This switchback can be difficult to find;

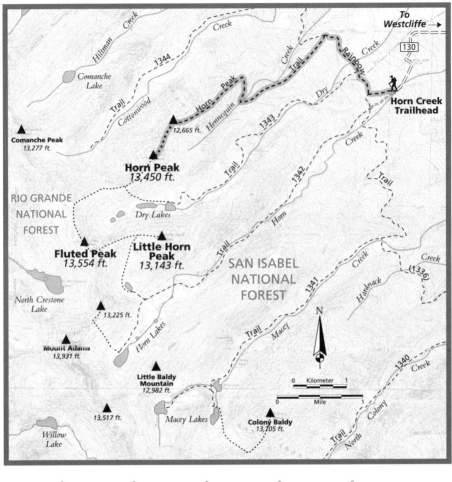

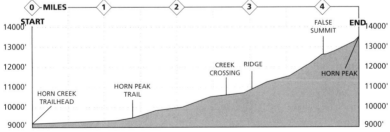

after crossing the stream, avoid continuing too far up the creek, where you might find some faint trails leading along its north bank.

Once on the ridge, the trail becomes thin in spots. It generally follows along the top of the ridge, with occasional switchbacks at steeper sections. Continue up past timberline on the faint rocky trail to Horn Peak's false summit, Point 12,665. The trail ceases beyond this point, but the route continues southwest on the ridgeline.

100

Comanche Peak from the summit of Horn Peak.

Avoid any difficult sections by staying left (south) of the crest, because the north face on the right drops precipitously down to Cottonwood Creek. Continue up solid talus to the summit.

There is very little camping between the creek crossing and the ridge.

Options: A viable descent option is to continue down Horn Peak's west ridge above the uppermost Dry Lake, hiking down over steep grassy slopes to the Dry Creek Trail (Hike 23). Ambitious climbers can link this hike with a climb of Fluted Peak and Little Horn Peak by continuing over the summit along the west ridge, where some easy scrambling leads to Fluted Peak's north ridge. From Fluted Peak's summit, descend south for 0.2 mile to the ridge connecting to Little Horn Peak, then hike east along the ridge to the summit. Return to the low point between Fluted Peak and Little Horn Peak before descending grassy slopes to the Horn Creek Trail (Hike 24). This loop adds only 2.6 miles but includes 4.5 miles of exposed strenuous hiking above timberline. The weather must be ideal; when it is, this loop is a classic. Don't forget your camera.

Snow season: Trailhead access is good, with regular road maintenance up to Horn Creek Ranch. This trail can be an enjoyable snowshoe or ski up to the ridge and possibly beyond. Above the tree line, the ridge tends to be windswept and bare, providing an avalanche safe route to the summit.

23 | Dry Creek

Highlights: *A steep and narrow valley up to high lakes surrounded by a steep cirque.*

Type of hike: Out-and-back day hike or overnight backpack.
Total distance: 8.4 miles.

Difficulty: Strenuous.
Best months: May to December.
Maps: USGS Horn Peak quad.

Finding the trailhead: From the intersection of Colorado Highways 69 and 96 in Westcliffe, drive south on CO 69 for 3.4 miles and turn right (west) on Schoolfield Road (County Road 140). After 0.9 mile, turn left (south) on Colfax Road (CR 129), then continue 2.0 miles and turn right (west) at Horn Creek Road (CR 130). Drive 2.2 miles and veer left, following the signs to Horn Creek Ranch. At the ranch entrance, stay right and continue 0.2 mile to Horn Creek Trailhead.

Parking and trailhead facilities: A parking area and toilet are available at the trailhead. Please respect the private property that lies southeast of the trailhead.

Key points:

- **0.0** Horn Creek Trailhead.
- **0.5** Rainbow Trail (1336); turn right.
- **0.8** Dry Creek Trail (1343); turn left.
- **1.5** Creek crossing.
- **3.0** Moraine.
- **4.2** Lower Dry Lake.

The hike: From the trailhead, hike along the trail to the right of the four-wheel-drive road on the left. At the Rainbow Trail (1336), turn right (north) and hike to the Dry Creek Trail (1343). Turn left (west) and climb steeply up the trail, which becomes narrow and rocky in places. The trail crosses over to the right (north) side of the creek and soon climbs up into an open valley. The hike becomes steeper

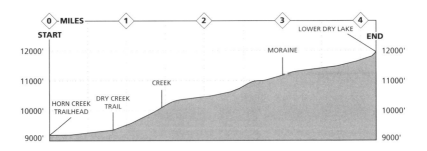

again as the trail leaves the creek and heads right into thicker forest to bypass the cliffs near the falls. As the trail winds back south toward the creek, look for the huge rocky moraine that comes into view and looms along the southern edge of the valley. As the trees grow thicker and taller, there are a few good campsites before the last climb to the lower lake just above the tree line, where camping is spectacular but much more exposed to the weather.

Options: It is possible to climb Horn Peak from the grassy slopes above the second lake. The loose scree above the lower lake leading straight up to the summit is to be avoided at all costs. Hike up the angling slopes above the second lake toward the low point on the ridge between Horn Peak and the range crest. Once on the ridge, turn right (east) to climb Horn Peak's summit. Descend northeast to the Horn Peak Trail (Hike 22), or turn left (west) and scramble up to the crest of the range and then left (south) to Fluted Peak. It is then possible to continue along the ridge toward Little Horn Peak and descend grassy slopes to Horn Creek (Hike 24).

Snow season: This is a difficult hike during snow season due to the steep grade below the upper basin. Otherwise, this is a fantastic, secluded hike with usually snow-free climbing up the south-facing slopes to Horn Peak.

Dry Lake with Colony Baldy and Humboldt Peak beyond from the summit of Horn Peak.

24

Horn Creek

Highlights: *A good trail to a large, open upper valley with access to Little Horn Peak, Mount Adams, and Little Baldy.*

Type of hike: Out-and-back day hike or overnight backpack.
Total distance: 11.0 miles.
Difficulty: Strenuous.

Best months: July to October, but access is good year-round.
Maps: USGS Horn Peak quad.

Finding the trailhead: From the intersection of Colorado Highways 69 and 96 in Westcliffe, drive south on CO 69 for 3.4 miles and turn right (west) on Schoolfield Road (County Road 140). After 0.9 mile, turn left (south) on Colfax Road (CR 129), then continue 2.0 miles and turn right (west) at Horn Creek Road (CR 130). Drive 2.2 miles and veer left, following the signs to Horn Creek Ranch. At the ranch entrance, stay right and continue 0.2 mile to Horn Creek Trailhead.

Parking and trailhead facilities: A parking area and toilet are available at the trailhead. Please respect the private property that lies southeast of the trailhead.

Key points:
0.0 Horn Creek Trailhead.
0.5 Rainbow Trail (1336); turn left.
0.8 Horn Creek Trail (1342); turn right.
2.8 Creek crossing.
4.5 Lower Horn Lakes.
5.5 Upper Horn Lakes.

The hike: Hike west to the Rainbow Trail (1336), turn left (south), and hike for 0.3 mile to the Horn Creek Trail (1342). Turn right and follow the trail as it climbs up the valley, far to the right (north) of the creek. Hike through aspens up the trail, which gets steeper as it enters evergreen forest and crosses over the creek to the left (south) side and up into the upper Horn Creek valley. The trail crosses to the right (north) side of the creek just before reaching the lowest lakes. Continue southwest on an obvious trail as it climbs into the upper valley. Below the lower lake, a spur trail on the right (north) leads to the lake below Fluted Peak's east face. Continue straight ahead into the upper Horn Creek valley to the lake below Unnamed 13,517 with Mount Adams and Unnamed 13,325 to the right. There is good camping along the lower valley and in the upper basins.

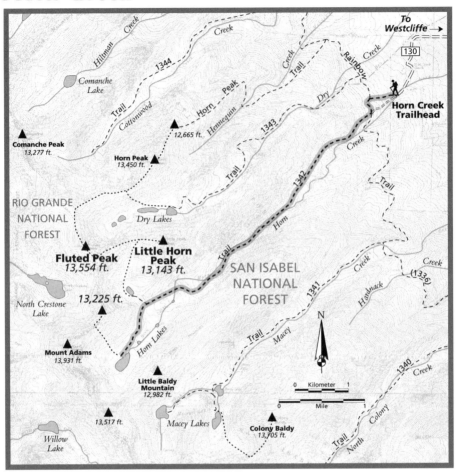

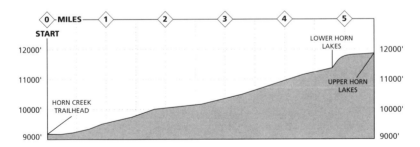

Options: From the largest and uppermost lake, climb northwest to the crest of the range and the summit of Unnamed 13,325.

From the spur trail and the lake below Fluted Peak, hike up a climbing traverse

View south from Little Baldy Mountain of Macey Lakes, Colony Baldy, and Humboldt Peak in the distance.

northeast to the ridge between Fluted Peak on the crest of the range and Little Horn Peak to the east. From this ridge, hike right (east) to the summit of Little Horn Peak or left (west) to Fluted Peak. As a long and strenuous option, continue north from Fluted Peak, then east to Horn Peak and descend via the Horn Peak Trail (Hike 22).

Snow season: This trail is a good snow-season hike, snowshoe, or ski into the upper valley before reaching the windswept areas of sparse snow cover near the upper lakes. The optional climb to Unnamed 13,325 climbs potentially dangerous east-facing wind-loaded slopes and should only be attempted during safe avalanche conditions. The climb of Little Horn Peak and the loop over Fluted Peak and Horn Peak can be safer because these slopes tend to be windswept.

25

Macey Creek

Highlights: *A lightly used trail to lakes surrounded by high peaks, with access to Colony Baldy.*

Type of hike: Long out-and-back day hike or overnight backpack.
Total distance: 14.0 miles.
Difficulty: Strenuous.

Best months: June to September.
Maps: USGS Crestone Peak and Horn Peak quads.

Special considerations: This hike lacks the steep climbs of most trails in this area, but its length requires being prepared for a long day.

Finding the trailhead: From the intersection of Colorado Highways 69 and 96 in Westcliffe, drive south on CO 69 for 3.4 miles and turn right (west) on Schoolfield Road (County Road 140). After 0.9 mile, turn left (south) on Colfax Road (CR 129), then continue 2.0 miles and turn right (west) at Horn Creek Road (CR 130). Drive 2.2 miles and veer left, following the signs to Horn Creek Ranch. At the ranch entrance, stay right and continue 0.2 mile to Horn Creek Trailhead.

For a longer hike, begin at the South Colony Lakes Road (see Hike 27) and hike 6.5 miles north on the Rainbow Trail to the Macey Lakes Trail.

Parking and trailhead facilities: A parking area and a toilet are available at the trailhead. Please respect the private property that lies south of the trailhead.

Key points:
- **0.0** Horn Creek Trailhead.
- **0.5** Rainbow Trail (1336); turn left.
- **3.5** Macey Lakes Trail (1341); turn right.
- **5.8** Copperstain Cliff.
- **6.0** Macey Falls.
- **6.2** Lower Macey Lake.
- **7.0** Upper Macey Lake.

The hike: From the Horn Creek Trailhead, hike up the spur trail to the right of the four-wheel-drive road to the Rainbow Trail (1336). Turn left (south) onto the Rainbow Trail, which climbs gently to a ridge and turns sharply to the right and down to Macey Creek. The Rainbow Trail has several outfitter camps at the Macey Lakes Trailhead. Turn right (west) on the Macey Lakes Trail (1341) and hike up the right (north) side of the creek while winding through dense forest. Cross the first

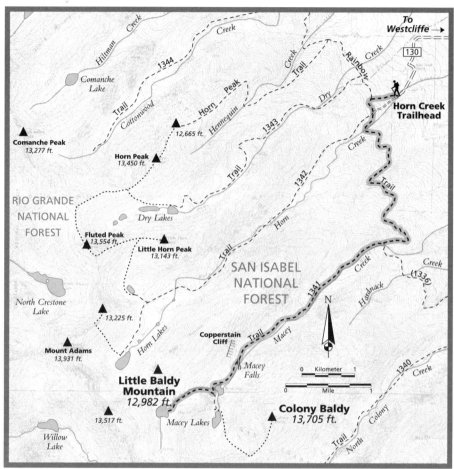

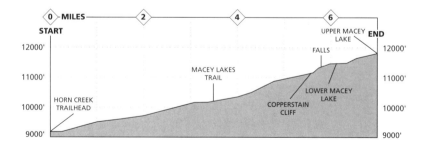

open area denuded by snowslides and hike straight across it back into the forest. As you enter another open area filled with downed timber and remnants of the winter season's snowslide, Copperstain Cliff comes into view on your right. Cross this slide path and rejoin the trail as it continues up the valley and skirts Macey Falls.

The trail winds through thick forest up along the creek to lower Macey Lake. From the lower lake, a trail continues around the right side, across the creek that feeds the lake, and past several campsites. It branches to the right to get to the highest lake and to the left to get to the lake sitting in the bench below (west of) Colony Baldy. Hike to the highest lake up the left side of the valley by picking up a decent trail into the upper cirque.

Options: To climb Colony Baldy, continue around the lower lake and up through willows to the high lake just above it and to the south. Stay to the left of the steeper slopes above the high lake and follow easier grassy slopes to the ridge between Point 12,995 and the summit of Colony Baldy. From the ridge leading to Colony Baldy's summit, there are excellent views of North Colony Creek, Humboldt Peak, Crestone Needle, and Crestone Peak to the south; Kit Carson Mountain, Challenger Point, and Mount Adams to the west; and north to Horn Peak and the northern range. This is a fantastic summit that is much less visited than the other peaks around it.

Snow season: The longer approach to this trail makes it very lightly used during snow season. The Rainbow Trail might not have enough snow cover for skiing, but the Macey Creek valley can be a very enjoyable snowshoe or ski up to the lakes. Colony Baldy is much harder to climb during periods of avalanche danger, but it can be a good spring to early summer snow climb when conditions are stable.

View south across Upper Macey Lake.

26

North Colony Creek

Highlights: *A longer trail to several very scenic lakes.*

Type of hike: Out-and-back overnight backpack.
Total distance: 15.0 miles.
Difficulty: Strenuous.

Best months: July to September.
Maps: USGS Crestone Peak, Horn Peak, and Beck Mountain quads.

Special considerations: Parts of South Colony Road (Forest Road 120) barely deserve to be classified as a road. Early in the season, runoff seems to use the road as much as the creek, and the snowpack can linger below the trailhead into June. Be prepared to stop and proceed on foot in spring or fall when the road conditions will require it.

Finding the trailhead: From the intersection of Colorado Highways 69 and 96 in Westcliffe, drive south on CO 69 for 4.6 miles, to where the road begins curving left (east). Turn right on County Road 119 (Colfax Lane) and drive south for 6.0 miles to a T intersection. Turn right (west) onto FR 120 and drive as far as your vehicle will allow. There is a small parking area on the right (north) side of the road, 1.4 miles past the T; after this point, passage requires a high-clearance vehicle. The road from the parking area up to the four-wheel-drive trailhead is very rough and tedious, and is one of the most difficult roads in the area.

For a longer hike, begin at the Horn Creek Trailhead (see Hike 22) and hike south about 6 miles on the Rainbow Trail.

Parking and trailhead facilities: Limited parking is available on South Colony Road near the intersection with the Rainbow Trail (1336).

Key points:
0.0 South Colony Road access to Rainbow Trail (1336).
3.5 North Colony Creek Trail (1340); turn left.
6.5 Lower North Colony Lake.
7.5 Upper North Colony Lakes.

The hike: From South Colony Road, hike 3.5 miles north along the gentle Rainbow Trail (1336) to the North Colony Creek Trail (1340); turn left (west). The trail continues climbing steadily up the valley before eventually leaving most of the trees behind. The trail thins above the tree line and becomes steeper, staying to the right (north) of the creek up to the lower lake. Continue up the North Colony Creek val-

111

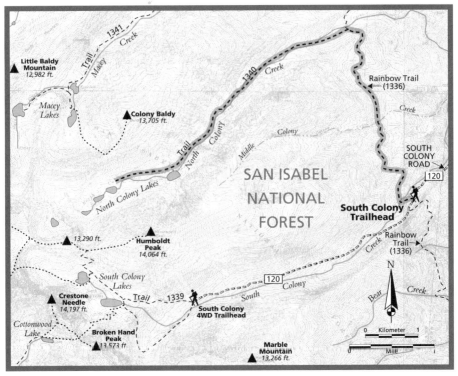

ley past smaller lakes up into the upper basin. Camping is available along the valley and in the upper basin.

Snow season: The long approach to this trail makes it a rarely hiked valley during snow season. The approach along the Rainbow Trail usually holds little snow.

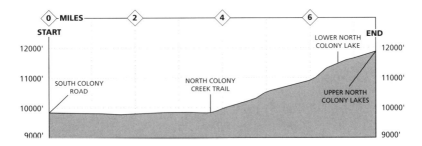

Colony Baldy and North Colony Lakes from Humboldt Peak's west ridge.

27

South Colony Lakes

Highlights: *A very popular trail to a pair of scenic lakes above the tree line.*

Type of hike: A short but steep out-and-back day hike or overnight backpack.
Total distance: 4.4 miles.
Difficulty: Easy.

Best months: Late June to September.
Maps: USGS Crestone Peak and Beck Mountain quads.

Special considerations: Parts of South Colony Road (Forest Road 120) barely deserve to be classified as a road. Early in the season, runoff seems to use the road as much as the creek, and the snowpack can linger below the trailhead into June. Be prepared to stop and proceed on foot in spring or fall when the road conditions will require it.

Finding the trailhead: From the intersection of Colorado Highways 69 and 96 in Westcliffe, drive south on CO 69 for 4.6 miles, to where the road begins curving left (east). Turn right on County Road 119 (Colfax Lane) and drive south for 6.0 miles to a T intersection. Turn right (west) onto CR 120 and drive as far as your vehicle will allow. There is a small parking area on the right (north) side of the road, 1.4 miles past the T; after this point, passage requires a high-clearance vehicle. The road from the lower parking area up to the four-wheel-drive trailhead is very rough and tedious, and is one of the most difficult roads in the area.

Parking and trailhead facilities: If you use the lower parking area, you will trade the wear on your car for tear on your knees, and add another 4.8 miles to the hike. There are a limited number of places to park and camp along the road past the national forest boundary, where it becomes FR 120. There are two good parking areas at the end of the road. Several heavily used camping areas exist near the end of the road on both sides of the creek.

Key points:
0.0 Four-wheel-drive trailhead.
1.1 Wilderness boundary.
1.5 Lower South Colony Lake.
2.2 Upper South Colony Lake.

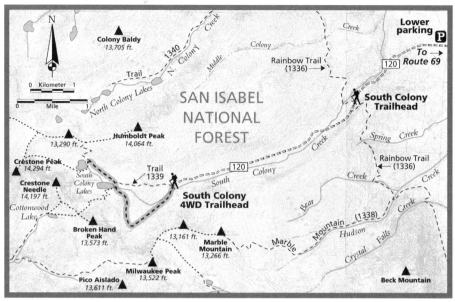

The hike: From the four-wheel-drive trailhead, hike past the gate closure up the left (south) side of the valley and past an old mine. Then curve right (north), past the wilderness boundary and continue climbing steadily into the upper valley. The trail enters the forest again and rejoins the creek below the lower lake. Here are the first good views of the very impressive Crestone Needle. Continue along the creek and then across it, using the stone stream crossing to get to the north side of the lower lake.

As an alternative approach to the lake, there is a shorter but steeper trail (1339) that starts from the north side of the creek just before the end of the four-wheel-drive road. This trail runs near some heavily used campsites and up through the trees along the right (north) side of the valley. It could be less snowcovered in early spring and late in the fall than the trail on the south side and therefore a better option.

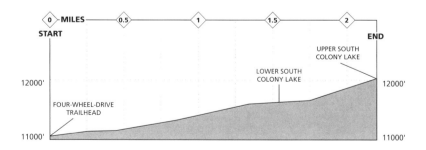

Crestone Needle and South Colony Creek.

From the lower lake, continue on the trail, which climbs gently to the upper lake at the base of Crestone Needle and Humboldt Peak, with Crestone Peak in the upper valley beyond.

Options: From the lower lake, a steep and rocky hike continues on a thin trail up to Broken Hand Pass, from where you can climb Crestone Needle or Broken Hand Peak (see Hike 30).

Hikes to Humboldt Peak, Kit Carson Mountain, and Crestone Peak (Hikes 28, 29, and 31) start on the north side of the upper lake. You can also continue west up the valley, find a thin trail along the left (east and south) side of the upper lake and enter the upper part of the valley, continuing to the small and scenic lake beyond. The optional access to Crestone Peak (Hike 31) is found here.

Snow season: When snow cuts off this popular road and deep drifts blanket the upper valley, the usual summer crowd becomes a distant memory and you are likely to have the entire valley to yourself. Park at the lower parking area and snowshoe or ski the 4.8 miles to the trailhead. Later in the snow season, the road can be a very enjoyable ski or snowshoe hike, although you will occasionally share it with snow machines. Even though the high peaks surrounding the upper valley are for more skilled winter climbers, the lakes and the valley can be a beautiful destination in winter.

28

Humboldt Peak

Highlights: *A popular trail to one of Colorado's easier 14,000-foot peaks with great summit views.*

Type of hike: Out-and-back day hike or overnight backpack.
Total distance: 8.0 miles.
Difficulty: Moderate.

Best months: Late June to September allows four-wheel-drive access.
Maps: USGS Crestone Peak and Beck Mountain quads.

Special considerations: This trail is mostly above the tree line, exposing hikers to thunderstorms and severe weather. Start this climb as early as possible to avoid the typical daily summer storm cycles.

Finding the trailhead: See South Colony Lakes (Hike 27) for trailhead description and the approach to the upper lake.

Key points:

0.0 Four-wheel-drive trailhead.
1.5 Lower South Colony Lake.
2.2 Upper South Colony Lake.
3.2 West ridge.
3.8 False summit.
4.0 Humboldt Peak.

The hike: From the upper South Colony Lake (Hike 27) turn right (north) and follow the well-built trail as it switchbacks up to the saddle onto Humboldt Peak's west ridge. From here, a thin trail leads directly up the ridge to the false summit

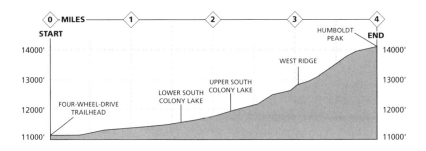

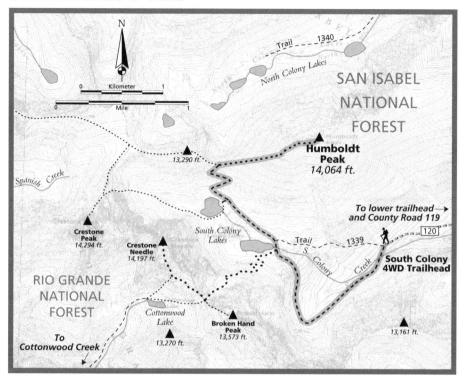

above. Take care to avoid being led left (north) of the ridge onto steeper terrain. From the false summit, continue along the right (south) side of the summit ridge across the almost level approach to the true summit.

Options: During spring and early summer, a long, continuous snowfield leads down from immediately east of the false summit to just above the end of the four-wheel-drive road. When snow conditions are safe, this can be an excellent glissade descent, if an ice ax is used.

Snow season: In winter, plan for a two- to three-day backpack, beginning at the lower parking area. The slopes above the upper lake may pose some avalanche danger. Check current conditions and be willing to turn back or alter your route to avoid dangerous slopes.

29

Kit Carson Mountain

Highlights: *A long, high traverse to one of Colorado's hardest 14,000-foot peaks.*

Type of hike: Long out-and-back day hike or overnight backpack.
Total distance: 12.0 miles.
Difficulty: Strenuous.

Best months: July to September.
Maps: USGS Crestone Peak and Beck Mountain quads.

Special considerations: This trail is mostly above the tree line, exposing hikers to thunderstorms and severe weather. Start this climb as early as possible to avoid the typical daily summer storm cycles. This is not a just hike—there are sections of steep scrambling (hand and foot climbing), with loose rock and possibly snow and ice. Wearing a helmet is recommended, and the use of an ice ax may be required in spring and fall. It is a nontechnical climb to one of Colorado's hardest 14,000-foot mountains, but it does require some route finding and is surrounded by technical terrain. Only those who are comfortable on steep rock should attempt it.

Finding the trailhead: See South Colony Lakes (Hike 27) for a description of the trailhead and the approach to the upper lake.

Key points:
0.0 Four-wheel-drive trailhead.
1.5 Lower South Colony Lake.
2.2 Upper South Colony Lake.
3.2 Humboldt's West Ridge.
4.2 Bear's Playground.
4.8 Unnamed 13,799.
5.5 False summit.
6.0 Kit Carson Mountain summit.

The hike: Hike to the upper South Colony Lake (Hike 27), then turn right (north) and switchback up to Humboldt's west ridge. Turn left (west) onto a thin trail that follows the ridge over Point 13,290. Stay generally to the left (south) of the ridge for about 0.5 mile, then cross over to the right (north) at a steep notch. Hike another 0.5 mile to the Bear's Playground, a flat tundra-covered saddle linking the connecting ridges of Humboldt Peak and Crestone Peak. Continue across tundra toward the high point leading to Kit Carson's east ridge, with views north over the upper basin of the Willow Creek valley and Mount Adams beyond. Proceed along

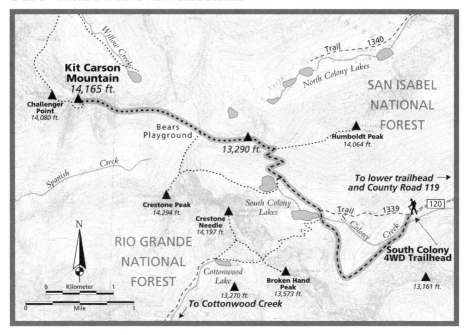

the crest of the ridge, dropping down before climbing more steeply up to Kit Carson's eastern false summit. From here, it is a difficult scramble down steep and loose rock before reaching the bottom of the notch. Climb up slightly easier slopes to the true summit.

Options: As a very strenuous addition, climb to the summit of Challenger Point by retracing the route back down the slope to the east. Descend until you reach the bottom of the notch. Turn right (south) and climb gradually to the west. Continue traversing southwest across the south buttress, then north along the Kit Carson Avenue ledges up to the saddle between Kit Carson Mountain and Challenger Point. Climb northwest up the easy slopes to the summit. With a car shuttle at the

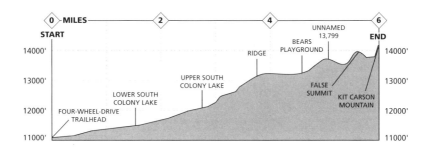

Kit Carson Mountain (far right) from the summit of Humboldt Peak.

South Crestone Trailhead, it would be an epic traverse to continue the descent north from Challenger Point to the Willow Creek valley; see Hikes 48 and 47 for route and trail descriptions.

Snow season: This is a difficult but reasonable route during safe avalanche conditions. The route begins at the lower parking area, adding almost 10 miles to the total distance. The length and the many high points along the ridge make this a very strenuous hike.

30

Crestone Needle

Highlights: *A challenging scramble up one of Colorado's hardest 14,000-foot peaks.*

Type of hike: Out-and-back day hike or overnight backpack.
Total distance: 6.4 miles.
Difficulty: Strenuous.

Best months: July to September.
Maps: USGS Crestone Peak and Beck Mountain quads.

Special considerations: This is not just a hike. It is a sustained, steep scramble (hand and foot climb) up a popular route with loose rock, running water, and possibly snow and ice. Wearing a helmet is recommended, and the use of an ice ax may be required in spring and fall. It is the only nontechnical way to climb one of Colorado's hardest 14,000-foot mountains, but it does require some route-finding skills and is surrounded by technical terrain. Only those who are comfortable on steep rock should attempt it.

Finding the trailhead: See South Colony Lakes (Hike 27) for trailhead description and the approach to the lower lake.

Key points:
0.0 Four-wheel-drive trailhead.
1.5 Lower South Colony Lake.
2.5 Pass.
2.8 Couloir.
3.1 False summit.
3.2 Crestone Needle.

The hike: From the trail at the lower South Colony Lake, turn left and find a crossing at the lake outlet. Wind your way through willows across to the base of the north-facing slope. Begin switchbacking up the trail on talus and scree high above the lake, toward the obvious low point on the ridge between Broken Hand Peak and Crestone Needle. There could be a snowfield here well into July. As you approach the pass, stay left of the sharp pinnacle above and find a narrow but easy scramble up to the ridge; turn right (west). From here it is possible to see the summit and most of the route ahead. Climb the couloir that extends from the lower left to the upper right, just right of the summit. Continue up the trail near the ridge, staying right at any forks in the braided trail.

The trail eventually gets harder to follow and crosses more and more broken ground. Enter the couloir above where it opens onto a scree slope that leads to

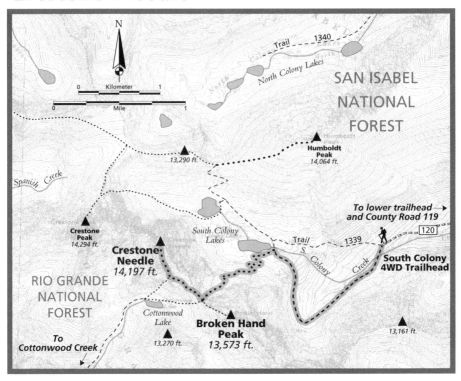

Cottonwood Lake below. If you get off the trail, it is possible to enter the couloir from the bottom over talus and scree above the lake. Climb and scramble up this couloir, directly up the center or along the sides, for about 1,000 vertical feet almost directly to the summit. Cross over the false summit and the final ridge to the true summit and enjoy the views from the top.

On the descent, take great care to retrace your steps all the way over the false summit and down the other side. You should be descending a couloir down toward

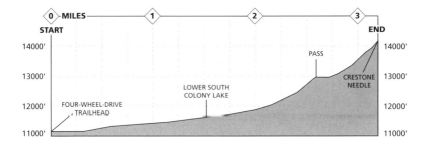

The trail leading to the couloir of Crestone Needle.

Broken Hand Peak (southeast), not the couloir above Cottonwood Lake (south), which becomes very steep and technical near the bottom. It is easy to mistake this for the correct route.

Options: Broken Hand Peak can also be climbed from this trail. At the pass, turn left (east) and climb up grassy slopes to the summit. As a difficult car shuttle backpacking trip, you can descend from Broken Hand Pass to Cottonwood Lake, then continue east over Milwaukee Pass, down the Sand Creek Trail (Hike 34), and then over Music Pass (Hike 33). Or descend from Cottonwood Lake west to the Cottonwood Creek Trailhead (Hike 49).

Snow season: This route is a hard technical climb when the couloir is filled with snow. It is a very enjoyable climb when avalanche conditions allow the approach to the pass to be made safely, but when the upper portions of Crestone Needle are covered with loose snow, this route is extremely difficult and potentially dangerous.

31

Crestone Peak

Highlights: *A challenging scramble up one of Colorado's hardest 14,000-foot peaks.*

Type of hike: Out-and-back day hike or overnight backpack.
Total distance: 10.0 miles.
Difficulty: Strenuous.

Best Months: July to September allow four-wheel drive access.
Maps: USGS Crestone Peak and Beck Mountain quads.

Special considerations: Like Crestone Needle, this hike involves some steep scrambling (hand and foot climbing) up a popular route with loose rock, running water, and possibly snow and ice. Wearing a helmet is recommended, and the use of an ice ax may be required most months of the year. It is a hard, semi-technical way to climb one of Colorado's hardest 14,000-foot mountains, but it does require some route-finding skills and is surrounded by technical terrain. Only those who are comfortable on steep rock should attempt it.

Finding the trailhead: See South Colony Lakes (Hike 27) for trailhead description and the approach to the upper lake.

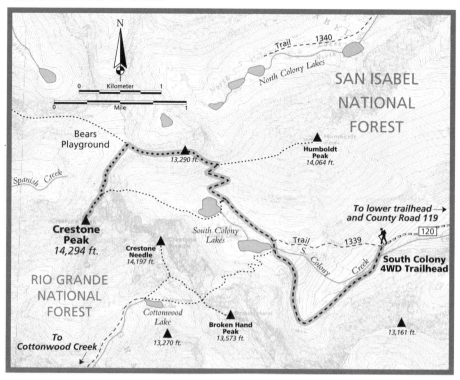

Key points:

- **0.0** Four-wheel-drive trailhead.
- **1.5** Lower South Colony Lake.
- **2.2** Upper South Colony Lake and optional approach trail.
- **3.2** Humboldt's west ridge.
- **4.2** Bear's Playground.
- **5.0** Crestone Peak.

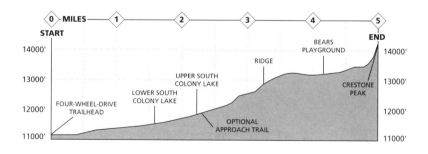

The hike: Hike to the upper South Colony Lake (Hike 27), then turn right (north) and switchback up onto Humboldt's west ridge. Turn left (west) onto a thin trail that follows the ridge over Point 13,290. Stay generally to the left (south) of the ridge for about 0.5 mile, then cross over to the right (north) at a steep notch. Hike another 0.5 mile to the Bear's Playground, a flat tundra-covered saddle linking the connecting ridges of Humboldt Peak and Crestone Peak. Hike south from here following a path to the right (west) of the rim of the cirque above the South Colony Creek drainage. An alternate approach from the upper lake crosses to the left (south) of the lake outlet and follows a thin trail up the valley and up one of several steep gullies at the end of the valley.

From the rim of the cirque, continue south up onto rocky ground as you climb toward Crestone Peak. Follow the path as it traverses across a rocky buttress that runs up toward the summit, and then follow the ledge into the gully that leads up between the twin spires that form the summit. The trail in the lower part of the couloir is not obvious until you climb a short way up into it where the entire route to the top becomes visible. It is possible to traverse too far beyond the lower entrance and end up on very steep and cliffy terrain beyond. The couloir is steep and loose, and running water, ice, and snow could clog the upper portions. Climb straight up through the center to the notch at the top of the couloir, turn right (south), and scramble along the ridge to the summit.

Crestone Peak.

128

Options: If the couloir is too loose or icy, it is possible to climb up the buttress to the left (north) up to the top and across to the summit. This is more difficult option and requires some semitechnical scrambling surrounded by technical terrain.

Crestone Peak can also be climbed from South Colony Lakes by following the route south over Broken Hand Pass (beginning of Hike 30) to Cottonwood Lake (Hike 49). This is an easier and more popular route than the Northwest Couloir.

Snow season: This route can actually be more desirable in spring snow than later in the summer when the snow gives way to loose rock and running water. Avalanche conditions must be favorable, however, and any mistakes above the steep cliffs at the lower end of the couloir could be costly. Climb this only with proper experience or a professional guide.

32 Marble Mountain Trail

Highlights: *A gentle trail to Marble Caves and Marble Mountain.*

Type of hike: Out-and-back day hike or overnight backpack.
Total distance: 12.0 miles.
Difficulty: Strenuous.

Best months: June to November.
Maps: USGS Crestone Peak and Beck Mountain quads.

Special considerations: When exploring the caves, take great care, go with an experienced guide, or turn back after the first couple hundred feet because there are obstacles beyond the entrance that require technical skills and equipment.

Parts of South Colony Road barely deserve to be classified as a road. Early in the season, runoff seems to use the road as much as the creek, and the snowpack can linger below the trailhead into June. Be prepared to stop and proceed on foot in spring or fall when the road conditions will require it.

Finding the trailhead: From the intersection of Colorado Highways 69 and 96 in Westcliffe, drive south on CO 69 for 4.6 miles, to where the road begins curving left (east). Turn right on County Road 119 (Colfax Lane) and drive south for 6.0 miles to a T intersection. Turn right (west) onto CR 120 and drive as far as your vehicle will allow. There is a small parking area on the right (north) side of the road, 1.4 miles past the T; after this point, passage requires a high-clearance vehicle. The road from the parking area up to the four-wheel-drive trailhead is very rough and tedious, and is one of the most difficult roads in the area.

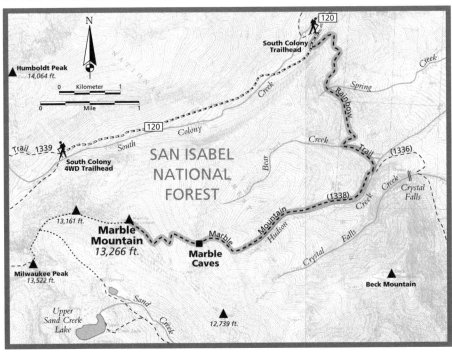

You can also begin at the lower Music Pass Trailhead (see Hike 33) and hike north about 7.5 miles on the Rainbow Trail. This longer approach requires more vertical gain, but the trailhead can usually be reached without a high-clearance vehicle.

Key points:
- **0.0** South Colony Road.
- **2.5** Marble Mountain Trail (1338); turn right.
- **5.0** Marble Caves.
- **6.0** Marble Mountain.

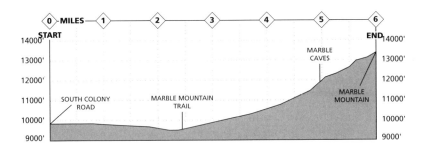

Jason Moore on Marble Mountain (October).

The hike: From the South Colony Road, hike northeast around a prominent ridge with views east over the Wet Mountain Valley and the Wet Mountains. Hike south as the trail slowly descends and crosses Bear Creek. Hike another 0.5 miles southeast along the Rainbow Trail (1336) to the Marble Mountain Trail (1338) and turn right (west). Continue up the trail, possibly also signed for Hudson Creek, along the right (north) side of the creek as it leads up to the tree line and the upper meadows. To find White Marble Hall Cave, look for a prominent rock buttress above the upper meadows. The entrance is on the left side just above its bottom. Marble Cave is on the right (north) side of this same buttress about 200 feet higher up. There are well-worn use trails in this area and some limited camping. Hike the Marble Mountain Trail northwest along a climbing traverse, switchbacking at times, to the crest of the range, and then right (north) to the summit of Marble Mountain.

Options: To reach Crystal Falls, continue south on the Rainbow Trail (1336) 1.0 mile beyond the intersection with the Marble Mountain Trail (1338). The falls are on the right, just above the creek crossing. This can be a good destination when conditions higher up are less than ideal.

With a car shuttle, an alternate descent from Marble Mountain can be made into the upper Sand Creek valley (Hike 34) by continuing west along the ridge, over Point 13,161, to the lowest point on the ridge east of Milwaukee Peak. Proceed southeast down to the drainage of the upper Sand Creek, then farther south on to Music Pass (Hike 33).

Snow season: Access up the South Colony Road can be limited by lower snow closures. The Music Pass Trailhead is usually easier to access but requires a longer approach. Snow cover can be thin along the open portions of the trail, thereby limiting good skiing. With good weather, ambitious hikers can climb Marble Mountain year-round.

33   Music Pass

Highlights: *An easy trail to a pass overlooking impressive peaks, with options for longer hikes and backpacking.*

Type of hike: Out-and-back day hike.
Total distance: 2.8 miles.
Difficulty: Easy.

Best months: May to December.
Maps: USGS Crestone Peak and Beck Mountain quads.

Finding the trailhead: From the intersection of Colorado Highways 69 and 96 in Westcliffe, drive south on CO 69 for 4.6 miles to where the road begins to curve left (west). Turn right on County Road 119 (Colfax Lane) and drive south for 6.0 miles to a T intersection. Turn left (east) onto CR 120. After 0.2 mile the road makes a sharp right and becomes CR 119. Continue about 5 miles, passing the national forest boundary, to the lower Music Pass Trailhead parking area at the intersection with the Rainbow Trail (1336). From this point, Forest Road 119 continues for another 2.5 miles, requiring a high-clearance vehicle. The road from the parking area up to the four-wheel-drive trailhead is rough and tedious, but it is usually passable to its end, where there is a small turnaround.

Parking and trailhead facilities: A parking area and a toilet are available at the lower trailhead. The upper trailhead has a large parking area and some heavily used campsites.

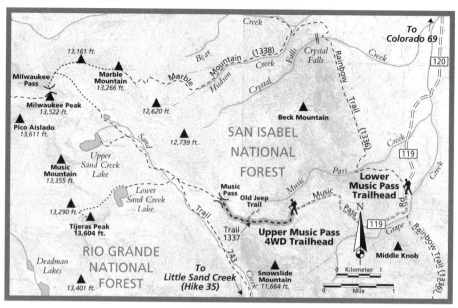

Key points:

0.0 Four-wheel-drive trailhead.
0.8 Jeep road.
1.4 Music Pass.

The hike: From the upper parking area, hike west up the gentle trail (1337) through an evergreen forest to an intersection with an old jeep road. Past the road, the trail becomes steeper and begins to switchback before reaching the pass at 1.4 miles.

Options: From the pass, descend west to the Sand Creek Trail (743) and the open meadows below. From the Sand Creek, you can turn left (south) to get to the Lit-

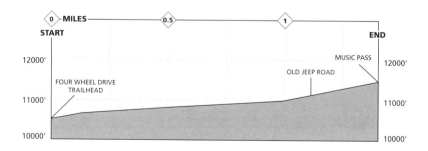

View of Tijeras Peak from Music Pass.

tle Sand Creek Lakes (Hike 35), or turn right (north) to approach the Sand Creek Lakes and the upper valley (Hike 34).

It is also possible to continue north along the crest of the range over three 12,000-foot points and on to the summit of Marble Mountain. This is a long and exposed hike above the tree line. Hike early in the day and only during good weather. The only good descent options are to return the way you came or continue up and over Marble Mountain. From Marble Mountain, you can continue along the ridge west to the saddle above Sand Creek's upper basin (Hike 34) and descend back south to Music Pass. This is a long and strenuous option, but the views south to the Sierra Blanca and west to the Crestones are spectacular.

It is also possible to continue south from Music Pass to the summits of Snowslide Mountain, Blueberry Peak, Blizzardine Peak, and beyond with long car shuttle options. These are strenuous off-trail routes that could require some route-finding skills and a willingness to cross downed timber and rough ground.

Snow season: The lower access to the Music Pass Road makes these hikes more difficult. The pass itself can be a good one-day snowshoe or ski route. The longer optional hikes beyond the pass usually require camping higher up the road, near its end.

34

Sand Creek Lakes

Highlights: *A good trail with access to two separate lakes, Tijeras Peak, Milwaukee Peak, Marble Mountain, and Cottonwood Creek (Hike 49).*

Type of hike: Out-and-back day hike or overnight backpack.
Total distance: 7.0 miles.
Difficulty: Moderate.

Best months: June to November.
Maps: USGS Crestone Peak and Beck Mountain quads.

Finding the trailhead: From the intersection of Colorado Highways 69 and 96 in Westcliffe, drive south on CO 69 for 4.6 miles, to where the road begins curving left (east). Turn right on County Road 119 (Colfax Lane) and drive south for 6.0 miles to a T intersection. Turn left (east) onto CR 120. After 0.2 mile the road makes a sharp right and becomes CR 119. Continue about 5 miles, passing the national forest boundary, to the lower Music Pass Trailhead parking area at the intersection with the Rainbow Trail (1336). From this point, Forest Road 119 continues for another 2.5 miles, requiring a high clearance vehicle. The road from the parking area up to the four-wheel-drive trailhead is rough and tedious, but it is usually passable to its end, where there is a small turnaround.

Parking and trailhead facilities: A parking area and a toilet are available at the lower trailhead. The upper trailhead has a large parking area and some heavily used campsites.

Key points:
0.0 Four-wheel-drive trailhead.
1.4 Music Pass.
2.2 Sand Creek Trail (743).
2.5 Lower Sand Creek Trail; continue straight.
3.1 Upper Sand Creek Trail.
3.5 Upper Sand Creek Lake.

The hike: From the upper parking area, hike west up the gentle trail (1337) through an evergreen forest to an intersection with an old jeep road. Past the road, the trail becomes steeper and begins to switchback before reaching the pass at 1.4 miles. Descend northwest into open meadows to the Sand Creek Trail (743) and hike northwest up the valley for 0.3 mile to the Lower Sand Creek Trail. Be aware

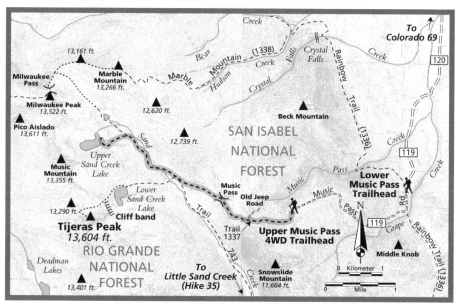

that this trail is farther south than shown on most maps. Continue north up the Sand Creek Trail 0.6 mile, crossing to the south side of the Sand Creek. Turn left (west) on the Upper Sand Creek Trail, which climbs up the west slope of the valley through evergreens to the Upper Sand Creek Lake. This trail is also misplaced on most maps, but it is usually well signed and easy to find. Camping is available in the Sand Creek Valley and at a limited number of sites around the lake.

Options: To visit Lower Sand Creek Lake and climb to the summit of Tijeras Peak, follow the Lower Sand Creek Trail west into evergreens as it crosses to the south side of Sand Creek and begins to switchback up to Lower Sand Creek Lake. There are good camping sites near the lake as well as in the meadows near the Sand Creek Trail. Hike around the north end of the lake, then northwest along the right

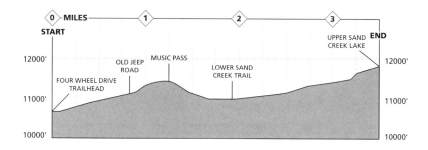

Looking toward Music Pass from the upper Sand Creek Valley.

(north) side of the willows, and climb up into the upper part of the basin. Traverse south through the thinning willows toward a prominent notch that leads from the lower right up to the left across the cliff band above. This slot ramps steeply up to the upper slopes of Tijeras's north face and requires fairly easy scrambling on solid rock with the possibility of steep snow or ice early in the summer. Once above the notch, hike up steep grassy slopes mixed with solid rock to the low point between the summit on the left (south) and Unnamed 13,290 on the right (west). From the saddle, stay left (north) of the jagged ridge across the steep rocky slope, and then move up on a more direct approach toward the summit. This is a steep scramble well above the tree line and requires good weather to be safe from thunderstorms.

You can continue on the Sand Creek Trail (743) past the Upper Sand Creek Trail over Milwaukee Pass to Cottonwood Creek (Hike 49). Do not follow the trail marked on most maps, which leads to steep technical terrain on the east face of Milwaukee Peak. Instead, follow the Sand Creek Trail north as it continues into the large upper valley. The trail thins and then eventually disappears as it enters the upper basin. Continue hiking up the gentle climb and around to the left (west) toward the saddle that lies to the left (west) of Unnamed 13,161. From here the views north across South Colony Creek, Humboldt Peak, Crestone Peak, and Crestone Needle are spectacular. To hike to the top of Marble Mountain, turn back to the right (east) and continue hiking along the ridge over Unnamed 13,161 before reaching the summit. To continue over the pass leading to Cottonwood Creek, turn left (south) on the ridge. Climb up the steep but solid rock and grass slopes to the left (east) of the high points directly to the south. This might look more intimidating than it is, because the climb up is fairly easy over solid ground. Find the trail leading up the last stretch to the pass north of Milwaukee Peak. From the pass, follow the trail west down to Cottonwood Creek (Hike 49).

Snow season: The lower access at the snow closure of the Music Pass road makes these hikes more difficult. The routes described to the upper and lower lakes or farther up into the upper basin can be excellent snowshoe day hikes or two- to three-day backpack trips. Climbing the optional hikes to Tijeras Peak or Milwaukee Pass should only be attempted with a safe spring snowpack because of the high potential for a serious avalanche. The climb to Marble Mountain may be possible year-round.

35

Little Sand Creek

Highlights: *A lesser-used trail to a high scenic lake.*

Type of hike: Two- to three-day out-and-back backpack.
Total distance: 17.0 miles.

Difficulty: Strenuous.
Best months: July to September.
Maps: USGS Crestone Peak and Liberty quads.

Finding the trailhead: See Music Pass (Hike 33) for trailhead access and the hike to Music Pass.

Key points:

0.0 Four-wheel-drive trailhead.
1.4 Music Pass.
2.2 Sand Creek Trail (743); turn left.
5.8 Little Sand Creek Trail (863); turn right.
8.5 Little Sand Creek Lakes.

The hike: From Music Pass (Hike 33), descend northwest to the Sand Creek Trail (743) and turn sharply left (south) down the valley. The descent along the Sand Creek requires frequent crossings. This trail is not used or maintained as often as the others in the area. You may have to bushwhack and cross over fallen timber in some places, but it is well worth it. Keep looking for the Little Sand Creek Trail (863) on the right, which climbs north near a large and well-used campsite just before you reach the Little Sand Creek. Turn right and climb steeply to the north as the trail stays high above and to the right (east) of the creek, then gradually levels off up into the upper valley. The trail stays to the right (east) of the creek before turning left (southwest) up into the upper basin and the lower Little Sand Creek Lake. There is limited but good camping near the lake.

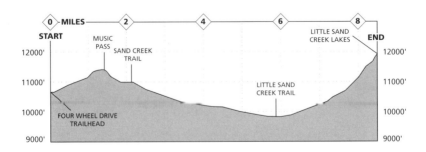

Lower Sand Creek from Music Pass.

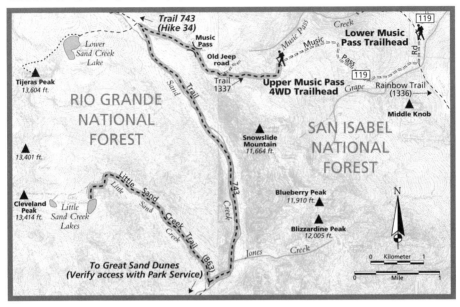

Options: As a continuation on a car shuttle loop, hike the lower Sand Creek valley past the Little Sand Creek Trail to the northern boundary of Great Sand Dunes National Park (Hike 54). This is a much more difficult trail than most because it is unmaintained and could be closed by private land at the bottom of the valley. Check with Great Sand Dunes National Park officials regarding the current status of access across the private Baca Grant. Acquisition of this land may allow for the expansion of Great Sand Dunes National Park and unrestricted access.

Snow season: Limited access makes this a much more difficult winter hike, snowshoe, or ski. It is a strenuous but very rewarding snow-season hike, almost ensuring total solitude.

36

Medano Lake

Highlights: *An easy trail up an open valley to a high lake and access to Mount Seven.*

Type of hike: Out-and-back day hike or overnight backpack.
Total distance: 7.0 miles.

Difficulty: Moderate.
Best months: June to September.
Maps: USGS Medano Pass quad.

Finding the trailhead: From the intersection of Colorado Highways 69 and 96 in Westcliffe, drive south for 24 miles on CO 69 and turn right (west) onto County Road 559, which usually has signs for Medano Pass. Drive west past private ranch land on a good dirt road for 7.0 miles to the national forest boundary. The road begins to climb more steeply and usually requires four-wheel drive for the last 2.0 miles to Medano Pass. Continue over the pass and down 0.5 mile to an open meadow and the spur road leading right (north) for another 0.2 mile to the Medano Lake Trailhead.

Alternatively, access the pass road from Great Sand Dunes National Park. Follow the signs for the Medano Pass Primitive Road, crossing Medano Creek before veering right (east) into the narrow canyon up to the spur road and the pass beyond. Deep sand near the dunes and the crossing of Medano Creek can make this a more difficult option.

Parking and trailhead facilities: A small turnaround is provided at the trailhead.

Key points:
0.0 Medano Lake Trailhead.
1.0 Creek crossing.
2.0 Slide path.
3.5 Medano Lake.

The hike: Hike immediately across Medano Creek to its west side and continue northwest up the valley through aspen and evergreen forests, open meadows, and thick patches of wildflowers. Follow the trail (887) as it curves left (west) and begins to climb steeply into the upper valley. Cross over to the left (south) side of the creek at an obvious slide path. (**Option:** Hike across the slide path, staying to the right of the creek, and continue to the lake.) After crossing the creek, the trail winds among the evergreens before eventually crossing to the right side of the creek and the final climb to the lake.

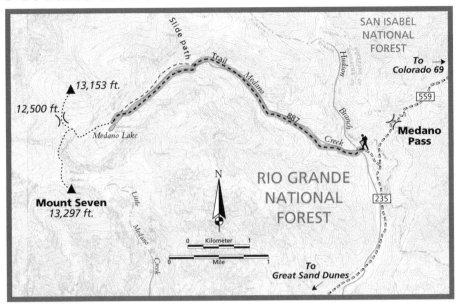

Options: From the lake, it is possible to continue into the upper basin to the north and the summit of Mount Seven, seen southwest at the head of the valley. Hike north of the lake outlet, then west up a ramp that forms a climbing traverse. The ramp takes you above the steep rock outcroppings that are situated above the lake but below the cliff face to the northwest. Follow a thin trail that you might find leading into the upper basin beyond the lake. Continue climbing west up to the ridge, left (south) of the low spot of the ridge, which is marked Point 12,500 on some maps. Once on the ridge, hike south to the large, broad summit of Mount Seven. It is also possible to climb north on the ridge from Point 12,500 to the summit of Unnamed 13,153.

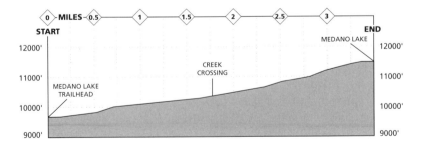

144

Mount Seven from Medano Lake.

Snow season: Access can be difficult during snow season, with the snow closure at about the national forest boundary on the east side. With a fairly easy snowshoe or ski up the road beyond the snow closure and a variety of camping options, this can be a good snow-season backpack trip. You can also continue over the pass to Great Sand Dunes National Park as a long day hike or overnight backpack with a car shuttle.

Central
SANGRE DE CRISTO,
WEST SIDE

Rising 7,000 vertical feet from the floor of the San Luis Valley, the mountains of the central Sangre de Cristo form an impressive sight, unlike any in Colorado. The valley itself, at more than 3,000 square miles, is the largest mountain valley in the world. It is an expansive plain of cattle and sheep ranchers and farmers. Potatoes, lettuce, organic carrots, broccoli, canola, hay, and barley are grown in the San Luis Valley.

There are only small towns scattered along the valley, and major services are limited. Saguache, Villa Grove, Moffat, and Crestone are small but delightful communities of agriculture, art, and spiritual retreats. Saguache has a grocery store, restaurants, a small number of inns, an RV park, and motels. *Saguache Crescent*, the local paper, is the last remaining hot-lead letterpress in Colorado; it has been family-owned since 1917. Crestone is host to several retreats, Buddhist stupas, and ashrams. It has a small store and a liquor store, but limited outdoor gear and accommodations. Hunting, fishing, hot springs (Valley View, Mineral, and the Sand Dunes Swimming Pool), biking on the many forest roads along the base of the mountains and near Bonanza, and world-class rock climbing in Penitente Canyon (see Falcon Guides *Rock Climbing Colorado's San Luis Valley*) round out a full plate of recreational opportunities in the area.

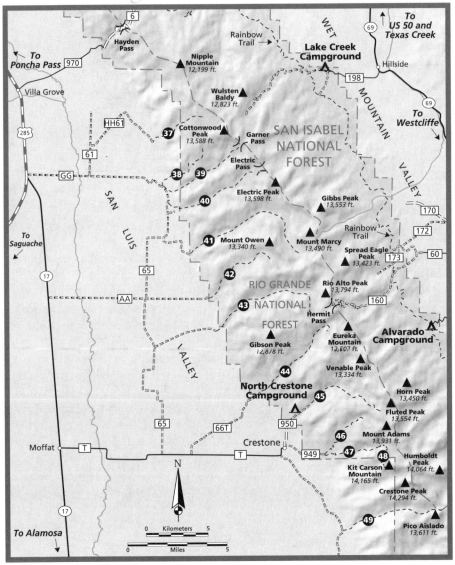

6

Hayden
Pass

Rainbow
Trail →

WET

69

To
US 50 and
Texas Creek

**To
Poncha Pass** 970

Nipple
Mountain
12,199 ft.

**Lake Creek
Campground**

Hillside

198

Villa Grove

Wulsten
Baldy
12,823 ft.

MOUNTAIN

69

To
Westcliffe

285

HH61

37

Cottonwood
Peak
13,588 ft.

Garner
Pass

SAN ISABEL
NATIONAL
FOREST

61

Electric
Pass

38 39

VALLEY

GG

SAN

40

Electric Peak
13,598 ft.

Gibbs Peak
13,553 ft.

Rainbow
Trail

170

172

To
Saguache

LUIS

41 Mount Owen
13,340 ft.

Mount Marcy
13,490 ft.

Spread Eagle
Peak
13,423 ft.

173

60

17

65

42

RIO GRANDE

Río Alto Peak
13,794 ft.

160

AA

43 NATIONAL
FOREST

Hermit
Pass

Eureka
Mountain
13,507 ft.

**Alvarado
Campground**

VALLEY

Gibson Peak
12,878 ft.

Venable Peak
13,334 ft.

44

**North Crestone
Campground**

45

Horn Peak
13,450 ft.

65

66T

950

Fluted Peak
13,554 ft.

Moffat

T

Crestone

949

46

47

Mount Adams
13,931 ft.

48

Humboldt
Peak
14,064 ft.

N

T

Kit Carson
Mountain
14,165 ft.

Crestone Peak
14,294 ft.

17

49

Pico Aislado
13,611 ft.

To Alamosa

0   Kilometers   5

0   Miles   5

37

Black Canyon

Highlights: *A short trail up a narrow valley with access to the Nipple Mountain Trail (Hike 7).*

Type of hike: Out-and-back day hike, or two- to three-day backpack.
Total distance: 7.0 miles.

Difficulty: Moderate.
Best months: May to October.
Maps: USGS Valley View Hot Springs quad.

Special considerations: Water is available throughout the lower valley but becomes scarce as you approach the tree line. Hunters frequent the valley during the fall; check with the Forest Service and the Colorado Division of Wildlife for more information.

Finding the trailhead: From Poncha Springs, drive 22 miles south on U.S. Highway 285 to Villa Grove, then 4 miles south to the intersection of US 285 and Colorado Highway 17. If coming from Alamosa, drive 50 miles north on CO 17 to US 285.

Immediately north of this intersection, turn east onto County Road GG. The road is hard to see as it turns off of US 285, but you might spot the small county road sign or other signs for Valley View Hot Springs. Drive east on CR GG for 3.2 miles and turn left (north) onto CR 61, which usually has a sign for the Black Canyon Trailhead. Drive north for 1.5 miles, then turn right (east) onto the rougher CR HH-61. Follow this road for 2.2 miles until it turns right and crosses a creek; continue straight another 2.5 miles to the Black Canyon Trailhead. Most cars can drive this road, except during winter months when snowdrifts could block the last mile or two.

Key points:
0.0 Black Canyon Trailhead.
1.0 Mines.
2.0 Wilderness Boundary.
2.5 Meadow.
3.0 Nipple Mountain Trail (754).
3.5 Upper meadow.

The hike: Hike along the rocky trail (754) up into the mouth of the narrow canyon along the small creek. Cross the creek several times before intersecting a larger trail/road on the left that leads up to a small bench with views of the San Luis Valley to the west and some small mine prospects. This area offers good camping,

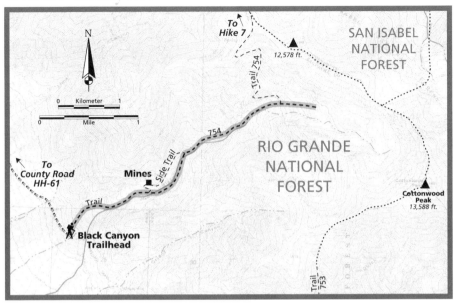

and the thin trail beyond continues up the valley to rejoin the main trail. If staying on the main trail, cross the creek to the left (north) side of the valley before rejoining the spur trail. Just after this intersection you cross the wilderness boundary. Continue hiking up the valley and pass a small meadow before intersecting the Nipple Mountain Trail (Hike 7) on the left. Continue following the trail as the valley curves to the right (south) and proceed to the upper meadows for views of Cottonwood Peak's northwest face.

Options: To continue on the Nipple Mountain Trail (Hike 7) to Point 12,503 and the crest of the range, hike north up the thin, gentle trail as it turns left off the main

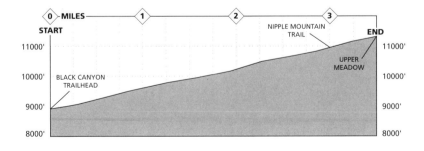

Cottonwood Peak from Black Canyon (February).

trail and ascends steeply up a seasonal creek to the ridge just below Point 12,503. See Hike 7 for a description of the trail from here over Nipple Mountain and north to Hayden Pass.

Where the Nipple Mountain Trail intersects with the crest of the range, you can turn right (south) and hike along the ridge to Cottonwood Peak. This is a more difficult approach than that from the Cloverdale Basin described in Hike 10 or from Hot Springs Canyon (Hike 38). This route requires some scrambling and prolonged exposure to the weather.

Snow season: During snow season, this canyon can be a good snowshoe up to the upper meadow and a challenging climb up to the crest of the range. Trailhead access may be slightly lower due to snow drifts.

38 Hot Springs Canyon

Highlights: *A trail up a narrow valley with access to Cottonwood Peak.*

Type of hike: Out-and-back day hike.
Total distance: 8.0 miles.
Difficulty: Easy.

Best months: Year-round.
Maps: USGS Valley View Hot Springs quad.

Special considerations: Water is available throughout the lower valley but becomes scarce as you approach the tree line. Some hunting is allowed in the valley during the fall; check with the Forest Service and the Colorado Division of Wildlife for more information.

Finding the trailhead: From Poncha Springs, drive 22 miles south on U.S. Highway 285 to Villa Grove, then 4 miles south to the intersection of US 285 and Colorado Highway 17. If coming from Alamosa, drive 50 miles north on CO 17 to US 285.

Immediately north of this intersection, turn east onto County Road GG. The road is hard to see as it turns off of US 285, but you might spot the small county road sign or other signs for Valley View Hot Springs. Drive east on CR GG for 8.2 miles, then turn right (south) onto CR 65. After 0.6 mile, turn left (east) and park at the Hot Springs Trailhead.

Parking and trailhead facilities: There is a good parking area at the trailhead, but no camping is available.

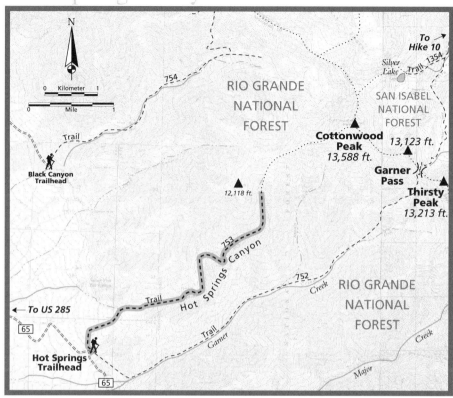

Key points:

0.0 Hot Springs Trailhead.
2.0 Meadow.
4.0 Tree line.

The hike: Follow the trail (753) as it climbs past pinion pine and juniper then up the canyon before narrowing beyond a small meadow. The trail becomes harder to

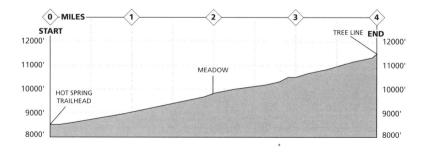

follow but mainly continues up the valley along the left side of the creek as the valley curves left (north) up to the tree line.

Options: After 4.0 miles the trail ceases to be recognizable, but continue climbing 0.5 mile along the creek up to the ridge ahead and to the left (north). This is Cottonwood Peak's west ridge, which has views of the northern section of the range and south over much of the central range. Hike east along the ridge 0.3 mile to the false summit, and continue 0.7 mile to Cottonwood Peak's true summit. Some camping is available along the lower valley.

It is possible to descend south from Cottonwood Peak along the crest of the range over Unnamed 13,123 to the pass north of Thirsty Peak. From the pass follow the thin trail west down to the Garner Creek Trail (Hike 39), or east down into Cloverdale Basin (Hike 10).

Snow season: Trailhead access is usually good year-round, and Cottonwood Peak's west ridge remains windswept with almost no avalanche danger. However, the slopes above the tree line approaching the ridge can slide and should be climbed with caution. The hikes to the ridge and Cottonwood Peak beyond are long and strenuous options that are well worth the effort.

North from Cottonwood Peak's west ridge (December).

39

Garner Creek

Highlights: *A trail up an aspen-filled valley with access to Thirsty Peak.*

Type of hike: Out-and-back day hike with loop and car shuttle options.
Total distance: 11.0 miles.
Difficulty: Moderate.

Best months: June to October.
Maps: USGS Electric Peak and Valley View Hot Springs quads.

Special considerations: Water is available throughout the lower valley but becomes scarce as you approach the tree line. Hunters frequent the valley during the fall; check with the Forest Service and the Colorado Division of Wildlife for more information.

Finding the trailhead: From Poncha Springs, drive 22 miles south on U.S. Highway 285 to Villa Grove, then 4 miles to the intersection of US 285 and Colorado Highway 17. If coming from Alamosa, drive 50 miles north on CO 17 to US 285.

Immediately north of this intersection, turn east onto County Road GG. The road is hard to see as it turns off of US 285, but you might spot the small county road sign or other signs for Valley View Hot Springs. Drive east on CR GG for 8.2 miles, then turn right (south) onto CR 65. After 0.6 mile, turn left (east) and park at the Hot Springs Trailhead.

Parking and trailhead facilities: There is a good parking area at the trailhead, but no camping is available.

Key points:
0.0 Hot Springs Trailhead.
0.6 Garner Creek valley.
2.6 Side stream.
4.2 Upper valley.
5.5 Garner Pass.

The hike: From the trailhead, hike to the right (south) and follow Trail 752 as it parallels private land and enters Garner Creek valley on the left. Climb gently along the creek through the extensive aspen forest as Thirsty Peak comes into view straight ahead. Continue past the smaller side streams on the left and hike east into the upper valley to Garner Pass. Good camping can be found up the valley below the steep uppermost sections approaching the pass that leads to Cloverdale Basin (Hike 10).

155

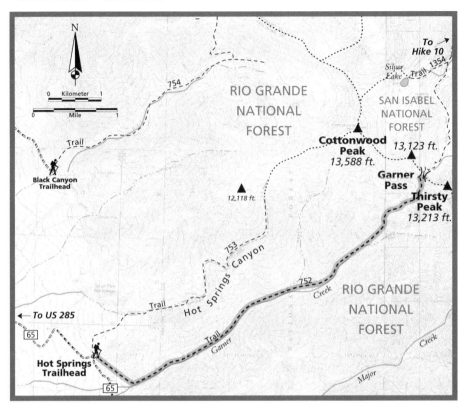

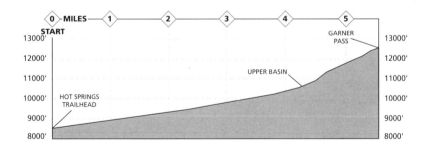

Thirsty Peak from Garner Pass.

Options: From the pass at the range crest, you can either hike directly down into the Cloverdale Basin, or climb north to Unnamed 13,123 and on to Cottonwood Peak, where you can descend east into Cloverdale Basin via Silver Lake. It is also possible to climb south of the pass to the summit of Thirsty Peak and return to the pass before descending, or continue south over Lakes Peak and descend into Major Creek (Hike 40).

Snow season: This is a very good snow-season ski or snowshoe up to the tree line. Beyond, the windswept slopes leading to the crest of the range can be climbed throughout most of the year.

40 Major Creek

Highlights: *A good trail past huge aspens and beaver ponds up to a high valley with access to Lakes Peak, Electric Peak, and Mount Niedhardt.*

Type of hike: Long out-and-back day hike or overnight backpack.
Total distance: 10.0 miles.
Difficulty: Strenuous.

Best months: May to November.
Maps: USGS Electric Peak and Valley View Hot Springs quads.

Special considerations: Treatable water is available up most of the valley but is limited in the upper basin. Hunters frequent the valley during the fall; check with the Forest Service and the Colorado Division of Wildlife for more information.

Finding the trailhead: From Poncha Springs, drive 22 miles south on U.S. Highway 285 to Villa Grove, then 4 miles south to the intersection of US 285 and Colorado Highway 17. If coming from Alamosa, drive 50 miles north on CO 17 to US 285.

Immediately north of this intersection, turn east onto County Road GG. The road is hard to see as it turns off of US 285, but you might spot the small county road sign or other signs for Valley View Hot Springs. Drive east on CR GG for 8.2 miles, then turn right (south) onto CR 65. Drive 1.0 mile, make a sharp left turn onto CR 66-FF, and continue 0.1 mile to the Major Creek Trailhead.

Parking and trailhead facilities: There is a small parking area at the trailhead, but no camping is available.

Key points:
- **0.0** Major Creek Trailhead.
- **1.5** Beaver ponds.
- **2.0** Lower meadows.
- **3.6** High meadows.
- **5.0** Upper valley.

The hike: From the trailhead, turn right (south) and hike past juniper and cactus to the ridge overlooking the Major Creek valley. Switchback down to the creek, taking care to avoid private land on the right (west). At the bottom of the descent, turn left (east) and follow the trail as it skirts and crosses the creek several times before passing to the left (north) around marshes and beaver ponds. Pass the ponds and hike the moderately steep trail up the lower meadows, where you can see Lakes Peak above the upper valley.

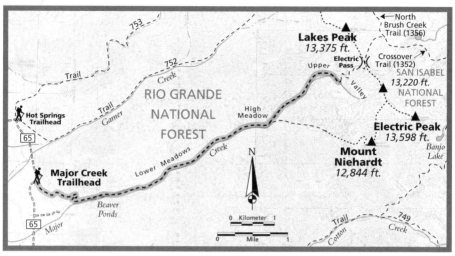

Continue up into thicker fir forest along a wide trail to open meadows and aspen tree stands. This high meadow is large and sometimes used by outfitters and horse and llama trekkers. Hike through the meadow to find the trail as it reenters the trees at the far end. At this point the trail gets rockier, winding in and out of the trees as it curves south up into the upper valley. From here, Lakes Peak is behind you and Electric Peak's north and west ridges are ahead to the south. A limited number of campsites are available along the lower valley with more sites at the lower and upper meadows.

Options: From the upper valley, you can climb to the summit of Lakes Peak, Unnamed 13,220, Electric Peak, or Mount Niedhardt. Climb to the pass from the meadow in the upper valley by following the rough trail that climbs up the switchbacks to the pass to the east. This trail may be hard to find, but it starts at the lower end of the upper valley and turns left (east) where it climbs the lower tree-covered slopes then up toward the pass. From the pass, turn left (north) and follow the broad ridge to Lakes Peak. Turn right (south) at the pass, to ascend to Unnamed

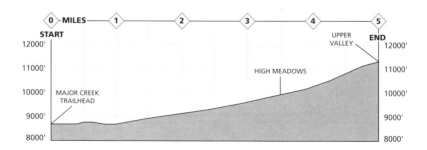

The upper meadow of Major Creek.

13,220, then continue down to the connecting ridge leading left (east) to Electric Peak's summit. To climb Mount Niedhardt, bypass Electric Peak's connecting ridge and turn right (west then south) to this lower summit overlooking the Cotton Creek basin to the south.

From Lakes Peak you can continue north along the ridge to Thirsty Peak and down to the west into the Garner Creek valley, or east to South Branch Lake, North Brush Lakes, or into the Cloverdale Basin. From Electric Peak you can descend north to South Branch Lake, or south to Banjo Lake.

An easier way to approach Electric Peak or Mount Niedhardt is to climb farther into the upper valley beyond where the main trail switchbacks up to Electric Pass. Trend to the right of the valley along a game trail that winds up to lower reaches of Electric Peak's east ridge. After the short climb to the ridge, hike up to the range crest between Unnamed 13,220 and Mount Niedhardt.

A more direct route to Mount Niedhardt follows a difficult path up the south fork of the creek that branches right (south) just below the high meadow. This trail immediately crosses the creek and climbs into the valley and meadows above, where it becomes increasingly difficult to follow. As it steepens along the approach, stay right of the creek and continue up steep grassy slopes to the summit of Mount Niedhardt. This path can be used as an emergency descent during bad weather, or descend from the summit southwest through a difficult bushwhack to the Cotton Creek Trail (Hike 41).

All of these options are off-trail and require a great deal of care to avoid excessive erosion. Please practice a strict zero impact policy when attempting any of these routes.

Snow season: Access to the trailhead is straightforward due to regular road maintenance. The best approach to the range crest from the upper valley may be along the alternate ridge approach on the game trail south of the upper valley as described above. It tends to be more windswept, with safer avalanche conditions than the direct climb to Electric Pass.

Cotton Creek

Highlights: *A long, gentle trail to a scenic lake.*

Type of hike: Long out-and-back day hike or overnight backpack.
Total distance: 16.0 miles.
Difficulty: Strenuous.

Best months: July to September.
Maps: USGS Valley View Hot Springs and Electric Peak quads.

Special considerations: The trail is wide and usually well maintained for much of its length. It is popular with horse and llama trekkers and outfitters. When wet, the last mile to the lake can be very muddy and rutted.

Finding the trailhead: From Poncha Springs, drive 26 miles south on U.S. Highway 285 to the intersection of Colorado Highway 17. Travel 6 miles south on CO 17 and turn left (east) onto County Road AA. From Alamosa, drive 44 miles north on CO 17 and turn right (east) onto CR AA.

Drive 6.0 miles on CR AA and turn left (north) onto CR 64. Continue for 2 miles to a right turn (east) onto a rougher road signed for the Cotton Creek Trailhead.

Parking and trailhead facilities: There is a small area for parking at the trailhead, but no camping is available.

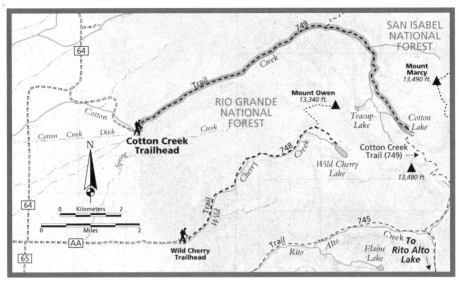

Key points:

- **0.0** Cotton Creek Trailhead.
- **3.0** Beaver ponds.
- **5.0** Banjo Lake Trail (856) goes left.
- **6.0** Middle Fork.
- **6.5** Henderson Gulch.
- **8.0** Cotton Lake.

The hike: This is one of the longest trails and largest drainages in the range. The valley carries one of the largest creeks and has the most extensive aspen groves. From the trailhead, hike east up the wide trail (749) to the right (south) of the creek. Then cross over to the left (north) side, using the usually good log or rock crossings. Climb up the gentle valley past remnants of beaver ponds and man-made

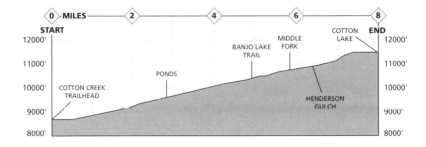

Cotton Lake.

reservoirs with views of De Anza Peak ahead to the left and Mount Marcy above to the right. As the valley begins to bend to the right (south), hike past several small meadows and beyond the Banjo Lake Trail (856) on the left (northeast) at 5.0 miles.

Continue up the valley, climbing gently to the south for about a mile. Cross the fairly large Middle Fork Creek and skirt a small willow-filled meadow before beginning a steep climb. After several switchbacks, the trail finally breaks out of the fir and spruce forest that surrounds Cotton Lake. Views of Mount Owen are to the right (south) along much of the trail below Cotton Lake. Camping is available in the upper portions of the valley near the lake, and outfitters heavily use many sites in the area. Camping is not allowed within 300 feet of the lake.

Options: To continue hiking up over the crest of the range to the South Brush Creek Trail (Hike 12), turn left (northeast) on the Banjo Lake trail (856) at mile 5.0. Hike up the steep switchbacking trail, past Horsethief Basin, and up to the top of the ridge.

As a car shuttle option, you can backpack south on established trails to Rito Alto Lake (Hike 43), then across the upper valley of San Isabel Creek (Hike 44), and down to the North Fork of North Crestone Creek (Hike 45). This is an excellent long backpacking trip that can be done from either direction. To get to Rito Alto Lake, continue on the trail as it wraps around the left (east) side of Cotton Lake. Cross the inlet at the foot of an impressive rockslide below the summit of Unnamed 13,513 and hike up the steep switchbacks above the west side of the lake. Continue to the crest of a prominent ridge that splits the upper Cotton Creek valley between the impressive faces of Unnamed 13,513 to the left and Unnamed 13,490 to the right. Follow the trail as it switchbacks up the final climb to the pass that leads to the Rito Alto Trail (Hike 43). The views to the north from the pass are spectacular.

Snow season: This is a good trail to the lake during snow season; the moderate grades are perfect for cross-country skiing or snowshoeing all the way to the lake. The optional hikes are much more challenging, but are still possible when the potential for avalanches is low. The climb up the last north-facing slopes of the high pass leading to Rito Alto Creek could be particularly unsafe after recent storms or high winds.

Wild Cherry Creek

Highlights: *A gentle aspen-lined trail to a large lake and access to Mount Owen.*

Type of hike: Out-and-back day hike or overnight backpack.
Total distance: 12.0 miles.
Difficulty: Moderate but long.

Best months: May to October.
Maps: USGS Electric Peak, Rito Alto, and Mirage quads.

Finding the trailhead: From Poncha Springs, drive 26 miles south on U.S. Highway 285 to the intersection of US 285 and Colorado Highway 17. Continue for 6.0 miles south on CO 17 and turn left (east) onto County Road AA. From Alamosa, drive 44 miles north on CO 17 and turn right (east) onto CR AA.

Drive east for 8.0 miles on CR AA past the intersection with the four-wheel-drive road that leads north to the Cotton Creek Trailhead. Continue straight on CR AA another 0.5 mile to the Wild Cherry Trailhead.

Parking and traihead facilities: A small parking area is provided at the turn-around near the trailhead.

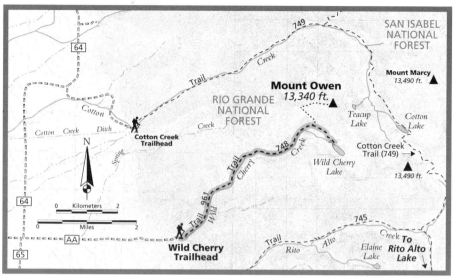

Key points:

0.0 Wild Cherry Trailhead.
2.0 Lower meadow.
4.5 Upper meadow.
6.0 Wild Cherry Lake.

The hike: Hike into the narrow valley up a gently climbing trail (961) on the left (north) side of the creek. The trail is shown crossing the creek on most maps, but it stays on the left (north) side, where it gets steeper and switchbacks up the valley. After the first steep section, pass a small meadow on the left. Continue up another steep and narrow climb to a gentler grade through aspens and open stands of evergreen. Hike up as the valley begins to curve to the right (south) and ascend into the upper meadows and up to the lake. Camping can be found along the upper valley below and around the lake.

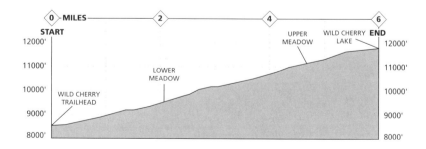

Wild Cherry Creek (March).

Options: To climb Mount Owen from the upper meadows below the lake, approach the west ridge near the saddle that lies east of Point 12,318, then continue east up to the summit.

Snow season: This can be a very good snowshoe or, during heavy winters, a good ski trail, with the exception of the few short but steep sections. Mount Owen's west ridge is usually windswept and safe to climb year-round, but care must be taken on the approaching slopes.

Rito Alto Creek

Highlights: *A long gentle trail to a scenic lake.*

Type of hike: Long out-and-back day hike or overnight backpack.
Total distance: 13.0 miles.

Difficulty: Strenuous.
Best months: July to September.
Maps: USGS Rito Alto Peak, Mirage quads.

Special considerations: The trail is well maintained and is popular with horse and llama trekkers and outfitters. When wet, the last mile to the lake can become very muddy and rutted.

Finding the trailhead: From Poncha Springs, drive 26 miles south on U.S. Highway 285 to the intersection of Colorado Highway 17. Continue for 6.0 miles south on CO 17 and turn left (east) onto County Road AA. From Alamosa, drive 44 miles north on CO 17 and turn right (east) onto CR AA.

Drive east for 5.5 miles and turn right (south) onto CR 64 for another 2.5 miles. Turn left (east) onto the rough road signed for Rito Alto Trailhead and continue east for 4 miles to the trailhead.

Parking and trailhead facilities: There is a small parking area at the trailhead.

Key points:
0.0 Rito Alto Trailhead.
3.0 Beaver ponds.
5.5 Cotton Creek Trail (749) goes left.
6.5 Rito Alto Lake.

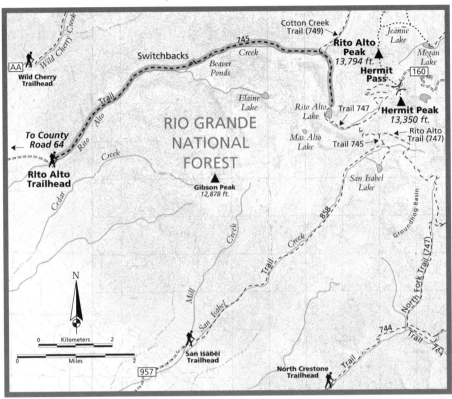

The hike: Hike up the trail (745) as it immediately crosses to the left (north) side of the creek and climbs gently up the narrow valley. Climb up the steeply switchbacking trail to a gentler stretch and past several small beaver ponds, then climb steeply again up to several open meadows on the right (south). At 5.5 miles the Cotton Creek Trail cuts sharply back to the left (north). Continue·up the valley as it turns to the right (south) and follow the gently climbing trail to the lake. Good camping can be found near the upper meadow and around the lake at least 300 feet from the shore.

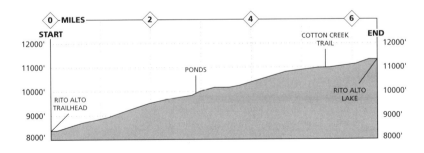

Options: To reach Cotton Lake, hike the Cotton Creek Trail (749) north into the upper valley. The trail passes high above and to the left (west) of several beaver ponds below Rito Alto Peak and Unnamed 13,524. Continue hiking up the valley before climbing left (west) across the upper slopes and switchback up to the pass above Cotton Lake (Hike 41). The views to the south along this portion of the trail are impressive. From the pass descend northwest along a prominent ridge that leads to steep switchbacks through the forest south of Cotton Lake.

From Rito Alto Lake, you can continue hiking south around the lake's west side and up past an impressive boulder field into the upper valley to the southeast. From here, hike east up an old road/trail (747) to Hermit Pass and Hermit Pass Road (Hike 16), or south to the pass that leads to San Isabel Creek (Hike 44).

Snow season: The length and steepness of this valley make it a rarely used snow-season trail. An ambitious backpacking trip would be rewarded with certain isolation in a beautiful high valley. The trail climbing up the southwest slopes of Rito Alto Peak to Hermit Pass Road (Hike 16) is usually windswept and safe from avalanche danger. The pass leading north to Cotton Creek (Hike 41) and the pass leading south to San Isabel Creek (Hike 44) should be climbed only during the safest of avalanche conditions.

Rito Alto Lake.

San Isabel Creek

Highlights: *A rarely used aspen-lined trail to an isolated high lake.*

Type of hike: Out-and-back day hike or overnight backpack.
Total distance: 11.0 miles.

Difficulty: Strenuous.
Best months: July to October.
Maps: USGS Rito Alto Peak quad.

Finding the trailhead: From Salida, drive 40 miles south over Poncha Pass on U.S. Highway 285. Turn left onto Colorado Highway 17 and drive south 13.2 miles to the small town of Moffat. Turn left (east) on County Road T, where there are signs for the town of Crestone. From Alamosa, drive 36 miles north on CO 17 to Moffat and turn right (east) on CR T.

Drive 8 miles and turn left (north) onto CR 66-T. Follow the main road as it becomes rougher beyond the national forest boundary. At the forest boundary the road becomes Forest Road 957. It will eventually become a four-wheel-drive road up to the San Isabel Trailhead. Slightly hard to find, the trail begins to the right (south) near the end of road where it enters a small meadow with a well-used campsite. The trailhead is across this meadow to the south.

Parking and trailhead facilities: A small parking area is provided at the turnaround near the trailhead.

Key points:

0.0 San Isabel Trailhead.
3.8 Meadow.
4.8 Upper meadow.
5.0 Rito Alto Lake Trail; continue straight.
5.5 San Isabel Lake.

The hike: Hike up the trail (858) as it climbs up the valley to the right (south) and above the creek. The valley begins to narrow, and the trail regularly crosses the creek. It also becomes rougher and climbs steadily before moderating through open aspen stands with views to the northeast to Hermit Peak. The trail becomes harder to follow as you hike farther into the meadows of the upper valley. Continue up the trail as views of the cirque that contains the lake begin to open up above on the right (south). Follow the thin trail until it reaches a T intersection, where Trail 745 heads left (north) up to the pass leading to Rito Alto Lake (see Hike 43). Continue right (south), following the trail as it crosses the willow-filled valley and up to

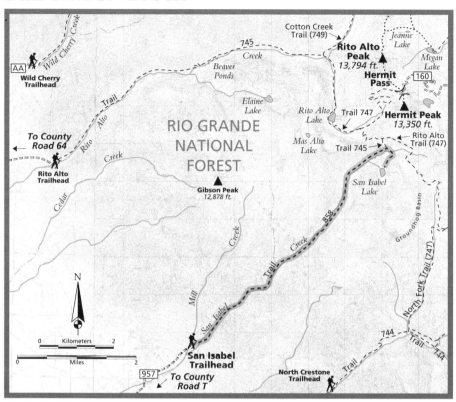

the left (east) of the trees leading into the cirque containing San Isabel Lake. Some camping is available along the upper portion of the trail and near the lake.

Options: Hike north at the T intersection and climb up to the Rito Alto Trail. At the next trail junction, hike left (west) to the pass and down to Rito Alto Lake (Hike 43), or turn right (east) and follow Trail 747 as it wraps south around the upper end of the San Isabel Creek Valley. This trail steadily descends and crosses the upper reaches of the creek that runs down the western slopes of Eureka Mountain. Hike

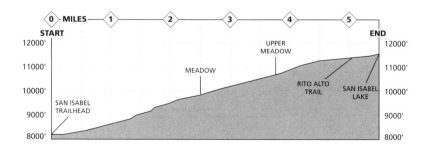

Upper San Isabel Valley.

south into the high basin east of San Isabel Lake and climb to the pass that leads to the North Fork of North Crestone Creek (Hike 45).

Snow season: With the rugged nature of this trail, it can be just as good or better when covered in deep snow. An enjoyable but difficult snowshoe leads high into the upper valley with incredibly isolated winter camping opportunities.

North Crestone Creek

Highlights: *A popular trail to a very scenic high lake and access to the North Fork and Middle Fork Trails.*

Type of hike: Out-and-back day hike or overnight backpack.
Total distance: 12.0 miles.

Difficulty: Moderate, but steep below the lake.
Best months: June to September.
Maps: USGS Horn Peak, Rito Alto Peak quads.

Special considerations: As one of the most popular trails in the area, the North Crestone Trail hosts day hikers, backpackers, and horse and llama trekkers in abundance on summer weekends and holidays. Take care to avoid increasing the already heavy impact on this beautiful valley by hiking early or late in the season, or on weekdays, and avoiding busy holidays.

Finding the trailhead: From Salida, drive 40 miles south over Poncha Pass on U.S. Highway 285. Turn left onto Colorado Highway 17 and drive south 13.2 miles to the small town of Moffat. Turn left (east) onto County Road T, where there are signs for the town of Crestone. From Alamosa, drive 36 miles north on CO 17 to Moffat and turn right (east) onto CR T.

Drive for 13 miles to the town of Crestone. Follow the main street north for 1.0 mile as it winds through town to the obvious signs for North Crestone Campground. Drive 1.0 mile past the campground entrance to the North Crestone Trailhead.

Parking and trailhead facilities: There is a large parking area at the trailhead.

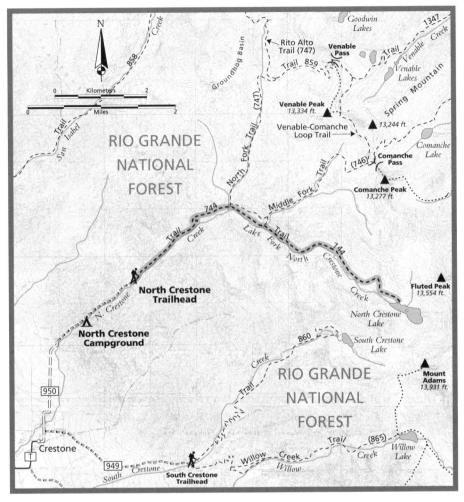

Key points:

0.0 North Crestone Trailhead.
3.0 North Fork Trail (747) and Middle Fork Trail (746); continue straight.
3.2 Lower camping area.
6.0 North Crestone Lake.

The hike: Hike the wide and gentle trail as it climbs up the valley on the left (north) side of the creek. The aspen-lined trail begins to switchback up to the left (north) and traverses high above the creek, offering fantastic views of the valley above and below to the San Luis Valley. Just after crossing the North Fork of North Crestone Creek, pass the North Fork and Middle Fork trails on your left. Continue up the main trail as it climbs past some well-used camping sites before climbing

Camping on the North Fork of North Crestone Creek.

steeply into the upper valley. After leaving the aspens behind, hike across alpine meadows to the upper bench containing North Crestone Lake.

Options: The North Fork Trail (747) provides access to Trail 859, which leads east to Venable Pass (Hike 19). This trail also continues over the pass that leads north to San Isabel Creek (Hike 44). From its intersection with the North Crestone Creek Trail (744), follow the North Fork Trail as it climbs north through aspen stands up into a beautiful high valley. The trail crosses over to the left (west) side of the creek and continues past the steep hike into Groundhog Basin, then crosses back to the east side of the creek and up to a large open meadow above the tree line.

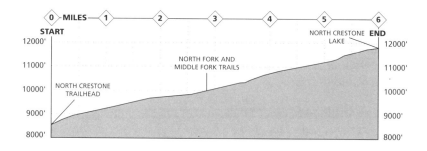

At this point the trail forks; go to the right (east) across the meadow and up a switchbacking climb to Venable Pass (Hike 19), or turn sharply left (west) to traverse high above the creek with views into Groundhog Basin and climb steadily up to the pass that leads to San Isabel Creek (Hike 44). The trail is popular with horse and llama trekkers and outfitters. When wet, it can become very muddy and rutted over the last couple of miles to the high meadow and up to the pass. Camping is available in the upper valley, Groundhog Basin, and the upper meadow near Venable Pass. These are all above the tree line and can be exposed to the wind and severe weather much more so than the areas closer to the North Crestone Trail.

From the North Fork trail intersection, hike the North Fork Trail about 50 feet and turn right (east) on the Middle Fork Trail (746) as it leads into a pleasant basin above the tree line and continues on to a steep section to gain the crest of the range. From this pass, continue down to the Comanche Creek Trail (Hike 20) or turn left and hike north to the Venable Creek Trail (Hike 19). Camping is available in the Middle Fork Valley's upper meadows and in the basin farther south of the trail in the upper valley southwest of Comanche Peak.

Snow season: Access becomes restricted for the last mile before the trailhead, at the gated entrance to North Crestone Campground. The lower valley can be a good snowshoe, but portions of the trail might not hold much snow during dry winters.

South Crestone Lake

Highlights: *A hike to a high lake surrounded by impressive peaks.*

Type of hike: Out-and-back day hike or easy overnight backpack.
Total distance: 11.0 miles.
Difficulty: Strenuous.

Best months: July to October.
Maps: USGS Rito Alto Peak, Crestone, and Horn Peak quads.

Special considerations: Most of this trail has been relocated and is not where it is shown on most maps.

Finding the trailhead: From Salida, drive 40 miles south over Poncha Pass on U.S. Highway 285. Turn left onto Colorado Highway 17 and drive south 13.2 miles to the small town of Moffat. Turn left (east) onto County Road T, where

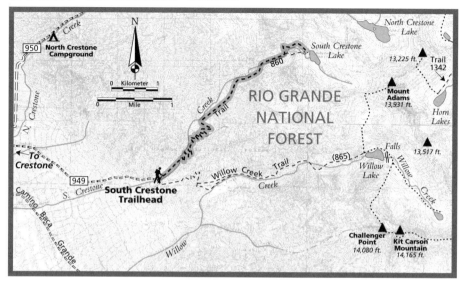

there are signs for the town of Crestone. From Alamosa, drive 36 miles north on CO 17 to Moffat and turn right (east) onto CR T.

Drive 13 miles to the town of Crestone and continue on CR T as it turns north into the center of town. Turn right (east) onto Galena Street at the stop sign just past the post office. Follow the dirt road for about 2 miles to the South Crestone Trailhead. The last mile or so may be too rough for some vehicles.

Parking and trailhead facilities: There is a large parking area at the trailhead as well as some heavily used campsites.

Key points:
- **0.0** South Crestone Trailhead.
- **0.5** First creek crossing.
- **2.8** Overlook.
- **3.2** Lower meadow.
- **3.6** Second creek crossing.
- **4.0** Cliff band.
- **5.0** Upper meadow.
- **5.5** South Crestone Lake.

The hike: From the trailhead, hike past the trail on the right that leads to Willow Creek (Hike 47), and climb up onto the open slopes that offer views back to the San Luis Valley. Continue up into the thick aspen groves and enter the valley, where the trail stays to the left of the creek. At 0.5 mile, the trail crosses to the right (east) side of the creek and switchbacks to the south. Hike several switchbacks as you climb

South Crestone Creek Trail.

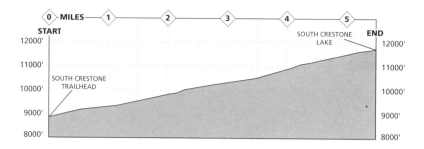

higher above the aspen-filled valley of South Crestone Creek. Hike north and return to a seasonal creek that runs down from the northeast. Cross to the north side of this seasonal creek and hike past the remains of an old cabin, then continue on a long traverse across open grassy slopes. Switchback several times up this open slope and enjoy the impressive views from the overlook at the top out to the San Luis Valley.

Reenter the aspen groves and evergreen forest on a gentle descent for 0.4 mile and return to South Crestone Creek at a small meadow. Do not cross this lower meadow, instead continue on the trail that stays to the right (southeast) and follow it through the trees before it crosses to the left (northwest) side of the South Crestone Creek. At 4.0 miles, climb up the trail to a prominent rock cliff, turn sharply to the left (west), and switchback up and return to the creek above the cliffs. After 5.0 miles, follow the trail into the upper meadows below the lake. Above the meadows, the trail follows a rough route that has been washed out. Cross over these loose gullies on the left (north) side of the valley, following the thin sections of trail between washouts. Hike steeply up to a point almost level with the upper basin that contains South Crestone Lake, then traverse to the right (southwest) and rejoin the trail where it descends to the lake.

Camping is available near the lower meadow and the upper meadows, but it is limited near South Crestone Lake.

Options: From the lake, climb southeast into the narrow but very scenic upper basin west of Mount Adams by hiking around the right (southwest) side of the lake and west along the creek that leads into the upper basin.

Snow season: Access up the road to the trailhead is usually good; the road rarely holds deep snow. The lower portions of the trail might hold only small amounts of snow. After entering the valley, expect more snow as you climb farther into the upper valley to the lake.

Highlights: *A difficult trail to a very scenic lake and access to Mount Adams, Challenger Point, and Kit Carson Mountain.*

Type of hike: Out-and-back day hike or overnight backpack.
Total distance: 10.0 miles.
Difficulty: Strenuous.

Best months: July to September.
Maps: USGS Crestone Peak, Crestone, and Horn Peak quads.

Finding the trailhead: From Salida, drive 40 miles south over Poncha Pass on U.S. Highway 285. Turn left onto Colorado Highway 17 and drive south 13.2 miles to the small town of Moffat. Turn left (east) onto County Road T, where there are signs for the town of Crestone. From Alamosa, drive 36 miles north on CO 17 to Moffat and turn right (east) onto CR T.

Drive 13 miles to the town of Crestone and continue on CR T as it turns north into the center of town. Turn right (east) onto Galena Street at the stop sign just past the post office. Follow the dirt road for about 2 miles to the South Crestone Trailhead. The last mile or so may be too rough for some vehicles.

Parking and trailhead facilities: There is a large parking area at the trailhead as well as some heavily used campsites.

Key points:
  0.0 South Crestone Trailhead.
  2.2 Spur trail to Willow Creek Park.
  3.5 Creek crossing.
  5.0 Willow Lake.

The hike: Hike up the South Crestone Creek Trail (860) for 200 feet, then turn right (south) onto the Willow Creek Trail (865) and cross over to the right (south) side of the creek. Turn left (east) and travel along the creek and then up a dozen or so switchbacks to the top of the ridge. At the top of the ridge, you enter the Willow Creek drainage. A spur trail splits off to the right down into Willow Creek Park, where there are many camping sites.

Continue left (east) past the park on the south-facing slope. The trail climbs high above the creek. As the valley narrows, the switchbacking trail becomes rockier and steeper. After 3.5 miles, cross the creek to its southern side and follow the trail across and to the top of a steep rocky slope overlooking the entire drainage and out over Crestone and the San Luis Valley. Above and to the right (south) looms the lower slope of Challenger Point's western flank.

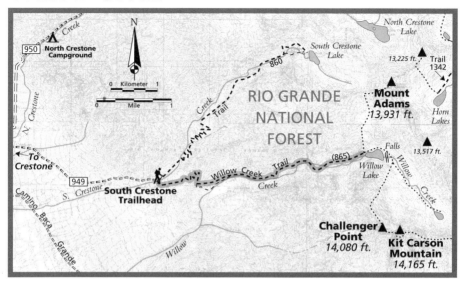

The trail becomes gentler as it winds up to the meadows below Willow Lake. These meadows are lush and full of wildflowers during the summer months. The lake is reached at 5.0 miles.

There are many well-used campsites near the creek west of the lake. Camping is prohibited within 300 feet of the lake's shore, preventing any camping in the narrow valley surrounding the lake.

Options: If you have the energy and camping is crowded below the lake, you can continue through the willows up the rough trail along the left (north) side of the lake. This trail climbs up and around the sheer headwall northwest of Willow Lake. Cross the creek at the top of the waterfall and follow a thin trail into the upper Willow Creek valley. The camping sites are limited and are more rocky and exposed to the weather in the upper valley, but the solitude can be worth the effort. The lake at the end of the valley is a good easy day hike from the lower lake. Past the falls

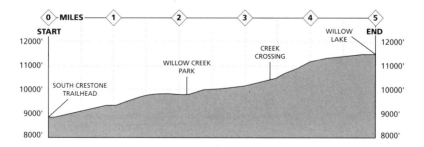

Falls along Willow Creek.

above the lake, follow the trail along the right side of the valley as it grows thinner and crosses over to the left side of the creek just below the outlet of the upper lake.

From a camp at the lower lake, it is also possible to climb to the summit of Mount Adams or either of the summits on the ridge to its west or south. From the outlet of the lower lake, proceed north on a thin trail along the right (east) side of a small stream into the upper basin. Cross the upper basin and continue steeply up to the low point of the ridge to the left (west) of Mount Adams. From the ridge, scramble just right (south) of the ridge crest to a prominent notch. Climb around and to the right of this step, then turn back up to the ridge for the final scramble to the summit.

Snow season: This trail provides an enjoyable but challenging winter hike. The lower part of the trail can be fairly dry along the south-facing slope until the steeper section below the lake. Some care should be taken along the rocky parts of the trail where it crosses the creek; they can be difficult to cross in deeper snow or when icy.

Kit Carson Mountain and Challenger Point

Highlights: *A challenging scramble up two of Colorado's 14,000-foot peaks.*

Type of hike: Out-and-back day hike from camp near Willow Lake.
Total distance: 5.2 miles.
Difficulty: Strenuous.

Best months: July to October.
Maps: USGS Crestone Peak and Crestone quads.

Special considerations: Like Crestone Needle and Crestone Peak, this is not a straightforward hike. It is a hard but nontechnical route climbing one of Colorado's hardest 14,000-foot mountains. It involves some scrambling (hand and foot climbing) up a route on steep rock that could be covered with snow and ice. Wearing a helmet is advisable, and the use of an ice ax may also be required during the spring and early summer months. It also requires some route-finding skills and is surrounded by technical terrain. Only those who are comfortable on steep rock and willing to turn back if conditions are less than ideal should attempt it.

Finding the trailhead: See Willow Creek (Hike 47) for directions to the trailhead and the hike description to Willow Lake.

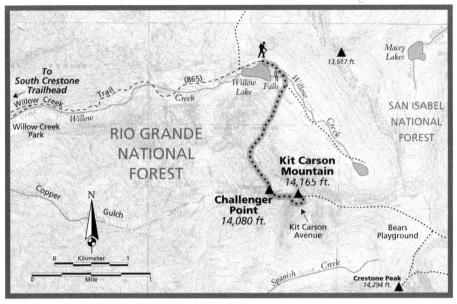

Key points:

- **0.0** Willow Lake.
- **0.6** Waterfall.
- **1.8** Summit ridge.
- **2.0** Challenger Point.
- **2.2** Kit Carson Avenue.
- **2.6** Kit Carson Summit.

The hike: From Willow Lake, hike the rough trail through the willows around the left (north) side of the lake and cross the creek at the top of the waterfall into the upper valley. A thin trail leads south quickly to the base of the climb up Challenger Point. Hike steeply to the right (southwest) up the rock and grass slopes to the left (south) of Challenger's northwest ridge that leads to the summit. Stay to the right

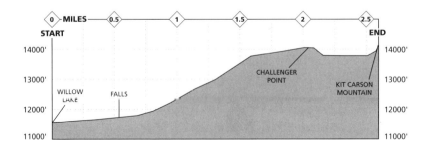

184

of a narrow couloir, usually filled with snow, that also leads to the summit ridge. Some cairns may be found along the way, which may mislead you onto steeper ground. Stay left of the ridge as you climb and trust your own judgment, choosing the easiest path as the conditions dictate. Once on the summit ridge, enjoy the views down across the San Luis Valley and back north to Mount Adams and a large section of the central range. If conditions are good, continue east over the summit of Challenger Point and descend the ridge to the saddle below Kit Carson Mountain. Find an obvious ledge system that leads south across the west face of Kit Carson. Follow "Kit Carson Avenue" around the south buttress and gently descend to the notch in Kit Carson's east ridge. Once all the way around to the east ridge, climb west up toward the true summit of Kit Carson Mountain.

Snow season: With stable spring snow, this is a very enjoyable but challenging route requiring the use of an ice ax and crampons. The couloir to the west of Kit Carson's summit can also be climbed as a semitechnical route. The couloir east of Kit Carson is even more difficult and thus climbed more rarely. These are steep snow climbs with the possibility of ice and significant avalanche danger. The routes should only be done with proper judgment, experience, and a stable spring snowpack.

Challenger Point and Kit Carson Mountain from near Crestone.

49

Cottonwood Creek

Highlights: *A lesser-used trail with access to Cottonwood Lake, Crestone Peak, Crestone Needle, and the Sand Creek Lakes (Hike 34).*

Type of hike: Out-and-back day hike or overnight backpack.
Total distance: 12.0 miles.
Difficulty: Strenuous.

Best months: July to September.
Maps: USGS Crestone Peak and Crestone quads.

Finding the trailhead: From Salida, drive 40 miles south over Poncha Pass on U.S. Highway 285. Turn left onto Colorado Highway 17 and drive south 13.2 miles to the small town of Moffat. Turn left (east) onto County Road T, where there are signs for the town of Crestone. From Alamosa, drive 36 miles north on CO 17 to Moffat and turn right (east) onto CR T.

Drive 13.2 miles on CR T and turn right onto Camino Baca Grande Road at the large sign for Baca Estates. Continue for approximately 5 miles as the road runs through a residential area. The pavement ends and the road becomes rougher and sandy before reaching a large water tank on the left (east). Park on the road, not on the property near the water tank, and hike up to the left of this property past an old mine to the closed road that leads to the Cottonwood Trail.

Parking and trailhead facilities: There is no official trailhead and no camping is allowed on the private land in the area. Please take care to park without blocking public right-of-way or the road to the water tank.

Key points:
0.0 Cottonwood Trailhead.
3.6 Cottonwood Lake spur trail; continue straight.
6.0 Milwaukee Pass.

The hike: Climb steadily up the valley on the trail that is on the left (north) side of the creek. The sometimes thin trail travels through mixed forest and becomes steeper before passing the thin Cottonwood Lake spur trail on the left (north). This trail is steep and stays to the left (west) side of the creek for 0.9 mile to the lake.

Continue east up the main fork of Cottonwood Creek. Hike between the impressive walls of the upper valley, with Unnamed 13,270 on the left (north), Milwaukee Pass ahead (east), and Pico Asilado to the right (south). From the upper basin it is a steep hike to Milwaukee Pass.

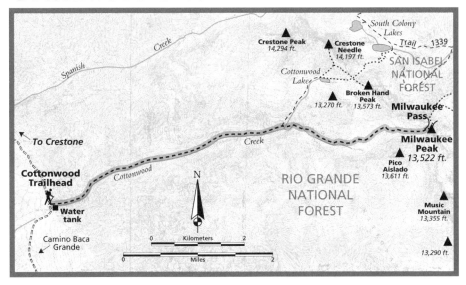

The first mile of the valley is broad and remains gentle below the steep climb up the pass. Camping along the east fork of Cottonwood Creek is easier and less exposed than at the end of the valley.

Options: Hike the spur trail to Cottonwood Lake to climb Crestone Needle, Crestone Peak, and Broken Hand Peak. To climb Crestone Needle, hike east and north from the lake over gentle terrain. Then begin a climbing traverse north to the base of the major couloir that leads almost directly up to the summit as described in the route to Crestone Needle (Hike 30). This is a difficult climb up steep and sometimes loose rock, requiring a helmet and sometimes an ice ax, depending on the conditions.

To climb Broken Hand Peak, continue the traverse up toward the saddle between Broken Hand Peak and Crestone Needle, then proceed southeast, climbing up the grassy slopes to this rarely visited summit with its spectacular views of the South Colony Lakes valley.

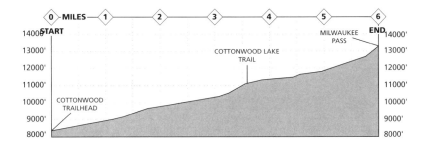

187

Unnamed 13,270 south of Cottonwood Lake.

Crestone Peak is commonly climbed from Cottonwood Lake and from South Colony Lakes over Broken Hand Pass to the north. From Cottonwood Lake hike the north shore on the thin trail to the west, back down Cottonwood Creek. After 0.2 miles take the side trail on the right (west) following a level trail into the basin southeast of Crestone Peak. Follow the trail to the left of the small seasonal creek as it enters the basin and approaches the boulder field to the north. From the basin it is usually easy to spot the rest of the route above: The prominent couloir cuts straight from lower left (south) to upper right (north). The trail leads to the right (east) of the lower end of this couloir where it is the narrowest and steepest. Follow the intermittent path as it winds through the rocks and turns sharply left back to the couloir. Depending on the conditions enter the couloir at about 1.0 mile or continue on the right side on the rocky rib another 400 vertical feet where steep rock forces you back into the gully. The route continues north to the narrow notch east of the main summit. From here, scramble left (west) below the ridge to the true summit.

Snow season: This can be an excellent snowshoe or ski up into the upper basin to Cottonwood Lake. A spring snow climb of Crestone Needle (Hike 30) without having to climb over the pass west of Broken Hand Peak makes this a good approach.

Great Sand Dunes
NATIONAL MONUMENT AND PRESERVE

Designated a National Monument by President Hoover in 1932, the original boundary of the Great Sand Dunes enclosed only the active dune field. Always associated with the dune system is the extensive sand sheet surrounding the dunes to the north and west, and the rare sabkha formations, hardened by salt and mineral deposits. Maybe the most crucial factor in maintaining this beautiful and unique formation is water. The high water table of the San Luis Valley has been an important resource for valley ranchers and farmers, as well as an essential component in the stability of the dune system. On November 22, 2000, President Clinton signed the Great Sand Dunes National Park and Preserve Act. In addition to expanding the size of the monument from about 39,000 acres to more than 150,000 acres and establishing a 92,000-acre wildlife refuge, this legislation also protects the water in the valley's aquifer from exportation. Call the National Park Service to get the latest update on the acquisition of private lands and to get current information about access to this newly expanded park and preserve.

The monument sees a moderate number of visitors—300,000 during the course of the year—most of those from June to September. The visitor center and the in-park services are available only during these months, but Alamosa is close enough to provide accommodations and necessities during an off-season visit. Most visitors come just for the day and get only a glimpse of the full depth and beauty and wonder the dunes have to offer. If you give yourself the time to slow down and enjoy the dunes, watch the wind blow sand across the ridges, see the water surge and flow and ripple down the creek, and listen to the gritty sounds of serenity, you will be rewarded with a sense of peace hard to come by anywhere else.

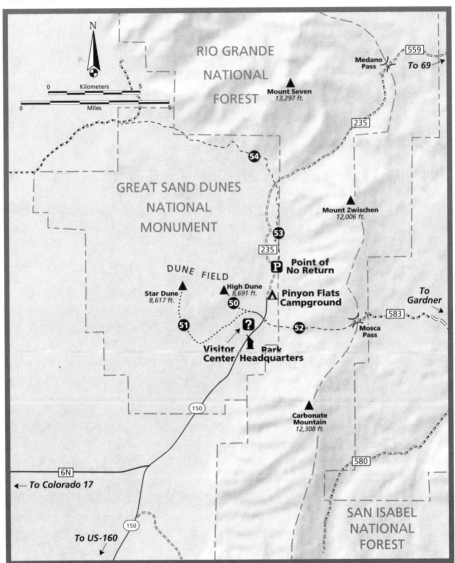

N

Kilometers
0   5

Miles
0   5

RIO GRANDE

NATIONAL

FOREST

Mount Seven
13,297 ft.

Medano
Pass

559

To 69

235

54

GREAT SAND DUNES

NATIONAL

MONUMENT

Mount Zwischen
12,006 ft.

53

235

DUNE FIELD

P Point of
No Return

Star Dune
8,617 ft.

High Dune
8,691 ft.

Pinyon Flats
Campground

To
Gardner

50

583

51

52

Mosca
Pass

?

Visitor
Center

Park
Headquarters

150

Carbonate
Mountain
12,308 ft.

6N

580

← To Colorado 17

150

SAN ISABEL

NATIONAL

FOREST

To US-160

50

High Dune

Highlights: *A popular, sandy ridge walk to the highest dunes in North America.*

Type of hike: Out-and-back day hike.
Total distance: 3.4 miles.
Difficulty: Easy.

Best months: Year-round access is reliable; spring and fall are the best seasons to hike.
Maps: USGS Zapata Ranch quad.

Special considerations: Even though this is usually done as a short hike, there are no trails or route markers. It can be harder than anticipated if the steady winds are stronger than usual or if the weather is hot and dry. Bring plenty of water and a windbreaker even during the best of weather. These dune hikes can be most enjoyable early and late in the day when the low light of the sun reveals the beautiful details of the dune structure.

Finding the trailhead: From the intersection of U.S. Highway 160 and Colorado Highway 150, 15 miles east of Alamosa, drive north on CO 150 for 16 miles to the entrance fee station of Great Sand Dunes Monument and preserve. Continue 1.0 mile north, past the visitor center, and turn left (west) at the sign for the Medano Creek and Picnic Area Access.

Parking and trailhead facilities: Parking throughout the monument is plentiful, and signage is clear and easy to follow. The nearest camping is located within the monument at the Pinyon Flats Campground, or just outside the park at the seasonal commercial campground on CO 150.

Key points:
0.0 Dunes Picnic Area.
0.1 Medano Creek.
1.0 Main dune mass.
1.7 High Dune.

The hike: From the parking lot, hike toward Medano Creek and enjoy its unique surging flow pattern before crossing out onto the flats that lead to the main dune mass. From here, identify the highest point to the northwest and the long sandy ridge to its right that leads to its summit. The sandy flats can be firm but are usually loose and more difficult to hike than you might expect. Once you reach the steeper dunes, stay along the ridges and follow the easiest route that connects them as they climb and curve to the left (west) before reaching the high point that overlooks the rest of the monument to the west and north.

191

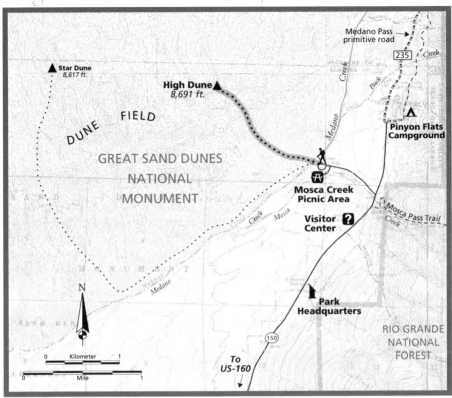

Options: If you find yourself off the route, continue hiking up to the highest nearby dune and you are likely to reach a point overlooking the main dune mass. The area to the right (east) of the High Dune has a pleasant summit area with great views and fewer crowds.

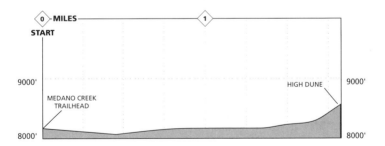

Dune fields north of the High Dune.

Snow season: The dunes are a great destination during snow season when the temperatures are low and the crowds are nonexistent. It can be extremely enjoyable to spend time out on the dunes when they are partially covered with a thin, windswept layer of snow. Winter winds keep the snow levels down and can also keep most visitors in their cars.

51

Star Dune

Highlights: *A less popular and difficult walk to a high dune overlooking miles of the main dune mass.*

Type of hike: Out-and-back day hike.
Total distance: 9.0 miles.
Difficulty: Strenuous.

Best months: Spring and fall can offer the best weather.
Maps: USGS Zapata Ranch quad.

Special considerations: Star Dune can be a challenging hike because it requires good navigational skills to locate. It is a long hike over loose and tiring sand. Bring plenty of water and protection from the sun and wind.

Finding the trailhead: From the intersection of U.S. Highway 160 and Colorado Highway 150, 15 miles east of Alamosa, drive north on CO 150 for 16 miles to the entrance fee station of Great Sand Dunes Monument and preserve. Continue 1.0 mile north, past the visitor center, and turn left (west) at the sign for the Medano Creek and Picnic Area Access.

Key points:
0.0 Dunes Picnic Area.
0.1 Medano Creek.
2.0 Cottonwoods.
4.5 Star Dune.

The hike: From the trailhead, cross over to the west side of Medano Creek and hike southwest over flat and fairly firm sand along the right side of the creek for about 2.0 miles. After you pass the last stands of cottonwoods on your left (south), start turning right (northwest) and hike toward the steeper dune slopes. Find the high point that is visible to the west of the High Dune area and beyond the broad sand gully that separates the Star Dune from the other high dune mass on the east. Hike about 2.0 miles and continue up the left (west) side of the dune ridges to the high point.

Options: The dune mass provides endless and sometimes demanding options. Short hikes across the dune mass can be exhausting; staying to the ridges makes it easier. This hike can be combined with the Sand Creek Trail (Hike 54) to complete an entire loop around the dunes. By hiking west from Star Dune it is possible to continue north then northeast along the base of the dune mass to the end of the Sand Creek Trail. No water is available along the way, making it a challenging and rarely hiked route.

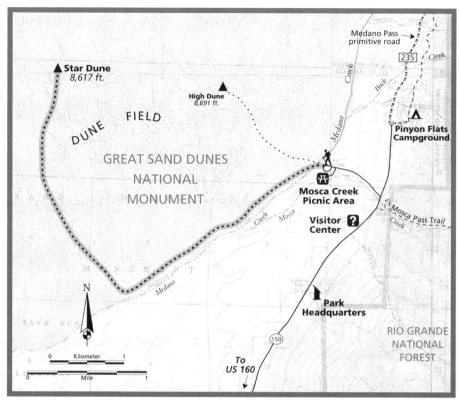

Snow season: When winter winds blow across the nearly frozen dunes, this hike becomes an exercise in solitude and endurance. Little snow remains after winter storms, but nothing can compare to a full moon over snow-dusted dunes. The sand can actually be more stable when temperatures drop, making snow season a cold but enjoyable time to explore the dunes.

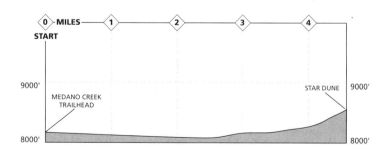

Medano Creek.

Mosca Pass Trail

Highlights: *An easy climb to a high pass on the crest of the range, with views of the San Luis and Wet Mountain Valleys.*

Type of hike: Out-and-back day hike or overnight backpack.
Total distance: 6.0 miles.
Difficulty: Easy.

Best months: Spring and fall can offer the best weather.
Maps: USGS Mosca Pass and Zapata Ranch quads.

Finding the trailhead: From the intersection of U.S. Highway 160 and Colorado Highway 150, 15 miles east of Alamosa, drive north on CO 150 for 16 miles to the entrance fee station of Great Sand Dunes Monument and Preserve. Drive 1.0 mile to the small parking area and the trailhead access for the Montville Nature Trail and Mosca Pass Trail (883) on the right (east) side of the road.

Alternatively, it is possible to drive to the top of the pass from the east side. From the town of Gardner on CO 69, drive west on County Road 550 to Redwing, continue straight on CR 580 and drive a total of 12 miles. Turn right (northwest) onto CR 583 at the sign for Mosca Pass. Passenger cars can drive all the way to the top of the pass on this dirt road when the conditions allow. A small parking area is provided at the end of the road south of the antenna tower, and there are a few camping sites in this area.

Key points:
0.0 Monteville Nature Trail Parking Area.
1.5 Meadows.
3.0 Mosca Pass.

The hike: From the Mosca Pass Trailhead on the west side of the range, Trail 883 starts at the Monteville self-guided trail and immediately crosses to the left (north) side of the creek. Climb east moderately up the narrow and steep-walled Mosca Creek valley for about 2 miles. For the last mile to the top of the pass, the valley becomes broader with some open meadows and the grade of the trail becomes flatter. Views of the dunes and the San Luis Valley to the west become more and more impressive as you approach the pass.

Camping areas are available throughout much of the valley.

Options: From the pass, continue along the crest of the range north to Mount Zwischen or south to Carbonate Mountain. Both of these routes are off-trail and

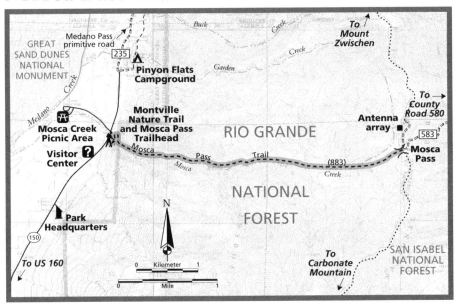

require the ability to navigate and bushwhack through downed timber. From the top of Mosca Pass, it is a 7.0-mile roundtrip to Carbonate Mountain and a 10.0-mile round trip to Mount Zwischen. Some camping is available along the ridge north and south of Mosca Pass, although sites are limited, rocky, and barely level. The solitude will reward your efforts.

Snow season: From the east side, the first mile of CR 583 could have some deeper snowdrifts requiring a four-wheel-drive vehicle. Beyond this point, the road is usually passable to within a half mile of the pass year-round. However, occasional heavy storms and wind drifts may limit your ability to drive the entire length of the road. Access from Great Sand Dunes National Park is reliable year-round.

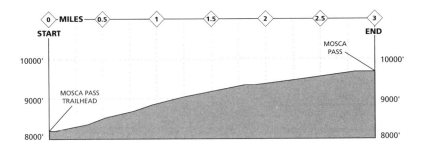

53

Little Medano Trail

Highlights: *An easy trail with views of the edge of the dunes.*

Type of hike: Out-and-back day hike.
Total distance: 6.0 miles.
Difficulty: Easy.

Best months: April to November.
Maps: USGS Liberty quad.

Special considerations: Even though this is an easy trail, it can be hot and there is no reliable source of water before Medano Creek. Bring plenty of water and protection from the sun and wind.

Finding the trailhead: From the intersection of U.S. Highway 160 and Colorado Highway 150, 15 miles east of Alamosa, drive north on CO 150 for 16 miles to the entrance fee station of Great Sand Dunes Monument and Preserve. Drive north 1.6 miles to the Medano Primitive Road and park at one of the parking areas along the road. Most cars can drive 0.6 mile to the Point of No Return parking area. With a high-clearance four-wheel-drive vehicle with low tire pressure, it is possible to continue north 4.0 miles over the sandy road past the Sand Pit and Castle Creek picnic areas to reach the Sand Creek Trailhead. From the picnic areas, drive north on the Medano Primitive Road along the edge of the dunes and across an open meadow to Medano Creek. The crossing of the creek can be difficult during periods of high water. Cross the creek and continue 0.2 mile to the small parking area. If you need to let some air out of your tires to drive through the loose sand, an air compressor is available at the Pinyon Flats Campground to fill them back up.

Parking and trailhead facilities: There is a parking area at the Point of No Return Trailhead. Picnic tables are provided at the Sand Pit and Castle Creek picnic areas. No water is available.

Key points:
0.0 Point of No Return Trailhead.
1.2 Escape Dunes designated camping area.
2.5 Indian Grove designated camping area.
3.0 Sand Creek Trailhead/Medano Pass Primitive Road.

The hike: From the Point of No Return parking area, hike north on the sandy and relatively flat trail through sage and rabbitbrush. The trail continues north across

Little Medano Trail

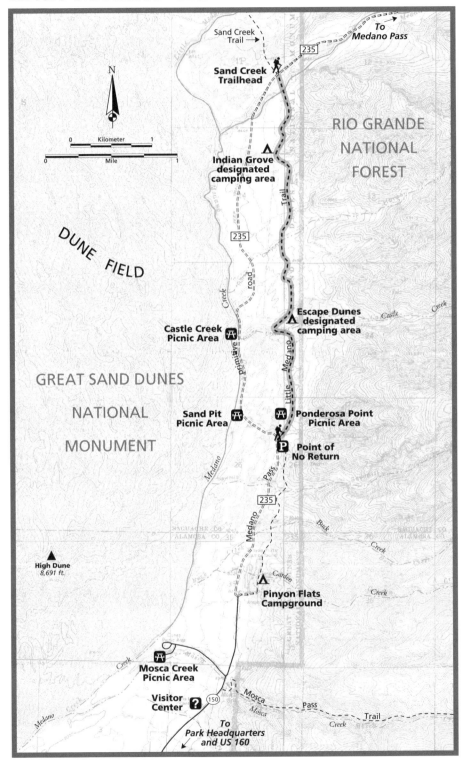

To
Medano Pass

235

Sand Creek
Trail →

Sand Creek
Trailhead

RIO GRANDE

NATIONAL

FOREST

Indian Grove
designated
camping area

235

DUNE FIELD

Escape Dunes
designated
camping area

Castle Creek
Picnic Area

GREAT SAND DUNES

NATIONAL

MONUMENT

Sand Pit
Picnic Area

Ponderosa Point
Picnic Area

Point of
No Return

235

High Dune
8,691 ft.

Pinyon Flats
Campground

Mosca Creek
Picnic Area

Visitor
Center

150

Mosca Pass

To
Park Headquarters
and US 160

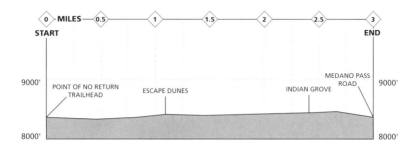

the seasonally dry Castle Creek bed to the small Escape Dunes and the designated backcountry camping site beyond. Proceed north across open meadows and small aspen and cottonwood stands before reaching the designated backcountry Indian Grove campsite. From here it is a quick jaunt to the Sand Creek Trailhead and access to the Medano Creek Primitive Road, the Sand Creek Trail (Hike 54), and Medano Pass Road.

Options: In the off-season (late fall till early spring), return to the Point of No Return Trailhead via the Medano Creek Primitive Road, which lies closer to the

Great Sand Dunes from the Little Medano Trail.

edge off the dune mass. Ambitious hikers can access the dune mass off-trail by hiking west from the Sand Creek Trailhead, returning to the Medano Primitive Road at any point as conditions dictate. You can also continue north on the trail from Sand Creek Trailhead on the Sand Creek Trail (Hike 54).

Snow season: The trail rarely holds much snow and can be a very good alternative to the sandy winds of the main dune mass.

54

Sand Creek Trail

Highlights: *A lesser-used trail along the northern edge of the dunes.*

Type of hike: Out-and-back day hike or two- to three-day backpack.
Total distance: 12.0 miles.
Difficulty: Moderate

Best months: April to September.
Maps: USGS Beck Mountain, Crestone Peak, and Liberty quads.

Special considerations: Water can be scarce along this route; it's a good idea to bring more than you think you need. The temperatures can be higher and the efforts more taxing than you anticipate.

Finding the trailhead: From the intersection of U.S. Highway 160 and Colorado Highway 150, 15 miles east of Alamosa, drive north on CO 150 for 16 miles to the entrance fee station of Great Sand Dunes Monument and Preserve. Drive north 1.6 miles to the Medano Primitive Road and park at one of the parking areas along the road. Most cars can drive 0.6 mile to the Point of No Return parking area. With a high-clearance four-wheel-drive vehicle with low tire pressure, it is possible to continue north 4.0 miles over the sandy road past the Sand Pit and Castle Creek picnic areas to reach the Sand Creek Trailhead. From the picnic areas, drive north on the Medano Primitive Road along the edge of the dunes and across an open meadow to Medano Creek. The crossing of the creek can be difficult during periods of high water. Cross the creek and continue 0.2 mile to the small parking area. If you need to let some air out of your tires to drive through the loose sand, an air compressor is available at the Pinyon Flats Campground to fill them back up.

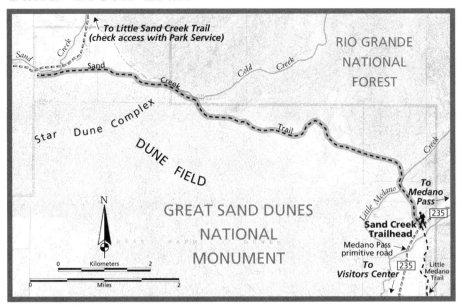

Key points:

0.0 Sand Creek Trailhead.

1.0 Little Medano Creek.

4.0 Cold Creek.

6.0 Sand Creek.

The hike: From the Sand Creek Trailhead, hike north on the trail as it skirts the edge of the dunes and passes stands of aspen and cottonwood. The trail crosses Little Medano Creek after 1.0 mile, then gently curves to the west as it climbs along the tree line. Cross the seasonally dry bed of Cold Creek at 4.0 miles, and continue west 2.0 miles on a gentle descent to Sand Creek.

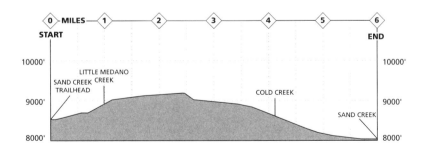

Northern edge of the dune field.

Options: Private land currently blocks access to the entrance of the Sand Creek valley, which climbs up to intersect the Little Sand Creek Trail (Hike 35) and on to Sand Creek Lakes (Hike 34) and Music Pass (Hike 33). Check with park officials regarding the current status of access across the private land; acquisition of the land for an expansion of the Great Sand Dunes National Park could allow future access.

A two- to three-day backpacking loop around the dune mass can be completed by continuing around the north end of the dunes and returning along the Medano Creek to the Visitor Center or the dunes access at the picnic grounds. This is a difficult and ambitious 20-mile loop that tours the entire dune area and is rarely done due to the lack of water.

Snow season: Significant snow cover in the dune area is rare, but cold temperatures and high winds are common. This is, however, still a good trail to consider because the cold temperatures can make the sand more firm and easier to walk on.

Sierra
BLANCA

The town of Alamosa, with a population of about 8,000, sits in the central San Luis Valley at an elevation of 7,500 feet. Along with Monte Vista to the west, it serves as the primary population and trade center for the valley. The semiarid San Luis Valley is primarily an agricultural area, with grain, alfalfa, hay, carrots, lettuce, and spinach the chief crops. There are excellent fishing and hunting opportunities as well as world-class rock climbing in Penitent Canyon (see Falcon Guides *Rock Climbing Colorado's San Luis Valley).* The spring and fall migrations of up to 20,000 sandhill cranes and 35,000 ducks are popular and impressive, attracting bird-watchers from around the world.

Fifteen miles east of Alamosa on U.S. Highway 160 is the intersection with Colorado Highway 150, which leads north to the Great Sand Dunes National Monument and Preserve, access to Lake Como and Blanca Peak, and Zapata Falls. Continuing east on US 160 over La Veta Pass is a beautiful drive, providing views of the Spanish Peaks to the south before reaching Walsenberg and Interstate 25. From Walsenburg drive west on CO 69 to Gardner and County Road 550 to access the hikes in the Huerfano Valley. For a more direct approach to CR 550 from just west of La Veta Pass, drive north on CR 29 over Pass Creek Pass, then continue north on CR 572.

Sierra Blanca

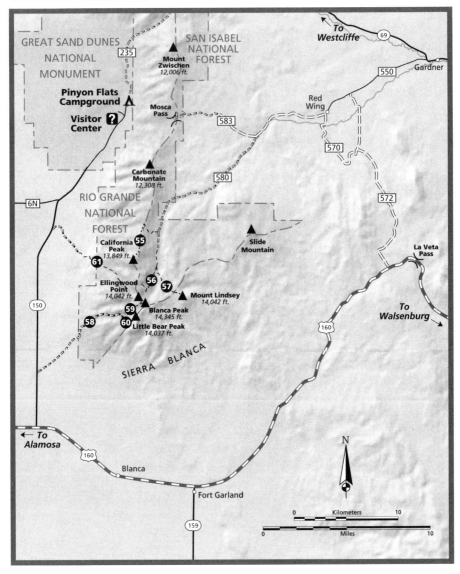

GREAT SAND DUNES
NATIONAL
MONUMENT

235

SAN ISABEL
NATIONAL
FOREST

Mount
Zwischen
12,006 ft.

To
Westcliffe

69

550

Gardner

Pinyon Flats
Campground

Visitor
Center

Mosca
Pass

Red
Wing

583

570

6N

Carbonate
Mountain
12,308 ft.

RIO GRANDE
NATIONAL
FOREST

580

572

California
Peak
13,849 ft.

55

Slide
Mountain

La Veta
Pass

61

150

Ellingwood
Point
14,042 ft.

56

57

Mount Lindsey
14,042 ft.

To
Walsenburg

58

59

60

Blanca Peak
14,345 ft.

Little Bear Peak
14,037 ft.

160

SIERRA BLANCA

To
Alamosa

160

Blanca

Fort Garland

159

N

0   Kilometers   10

0   Miles   10

California Peak

Highlights: *A straightforward hike to a high summit.*

Type of hike: Out-and-back day hike.
Total distance: 7.2 miles.
Difficulty: Moderate.

Best months: July to September.
Maps: USGS Mosca Pass and Blanca Peak quads.

Special considerations: Compared to the other summit hikes in the Sangre de Cristo range, this is an easy and straightforward climb. Most of it is above the tree line on a ridge that is exposed to severe winds and weather. Make your descent early to avoid the typical summer afternoon thunderstorms.

Finding the trailhead: From Colorado Highway 69 just north of Gardner, turn west onto County Road 550, which usually has a sign for Red Wing. At Red Wing, stay right at the fork in the road that turns toward the small town and continue 8 miles on CR 580. Drive through the Huerfano State Wildlife Area to the entrance of the Singing River Ranch, where a parking area is provided. The road is passable by most cars for another mile or two. If it is too rough for your vehicle, park here and hike the road. From this point it is 4.9 miles to the national forest boundary. Both sides of this stretch of road are private property. Do not camp or park along the road before you cross south of the forest boundary. Depending on the road conditions and frequency of maintenance, the road may get rougher along the last 2.5 miles before the forest boundary. The road could be muddy, rutted, or snow covered into June or July. With ideal road conditions, high-clearance two-wheel-drive vehicles may be able to reach the trailhead if driven carefully. The trailhead is on the right, 0.7 mile past the forest boundary. There is a small sign on the right side of the road at a small clearing indicating the beginning of the Huerfano Trail.

Parking and trailhead facilities: Some parking is available on the left side of the road past the trailhead. There are some well-used camping sites along the road from the Huerfano Trailhead to the Lily Lake Trailhead at the end of the road.

Key points:
- **0.0** Huerfano Trailhead.
- **0.4** Meadow.
- **1.5** Ridge.
- **3.0** Point 13,476.
- **3.6** Summit California Peak.

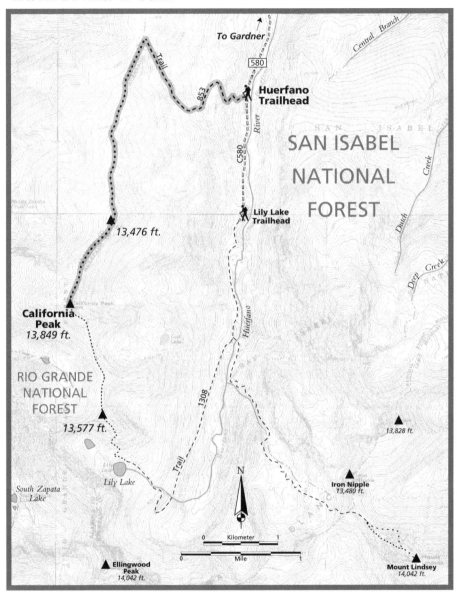

To Gardner

580

Huerfano
Trailhead

Central Branch

Trail

853

River

C580

SAN ISABEL

Creek

Dutch

NATIONAL

Lily Lake
Trailhead

FOREST

13,476 ft.

Deep Creek

California
Peak
13,849 ft.

Huerfano

Loaf
Lake

RIO GRANDE
NATIONAL
FOREST

13,577 ft.

1308

13,828 ft.

Trail

Lily Lake

South Zapata
Lake

Iron Nipple
13,480 ft.

N

0   Kilometer   1

0   Mile   1

Ellingwood
Peak
14,042 ft.

Mount Lindsey
14,042 ft.

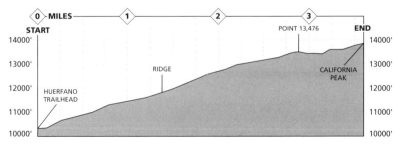

0 MILES   1   2   3

START   POINT 13,476   END

14000'   14000'

13000'   RIDGE   CALIFORNIA   13000'
                                                              PEAK

12000'   12000'
          HUERFANO
          TRAILHEAD
11000'   11000'

10000'   10000'

California Peak.

The hike: Hike Trail 853 to the west up through the aspen forest and switchback up to an open meadow. Proceed southwest on the thin trail, then turn sharply to the right (north) and climb steadily up to the ridge and the crest of the range. Turn left (south) and follow the broad ridge up to Point 13,476, then drop slightly a short distance before climbing to the summit of California Peak. The views from the summit include Mount Lindsey, Blanca Peak, Ellingwood Peak, and Twin Peaks to the south, and the Great Sand Dunes and the Crestone Group to the north.

Options: Continue hiking south along the ridge over Point 13,577 and down over steep talus slopes to Lily Lake. Descend on the Lily Lake Trail (Hike 56), eventually completing a loop back to the Huerfano Trailhead. This is a strenuous option that should only be attempted during good weather.

Snow season: Access to this hike can be difficult during snow season due to the private land along both sides of the road. If snow closes the road before reaching the forest boundary, park at the ranch entrance and walk up the road to the trailhead. With a four-wheel-drive vehicle, you might be able to drive to the trailhead well into November, depending on snow conditions.

Lily Lake

Highlights: *A popular trail to a very scenic high lake.*

Type of hike: Out-and-back day hike or overnight backpack.
Total distance: 6.4 miles.

Difficulty: Moderate.
Best months: July to September.
Maps: USGS Blanca Peak quad.

Finding the trailhead: From Colorado Highway 69 just north of Gardner, turn west onto County Road 550, which usually has a sign for Red Wing. At Red Wing, stay right at the fork in the road that turns toward the small town and continue 8 miles on CR 580. Drive through the Huerfano State Wildlife Area to the entrance of the Singing River Ranch, where a parking area is provided. The road is passable by most cars for another mile or two. If it is too rough for your vehicle, park here and hike the road.

From this point it is 4.9 miles to the national forest boundary. Both sides of this stretch of road are private property. Do not camp or park along the road before you cross south of the forest boundary. Depending on the road conditions and fre-

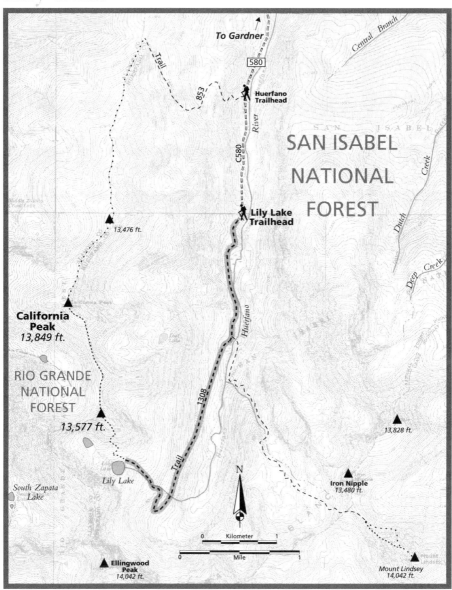

quency of maintenance, the road may get rougher along the last 2.5 miles before the forest boundary, then the rest of the way to the Lily Lake Trailhead. The road could be muddy, rutted, or snow covered into June or July. Continue on CR 580 for 2.0 miles past the forest boundary to the end of the road and the Lily Lake Trailhead. The road is rough and steep in spots and may require a four-wheel-drive vehicle throughout much of the year

Jon Funk at Lily Lake with Iron Nipple and Mount Lindsey beyond.

Parking and trailhead facilities: A turnaround is available for parking at the Lily Lake Trailhead. There are plenty of camping spots along the road between the Huerfano Trailhead and the end of the road, but camping is best after a short backpack up the valley along the first gentle mile or two of the trail.

Key points:
- **0.0** Lily Lake Trailhead.
- **1.0** Trail fork; keep right.
- **2.4** Creek crossing.
- **3.2** Lily Lake.

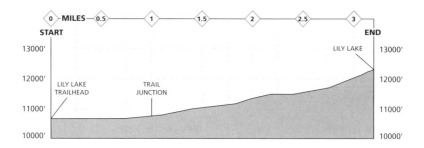

The hike: From the trailhead, descend along the right (west) side of the Huerfano River valley to a broad meadow and up the Lily Lake Trail (1308) into the forest ahead. Continue south up the valley and into a smaller open meadow. Just as you enter the trees, watch for a fork in the trail and continue up to the right. If you cross over to the east side of the river you have taken the wrong fork. The trail is almost flat as it leads through an open meadow before curving sharply to the right (northwest). Hike toward the east edge of the meadow and follow the trail as it switches back sharply to the left, then begins to climb gently but steadily up the right (west) side of the valley. As the trail continues to climb to the south, the views of Blanca Peak's north face become more impressive. The trail crosses the creek and begins to switchback to the northwest past several campsites with awesome views of the Blanca headwall. Follow the trail across to the north side of the creek above the tree line and continue to Lily Lake.

Options: From the lake, hike north on talus slopes toward Unnamed 13,577 and then along the ridge north to California Peak (see Hike 55). This is an ambitious option and requires good weather to be safe.

Snow season: Access to this trailhead is limited (see Hike 55 for additional notes), but the area is extremely enjoyable during snow season. If solitude is your goal, try this valley in February or March.

57

Mount Lindsey

Highlights: *A difficult hike to one of Colorado's 14,000-foot peaks.*

Type of hike: Out-and-back day hike or overnight backpack.
Total distance: 8.0 miles.

Difficulty: Strenuous.
Best months: July to September.
Maps: USGS Blanca Peak quad.

Special considerations: Even though this is considered to be one of the easier 14,000-foot mountains in Colorado, it is still a difficult hike and should not be attempted without adequate skills. Parts of the upper route are loose and rocky. If you knock a rock loose, warn the hikers below you by calling out "Rock!" until you see it stop.

Finding the trailhead: From Colorado Highway 69 just north of Gardner, turn west onto County Road 550, which usually has a sign for Red Wing. At Red Wing, stay right at the fork in the road that turns toward the small town and continue 8 miles on CR 580. Drive through the Huerfano State Wildlife Area to the entrance of the Singing River Ranch, where a parking area is provided. The road is passable by most cars for another mile or two. If it is too rough for your vehicle, park here and hike the road.

From this point it is 4.9 miles to the national forest boundary. Both sides of this stretch of road are private property. Do not camp or park along the road before you cross south of the forest boundary. Depending on the road conditions and frequency of maintenance, the road may get rougher along the last 2.5 miles before the forest boundary, then the rest of the way to the Lily Lake Trailhead. The road could be muddy, rutted, or snow covered into June or July. Continue on CR 580 for 2.0 miles past the forest boundary to the end of the road and the Lily Lake Trailhead. The road is rough and steep in spots and may require a four-wheel-drive vehicle throughout much of the year.

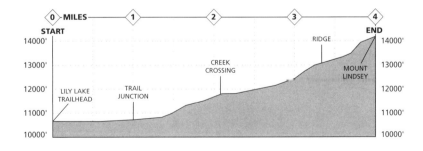

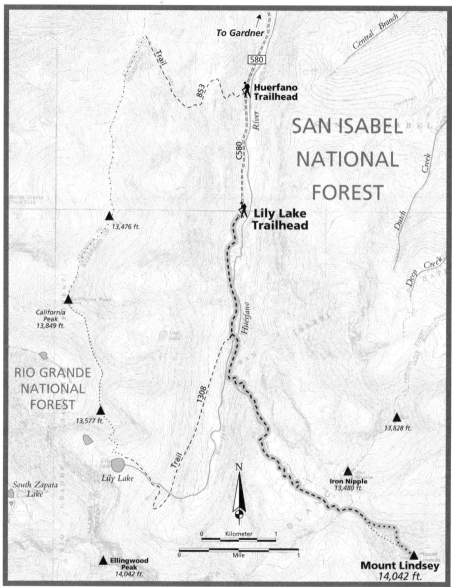

Key points:

- **0.0** Lily Lake Trailhead.
- **1.0** Trail junction; continue straight.
- **1.2** Boulder field.
- **2.0** Creek crossing.
- **3.2** Ridge.
- **4.0** Mount Lindsey.

North face of Mount Lindsey (November).

The hike: Hike up the trail past the first large meadow and up through the trees to a smaller clearing where the trail forks right (west) for Lily Lake (Hike 56). Continue straight past this turnoff and cross over to the left (east) side of the creek, where the trail becomes narrower and harder to find as it winds through the trees. Follow the thin trail as best you can, trending upslope and left (east) toward the lower edge of the boulder field that leads up to Iron Nipple's west ridge. Stay below and to the right (south) of the boulder field to find the trail, which intersects the creek that runs steeply from the east. Stay to the left (north) of the creek and wind up along the steep switchbacks into the upper valley.

As the trail levels off and the upper valley comes into view, look for the second creek crossing that leads over to the right (south) side of the creek. Hike along the twisted pines before the tree line, where the gentle trail crosses the broad upper valley southeast toward the saddle between Iron Nipple on the left and Mount Lindsey's summit, which is now visible above and behind the ridge. Climb up the good trail on the steep slopes and the occasional switchback to the ridge, where the trail thins out in spots. From this ridge, Mount Lindsey's impressive north face is visible and the rest of the route can be seen.

Follow the thin trail southeast along the ridge to the point where the trail begins to traverse the north face and enter the prominent couloir that leads to the summit ridge. This gully gets loose and rocky in places and has claimed the life of a climber in recent years. Take great care not to dislodge rocks when other hikers are below you, and avoid climbing when others are above. The use of a helmet is recommended. From the top of the couloir, it is a gradual traverse south to the true summit.

Options: From the point where the trail starts crossing Mount Lindsey's north face, continue directly up the ridge to the summit. This is a hand-and-foot scramble that avoids the loose rock chute and can be very enjoyable if your comfort level and skill level allow. This option can become much more difficult when conditions or weather are not ideal.

Snow season: With difficult access, this becomes a virtual expedition with a low camp near either of the lower meadows just past the trailhead. Snow conditions need to be safe to cross the north face, or you can climb the more difficult but avalanche-free west ridge. When ice and snow conditions are less than ideal, this becomes a highly technical climb.

58

Lake Como

Highlights: *A difficult hike with the option to attempt Little Bear Peak, Ellingwood Point, and Blanca Peak.*

Type of hike: Out-and-back overnight backpack.
Total distance: 8.4 from the forest boundary.
Difficulty: Strenuous.

Best months: May to September.
Maps: USGS Blanca Peak and Twin Peaks quads.

Special considerations: This is one of the most difficult four-wheel-drive roads in Colorado. Only experienced drivers with appropriately equipped vehicles should attempt to drive the entire road to Lake Como. It is recommended that you park early and hike a little farther to save your vehicle excessive wear and tear.

Finding the trailhead: From the intersection of U.S. Highway 160 and Colorado Highway 150, 15 miles east of Alamosa, drive north on CO 150 for 3.2 miles to Forest Road 975 (Holbrook Gulch). This road can be difficult to spot and may not have a readable sign at the intersection. Turn off to the right (east) on the small dirt road and continue on a diagonal northeast toward Blanca Peak.

The first 2.0 miles of FR 975 are sandy but usually passable by most cars. Afterward, the road begins to rise above the valley floor. The road gets rougher, with sections of loose rock before reaching the national forest boundary at 3.2 miles. Park off to the side of the road at the point where you judge your vehicle has gone far enough and start hiking up the road. High-clearance four-wheel-drive vehicles can continue up to the forest boundary, where a small parking area is provided. Expert drivers with serious machines may attempt to drive the entire road up to the lake. The hike description starts at the lower parking area where the road enters the national forest.

Key points:

0.0 Forest boundary.
1.5 Ridge.
2.8 Creek crossing.
4.2 Lake Como.

The hike: From the lower parking area, hike up the rocky road through juniper and pinion pine, then switchback up to the top of the ridge above and to the left (west) of Chokecherry Canyon. Hike north over the ridge, through the trees and down into the narrow Holbrook Creek valley. Gently descend along the right

218

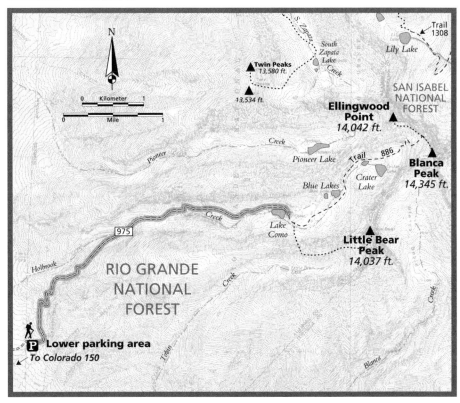

(south) side of the creek before crossing to its north side. Continue east along the road as it climbs above the creek and past several difficult four-wheel-drive steps that are stained by oil pan sacrifices and littered with the rusty remains of failed attempts to drive the road. Continue up the north side of the valley to the last turn-around at the road closure at the lake. There are several places to camp around Lake Como, but the best camping may be farther up the trail in the open meadows around Blue Lakes.

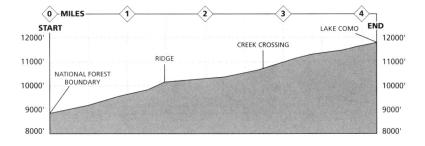

Falls above Blue Lakes.

Options: From Lake Como, continue east up the valley and climb Ellingwood Point and Blanca Peak (Hike 59), or the much harder Little Bear Peak (Hike 60). You can also follow the trail up into the upper valley to Blue Lakes and grand views of the peaks beyond.

Snow season: This can be a good snow-season hike to avoid the summer crowds and the temptation to damage your vehicle. It is more difficult to drive up the road to the ridge, but it might not hold enough snow to justify the use of skis or snowshoes. The valley near the lake, and the upper basin beyond, are good snowshoe destinations as long day hikes or two- to three-day backpack trips.

59 Blanca Peak and Ellingwood Point

Highlights: *A popular hike from camp near Lake Como (Hike 58) to two of Colorado's 14,000-foot peaks.*

Type of hike: Out-and-back day hike from Lake Como.
Total distance: 8.0 miles.
Difficulty: Strenuous.

Best months: June to September.
Maps: USGS Blanca Peak and Twin Peaks quads.

Special considerations: Even though these are considered moderately difficult 14,000-foot mountains, they are still difficult hikes and should not be done without adequate skills. Parts of the upper route are loose and rocky. If you knock a rock loose, warn the hikers below you by calling out "Rock!" until you see it stop.

Finding the trailhead: See Lake Como (Hike 58) for access to the Holbrook Gulch road and the hike to Lake Como.

Key points:
- **0.0** Lake Como.
- **1.0** Blue Lakes.
- **2.0** Crater Lake.
- **3.0** Ridge.
- **3.2** Blanca Peak.
- **3.4** Ridge.
- **4.0** Ellingwood Point.

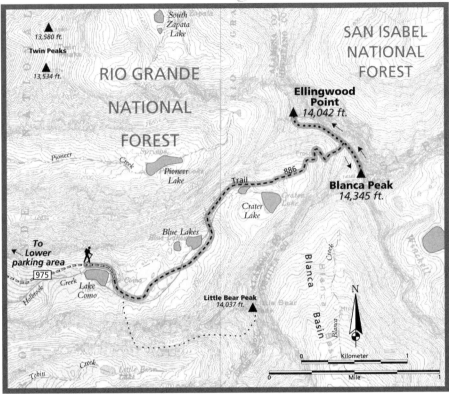

The hike: To reach these summits as a day hike, the usual method is to begin from a high camp near Lake Como or Blue Lakes. Starting below Lake Como makes this a two- to three-day backpack trip or an extremely long day hike. From Lake Como (Hike 58), hike around the left (north) side and follow the road until it crosses the seasonal inlet creek. At this point, the road is blocked and becomes a trail (886) on the south side of the creek. Hike steeply to the tree line and northeast up into the upper valley, across the creek and past several small lakes and marshes. Here you

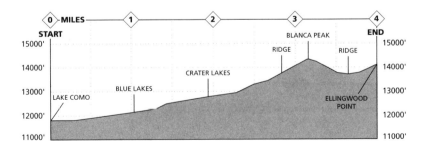

Lake Como from Blanca Peak.

encounter the first open views to the end of the valley, with Ellingwood Point on the left, Blanca Peak and Little Bear Peak on the right, and the spectacular Blanca-Little Bear ridge looming in between.

The trail becomes thinner as it passes to the right (east) of Blue Lakes. Cross to the left (north) side of the creek at the inlet and continue past the lake. Follow the trail as it curves left (west) toward the falls from Crater Lake, then climbs steeply along the left (west) side of the falls and into the upper valley past the lake. From here, find the ever-steepening trail as it winds up to the ledges and benches that lie below the ridge between Ellingwood Point and Blanca Peak. Climb up the easy snowfield above and generally head toward the right of the low point of the ridge. Do not climb straight up the loose rocky slopes that lead directly toward the summit of Blanca Peak; it is strenuous and potentially dangerous to those below you.

Once on the ridge, turn right (south) and climb the solid talus and boulder slope to Blanca Peak. Retrace your route to and continue north, following a ledge trail across the slopes and up toward Ellingwood Point. The route to Ellingwood Point is near and to the left (west) side of the ridge, crossing many rock ribs. It could be difficult to find, but it is easy to follow once located. You may have to start up the steep talus slope before finding a thin trail, marked by infrequent cairns, up to the summit.

Options: If you attempt this route during the summer, take care to watch for afternoon thunderstorms. From the summit of Blanca Peak, you can view the technical climb of the ridge that traverses west to Little Bear Peak (Hike 60). This is usually done by coming from Little Bear Peak to arrive at and descend via Blanca Peak.

Snow season: These are reasonable routes during snow season and are actually quite enjoyable during spring snow before the summer crowds file in. The slopes leading up to the Ellingwood Point–Blanca Peak ridge need to be stable, and the south face of Ellingwood Point should be climbed only during the best of avalanche conditions.

Little Bear Peak

Highlights: *A semitechnical climb of one of Colorado's most difficult 14,000-foot peaks, with the option of climbing the connecting ridge to Blanca Peak (Hike 59).*

Type of hike: Out-and-back day hike from Lake Como.
Total distance: 4.0 miles.
Difficulty: Moderate but semitechnical.

Best months: June to September.
Maps: USGS Blanca Peak and Twin Peaks quads.

Special considerations: This is not merely a hike. In the best conditions, it is a challenging hand-and-foot scramble with loose rock, running water, and possibly technical terrain. Wear a helmet and consider carrying equipment to rappel back down from the summit. Even though this is commonly done as a nontechnical scramble, do not attempt this route without previous climbing experience. Go with an experienced friend or hire a professional guide.

Finding the trailhead: See the description for Lake Como (Hike 58) for access to the trail and the initial approach.

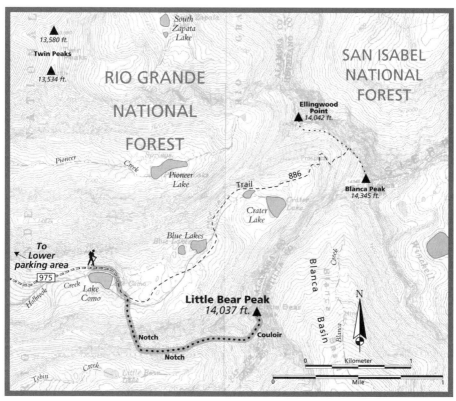

Key points:

- **0.0** Lake Como.
- **0.2** Turn right off trail.
- **0.5** Boulder field.
- **0.8** Ridge.
- **1.1** Second notch.
- **2.0** Little Bear Peak.

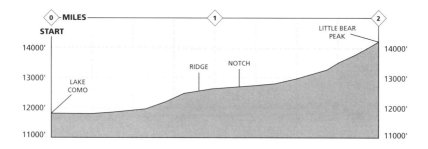

Little Bear Peak from Ellingwood Point.

The hike: Hike around the left (north) side of Lake Como and follow the road as it crosses to the south side of the seasonal inlet creek. At this point, the road is blocked and becomes a trail (886) on the south side of the creek. After 0.2 mile and still below the tree line, turn right off the trail and scramble to the base of a large boulder field leading to Little Bear's west ridge on the right (south). Cross the lower section of this boulder field and begin climbing up the stable talus slope toward the notch in the ridge above. Continue east near the top of the ridge, then drop to its right (south) side where you may find a cairned route before another steep and prominent notch from which you can see the rest of the route.

Descend east of the ridge for about 100 feet. Head east across the southwest face of Little Bear Peak and up toward the bottom of the prominent hourglass-shaped couloir that leads just to the right of the summit. This couloir is an obvious funnel-shaped rock chute commonly rated as a fourth-class climb. It often contains loose rock, ice, and running water, and can be dangerous when there are other climbers above you. Take great care to avoid loosening any rocks; if you do, call "Rock!" until you see it stop. Climb up as the gully narrows then widens again, becoming easier on its left side before reaching the summit ridge.

Options: From the summit of Little Bear, experienced climbers can traverse the jagged northeast ridge to the summit of Blanca Peak. This requires a rappel from the summit of Little Bear, north down to the ridge where the climb is generally a moderate scramble with only an occasional fourth- or fifth-class climbing move. Avoid the most difficult sections by staying to the right (southeast) of the ridge. From Blanca Peak, descend to the northwest as described in Hike 59. Although not difficult, this is a technical climb that requires appropriate skills and ideal weather conditions.

Snow season: From a camp near Lake Como, this hike can be a reasonable but challenging route requiring technical climbing skills and comfort on steep snow. The danger of rockfall can be avoided when stable snow fills the hourglass couloir that leads to the summit.

61

South Zapata Creek

Highlights: *A scenic trail up to high lakes above the tree line, with access to Twin Peaks.*

Type of hike: Two- to three-day out-and-back backpack.
Total distance: 9.0 miles.

Difficulty: Strenuous.
Best months: May to September.
Maps: USGS Twin Peaks quads.

Finding the trailhead: From Alamosa, drive east for 15 miles on U.S. Highway 160 to Colorado Highway 150. Alternatively, from La Veta Pass, drive west for 28 miles on US 160 and turn north onto CO 150.

Drive north on CO 150 for 10.6 miles and turn right (east) at the dirt road signed for Zapata Falls. Follow the dirt road east for about 4 miles as it winds up to a small parking area at the end of the road.

Parking and trailhead facilities: There are rest rooms and a picnic ground near the end of the road, but no camping is allowed.

Key points:

0.0 Zapata Falls Trailhead.
0.5 Zapata Falls; turn right.
0.8 Creek crossing.
2.2 California Gulch.
2.5 North Fork.
3.5 Creek crossing.
4.5 South Zapata Lake.

The hike: Hike the Zapata Falls Trail starting right (south) of the rest rooms and continuing east along a good trail with periodic views of the Great Sand Dunes and several benches along the way. After a gentle 0.5 mile you reach Zapata Falls, which can only be viewed by wading the creek into the secluded pocket that actually contains the falls. This trail is easy, however, and it's a good destination for families and picnics.

Continuing up the valley to South Zapata Lake, is a longer and more ambitious hike. Trail 852 forks right (south) from the Zapata Falls Trail just before it reaches the creek traveling south then southeast by switchbacking up a broad ridge before continuing left (north) to the South Zapata Creek and across to its north side. The trail ascends high above the creek, with views to the peaks that surround the

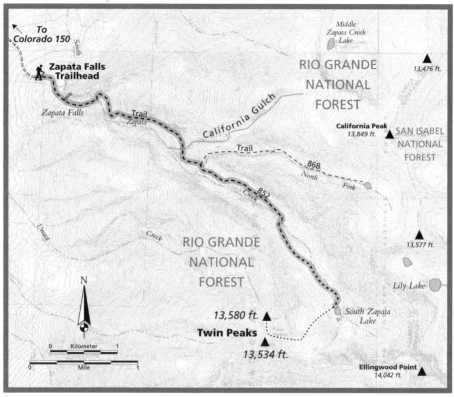

upper valley. Cross the creeks from California Gulch and the North Fork, and pass the thin trail leading up the North Fork to the left. Continue east on the main trail that tracks farther up the South Zapata Creek valley as it curves to the right (southeast). Cross over to the right (south) side of the creek and hike steeply to the tree line. The trail ends here, but the route continues over a gentle grassy meadow to the lakes. There is good camping near the lakes and beyond them in the upper basin.

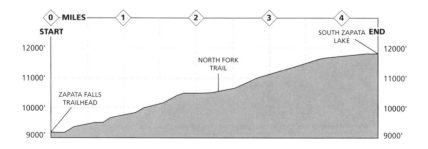

Zapata Falls.

Options: Follow the very thin and difficult Trail 868 up the North Fork from where it intersects the South Zapata Creek Trail. The trail runs north through heavy timber, then east above the tree line to a small unnamed lake below the crest of the range and a limited number of campsites.

To climb the summits of Twin Peaks from South Zapata Lake, hike around to the right (west) side of the lake outlet and climb west then southwest up grassy slopes to a prominent ridge above the lake and a small upper basin. Climb west up steeper slopes to the low point between the two summits. The northern point is the higher peak.

Snow season: This can be a good snow-season hike, although portions of the trail will be free of snow cover throughout the year.

Spanish Peaks
WILDERNESS AREA

Used as major landmarks by the Indians, and later by Spanish and European emigrants moving west on the Santa Fe Trail, the Wahatoya (Indian for "two breasts" or "breasts of the world") are still an unmistakably important and impressive part of the landscape. Known today as the Spanish Peaks, these paired mountains dominate the surrounding valley and its unique intrusive rock formations, the Great Dikes of the Spanish Peaks. These radial dike formations are an important and world-renowned geologic formation that occurs nowhere else on the planet in the quantity and pattern found here.

Walsenburg, just west of Interstate 25, is the nearest major town. Drive west on U.S. Highway 160 to Colorado Highway 12, then south to La Veta, a small but character-rich town of about 800 people. Established in 1876, this small town offers several motels, inns, and bed-and-breakfasts. Continuing south on CO 12, the Scenic Highway of Legends, leads to the small resort town of Cuchara. The local ski area has struggled at times to stay afloat, so call to check on the current status before showing up with your skis. During the summer months, there are opportunities to bike, fish, sightsee, camp, and hike the trails on the west side of the valley not described here. In winter, even without the local runs, there is cross-country skiing on the local trails in addition to the routes to the high peaks in this chapter.

Spanish Peaks

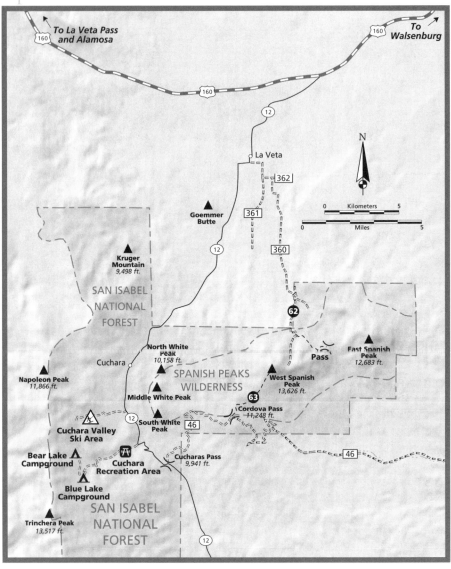

62 Wahatoya Trail

Highlights: *A scenic trail to a high pass with access to East Spanish and West Spanish Peaks.*

Type of hike: Out-and-back day hike or overnight backpack.
Total distance: 8.0 miles.

Difficulty: Moderate.
Best months: May to October.
Maps: USGS Spanish Peaks quads.

Finding the trailhead: From Walsenburg, drive west 11 miles on U.S. Highway 160 to Colorado Highway 12. From Alamosa, drive east on US 160 for 56 miles to CO 12.

Turn south on CO 12 and drive 5 miles to the town of La Veta. From the south end of town, at the T intersection where CO 12 turns sharply to the right, turn left (east) onto a dirt road signed as Grand Avenue. This dirt road (Country Road 361) winds up toward the Spanish Peaks until just past a small reservoir on the right, where it becomes CR 362 and CR 360. The road continues south for 5 miles to the top of a gentle climb just before dropping sharply down to the creek and the private cabins of Wahatoya Camp. The Wahatoya Trail (1304) leads south from the road at the crest of the ridge near the area marked as Lover's Leap on most maps.

Parking and trailhead facilities: Park off to the side of the road. There is no camping near the trailhead, nor is camping allowed farther up the road toward Wahatoya Camp.

Key points:
- **0.0** Wahatoya Trailhead.
- **2.0** Bulls Eye Mine Road.
- **2.8** Slide path.
- **4.0** Pass.

The hike: Hike south along an old closed road (Forest Road 442) as it climbs steadily for 1.8 miles, then turns sharply to the left (southeast) across a north-facing slope. Follow the trail another 0.2 mile to the road leading to the Bulls Eye Mine. From this intersection, continue southeast, climbing gently along the single-track trail (1304) as it crosses several small creeks and a prominent avalanche path before it reaches the pass between the two peaks. There is good camping along the trail and near the pass.

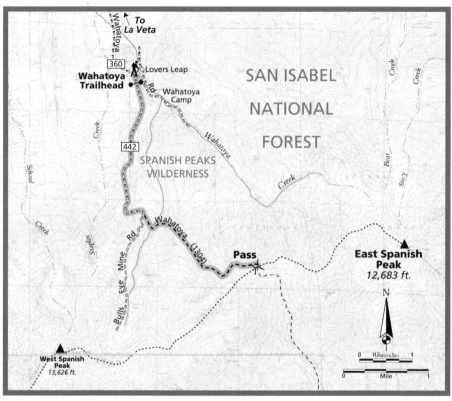

Options: From the pass, climb east for 2.0 miles along the ridge to the summit of East Spanish Peak. This is the lower of the two Spanish Peaks and is climbed less often than its western companion. From the pass, hike 3.0 miles west along the ridge to reach the summit of West Spanish Peak. Both of these routes are moderate but steep and sometimes cross loose rock.

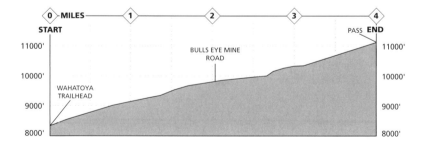

Great Dikes of the Spanish Peaks.

Snow season: Access to the trailhead is usually reliable for passenger cars, except after heavy storms when road maintenance fails to clear the road for the last mile or two. The fairly easy hike could require snowshoes beyond the first mile or two. Crossing the slide path on the north face of West Spanish Peak should only be attempted when conditions are absolutely ideal.

63

West Spanish Peak

Highlights: *An easy hike and scramble to a beautiful summit.*

Type of hike: Out-and-back day hike or overnight backpack.
Total distance: 6.4 miles.
Difficulty: Moderate.

Best months: March to December.
Maps: USGS Spanish Peaks, Cucharas Pass, and Herlick Canyon quads.

Finding the trailhead: From Walsenburg, drive 11 miles west on U.S. Highway 160 to Colorado Highway 12. From Alamosa, drive 56 miles east on US 160 to CO 12 and turn right (south).

Drive south on CO 12 for 5 miles to the town of La Veta. Continue south on CO 12 as it winds through town then up the valley along the Cucharas River and past several of the Spanish Peak's Great Dikes. The most notable of these dikes is the Devil's Stairsteps, with views all the way along it up to the summit of West Spanish Peak. Drive through the small town of Cuchara and past the ski area up to Cucharas Pass. At the top of the pass, turn left (east) on the dirt road and drive 6 miles to Cordova Pass (shown as Apishapa Pass on older maps).

Parking and trailhead facilities: Roadside parking and rest rooms are provided at Cordova Pass.

Key points:

- **0.0** Cordova Pass.
- **1.2** Ridge.
- **1.6** Apishapa Trail (1324); continue straight.
- **2.2** Tree line.
- **3.2** West Spanish Peak.

The hike: At Cordova Pass, turn left (north) onto Trail 1324 as it starts off through forest then open meadows along a gentle ridge. Just before the trail begins to climb, it joins the ridge and offers distant views north over the Cucharas River valley. As the trail begins to steepen it meets the Apishapa Trail, which descends to the right. Follow the switchbacks and hike up through the thinning trees and past some impressive bristlecone pines just below the tree line and the first open views of West Spanish Peak above. Continue just to the right (south) of the ridge and fol-

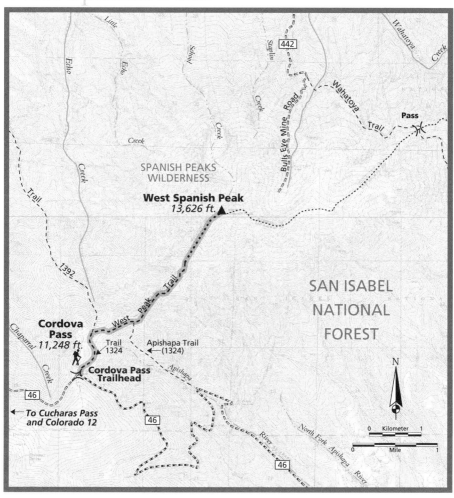

West Spanish Peak
13,626 ft.

SPANISH PEAKS
WILDERNESS

Pass

SAN ISABEL
NATIONAL
FOREST

Cordova
Pass
11,248 ft.

Trail
1324

Apishapa Trail
(1324)

Cordova Pass
Trailhead

← To Cucharas Pass
and Colorado 12

46

46

46

N

Kilometer

Mile

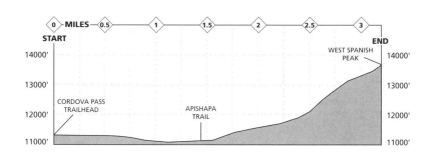

MILES

0   0.5   1   1.5   2   2.5   3

START

END

WEST SPANISH
PEAK

14000'

13000'

12000'

11000'

CORDOVA PASS
TRAILHEAD

APISHAPA
TRAIL

Bristlecone pine on West Spanish Peak.

low a rough and sometimes loose trail to the summit. The trail can be hard to follow, but generally stays to the right (south) of the prominent ridge before it traverses to the right (east) across the upper slopes just below the false summit. From the false summit, hike the last rocky ridge to the top and enjoy the views of the Cucharas River valley, East Spanish Peak, and the spokelike volcanic dikes that radiate from the summits of both peaks. Limited camping sites are available along the ridge before the Apishapa Trail, though water is sparse. By descending the Apishapa Trail about 2.0 miles, you can find additional sites and more water will be available. Very rocky and limited camping can be found on the West Spanish Peak Trail beyond the Apishapa Trail just below the tree line.

Options: Descend east from the summit along the ridge to the pass between East and West Spanish Peaks. From the pass, you can climb up to the summit of East Spanish Peak or, with a car shuttle, descend north on the Wahatoya Trail (Hike 62). This car shuttle option is 10.0 miles and is an extremely long day hike or a very difficult backpacking trip when carrying a full pack over the summit of West Spanish Peak.

Snow season: The Cordova Pass road may be maintained well into November or even December. After that, a light snow year might allow four-wheel-drive access to within a mile or so of the pass. Even with lower access, this remains a good but challenging climb in winter. Some avalanche danger can exist on the upper part of the route; staying near the ridge helps to avoid most of it.

Appendix A

Contacts

Land and resource
management agencies

Colorado Division of Wildlife
wildlife.state.co.us
Denver Headquarters and Central Region Office
6060 Broadway
Denver, CO 80216
(303) 297–1192
For fishing and hunting information, rules and regulations.

Southeast Regional Office
2126 North Weber Street
Colorado Springs, CO 80907
(719) 473–2945

Great Sand Dunes National Monument and Preserve
11999 Highway 150
Mosca, CO 81146–9798
(719) 378–2312
www.nps.gov.grsa

Rio Grande National Forest
Forest Supervisor, Main Office
(719) 852–5941

Conejos Peak Ranger District
15571 County Road T-5
La Jara, CO 81140
(719) 274–8971
Jurisdiction includes the west side of the southern range from Medano Pass
south to the Sierra Blanca.

Saguache Ranger District
46525 State Highway 114
Saguache, CO 81149
(719) 655–2553
Jurisdiction over the central range, west side, from Poncha Pass to Medano Pass.

San Isabel National Forest
Forest Supervisor, Main Office
1920 Valley Drive
Pueblo, CO 81008
(719) 545–8737
Pike and San Isabel National Forests
Comanche and Cimmeron National Grasslands

Salida Ranger District
U.S. Forest Service
325 West Rainbow Boulevard
Salida, CO 81210
(719) 539–3591
Jurisdiction includes the east side of the Northern Sangre de Cristo south to
the Cloverdale Basin.

San Carlos Ranger District
U.S. Forest Service
3170 East Main
Canon City, CO 81212
(719) 269–8500
Jurisdiction of the central range, east side, from the Cloverdale Basin south to
the Huerfano Valley and the Spanish Peaks.

Law enforcement agencies
(includes search and rescue)

Custer County Sheriff
(719) 783–2270

Fremont County Sheriff
(719) 276–5555

Huerfano County Sheriff
(719) 738–1600

Saguache County Sheriff
(719) 655–2544

Avalanche forecasting hotlines

Statewide:
Denver/Boulder, (303) 275–5360
Fort Collins, (970) 482–0457
Colorado Springs, (719) 520–0020

Local:
Summit County, (970) 668–0600
Durango/Southern Mountains, (970) 247–8187
Aspen, (970) 920–1664
Vail, (970) 479–4652

Internet resources

General weather forecasts
www.weather.com
www.crh.noaa.gov/pub/zone.htm

Avalanche warnings and mountain weather
geosurvey.state.co.us/avalanche
www.firstrax.com/index.htm

Colorado Department of Transportation road conditions and weather
www.cotrip.org

Topographic Maps
Free on-line maps:
maptech.com
www.topozone.com
terraserver.homeadvisor.msn.com
Maps for purchase on CD-ROM:
maps.nationalgeographic.com/topo
www.mapsoftware.com/toposcout/toposcout.html
Hard copy maps for purchase:
www.bouldermapgallery.com

General Area Information
peaksnewsnet.com
saguachecounty.org
sangre-de-cristo.com
www.alamosa.org
www.campcolorado.com
www.coloradoadventure.net

www.coloradocampgrounds.com
www.coloradodirectory.com
www.coloradovacation.com
www.miningcamps.com
www.sangres.com

Other organizations

Colorado Division of Wildlife, wildlife.state.co.us

Colorado Mountain Club, www.cmc.org

Mission Wolf, www.missionwolf.com

The Fourteener Initiative, www.coloradofourteeners.org

The Nature Conservancy, nature.org

The Wilderness Society, www.wilderness.org

Appendix B

Further Reading

Avalanche evaluation

Atkins, Dale, and Knox Williams. *Avalanche Wise: Your Guide to Avalanche Safety in Colorado*. Denver: Colorado Geological Survey, 1999.

Fredston, Jill, Doug Fesler and Douglas S. Fesler. *Snow Sense: A Guide to Evaluating Snow Avalanche Hazard*. Alaska Mountain Safety Center, 2001.

Moynier, John. Avalanche Aware, *Safe Travel in Avalanche Country*. Guilford, Conn.: The Globe Pequot Press, 1998.

Tilton, Buck. *Basic Essentials of Avalanche Safety*. Guilford, Conn.: The Globe Pequot Press, 1993.

Backpacking and wilderness travel skills

Gilbert, Preston. *Wilderness First Aid*. Guilford, Conn.: The Globe Pequot Press, 1997

Gorman, Stephen. *Winter Camping*. 2nd ed. Boston: Appalachian Mountain Club, 1999.

Harmon, Will. *Leave No Trace, Minimum Impact Outdoor Recreation*. Guilford, Conn.: The Globe Pequot Press, 1997.

Harmon, Will. *Wild Country Companion*. Guilford, Conn.: The Globe Pequot Press, 1994.

Karr, Paul. *Compass and Map Navigator*. 2nd ed. Guilford, Conn.: The Globe Pequot Press, 2000.

Logue, Victoria Steele. *Backpacking: Essential Skills to Advanced Techniques*. Birmingham, Ala.: Menasha Ridge Press, 2000.

Roberts, Harry. *Basic Essentials Backpacking*. 2nd ed. Guilford, Conn.: The Globe Pequot Press, 1999.

Schneider, Bill. *Bear Aware: Hiking and Camping in Bear Country.* Guilford, Conn.: The Globe Pequot Press, 1996.

Tawrell, Paul. *Camping and Wilderness Survival, The Ultimate Outdoors Book.* Paul Tawrell, 1996.

Car and RV camping

Crow, Melinda. *Camping Colorado.* 2nd ed. Guilford, Conn.: The Globe Pequot Press, 2001.

Woodall Press. *2001 Western America Campground Directory.* Woodall Publications Corporation, 2001.

Woodall Press. *2001 Frontier West/Great Plains and Mountain Region Campground Guide.* Woodall Publications Corporation, 2001.

History, ecology, and geology

Cushman, Carol Ruth, and Stephan R. Jones. *Colorado Nature Almanac.* Boulder, Colo.: Pruett Publishing Company, 1998.

Kavanaugh, James and Raymond Leung (illustrator). *Colorado Trees & Wildflowers: An Introduction to Familiar Species.* Whitefish Mont.: Waterford Press, 2000.

———*Rocky Mountain Wildlife: An Introduction to Familiar Species.* Whitefish, Mont.: Waterford Press, 2001.

Waterford Press. *Colorado Birds: An Introduction to Familiar Species.* Whitefish, Mont.: Waterford Press, 2001.

Wolf, Tom. *Colorado's Sangre de Cristo Mountains.* Bouder, Colo.: University Press of Colorado, 1995.

Mountain weather

Hodgson, Michael. *Basic Essentials Weather Forecasting.* 2nd ed. Guilford, Conn.: The Globe Pequot Press, 1999.

Rock climbing in the area

D'Antonio, Bob. *Rock Climbing the San Luis Valley.* Guilford, Conn.: The Globe Pequot Press, 1999.

Horn, Mark Van. *Rock Climbing Shelf Road.* Guilford, Conn.: The Globe Pequot Press, 1998.

Appendix C

Hiker Checklist

The following is a typical checklist that I use on a regular basis. I always add items as I feel necessary. In fact, I have a packed duffel bag with almost all of my hiking gear in it. I bring it all with me to the trailhead and decide on the spot what I need to bring based on the weather, start time, and the day's hike or backpacking goals. If I am hiking with friends, I find I often save the day with an extra pair of socks or a hat when someone forgets something. All of my clothing is polypropylene, polyester, acrylic and wool blends, nylon, and Gore-Tex. I never wear cotton, not even underwear. See Being Prepared: Backcountry Safety and Hazards in the Introduction for more information on clothing.

The ten essentials:

❑ Map
❑ Compass
❑ Extra water
❑ Extra food
❑ Sunscreen (SPF 30, minimum) and sunglasses
❑ Knife (multifunction)
❑ Fire kit (waterproof matches and fire starter)
❑ Emergency space blanket
❑ Mirror and whistle
❑ First-aid kit

Day hikes (add the following):

❑ Backpack
❑ Boots
❑ Socks
❑ Shorts
❑ Long underwear or tights
❑ Light short-sleeved shirt
❑ Medium-weight long-sleeved shirt
❑ Fleece jacket
❑ Extra long-sleeved shirt or fleece vest
❑ Water- and windproof shell
❑ Windproof pants
❑ Extra socks
❑ Hat and gloves (lightweight in summer)

- ❑ Trekking poles
- ❑ Toilet kit (toilet paper, trowel, sanitary wipes)
- ❑ Trash bag (resealable is best)
- ❑ Camera, extra film, minitripod

Optional:
- ❑ Water filter or iodine tablets
- ❑ Altimeter watch
- ❑ GPS

Overnight backpack (add the following):

- ❑ Tent (ground cloth, stakes, fly)
- ❑ Sleeping bag and pillow
- ❑ Sleeping pad
- ❑ Extra food
- ❑ Stove kit (pot, stove, fuel, spoon, lighter)
- ❑ Drinks (sport mix, tea, apple cider, sugar)
- ❑ Trash bag and airtight bear bag
- ❑ Biodegradable soap and/or antibacterial gel
- ❑ 50-foot nylon cord to hang food and trash in bear bag
- ❑ Water filter and iodine backup
- ❑ Water bladder and collapsible canteen
- ❑ Headlamp and extra batteries
- ❑ Warm hat
- ❑ Warm gloves
- ❑ Extra socks
- ❑ Toothbrush and tooth powder
- ❑ Lip balm (SPF 30)
- ❑ Bug repellent

Optional:
- ❑ Camp shoes
- ❑ Book
- ❑ Playing cards
- ❑ Watch
- ❑ Star chart
- ❑ Hand towel

Multiday backpack (add the following):

- ❑ More food
- ❑ Extra socks
- ❑ Book or magazine
- ❑ Tent and backpack patch, sewing, and general fix kit

Appendix D

Summit List with GPS Coordinates

Sixty summits are included in the following list of peaks. They can all be climbed using the routes described in this guidebook. The hike number listed in the table corresponds to the hike chapter describing the approach to the peak and the subsequent optional route to climb it. The elevations noted are those found on USGS 7.5-minute quads. You might find some maps that show variations of the names listed below, and some maps that show unofficial names not recognized by the United States Board of Geographic Names. These labels have not been included.

In general, the GPS coordinates that are listed are accurate to within 2 or 3 seconds, about 100 feet, and well within the accuracy range for a consumer GPS unit. Be cautious when using a GPS or an altimeter while traveling in the mountains. The ability to navigate by using a map and compass should always be your primary tool when hiking. The accuracy and reliability of any electronic device should be questioned when venturing into the wildland of rain, snow, ice, mud, and rock. Altimeters, electronic and mechanical, can also give deceiving elevation readings. The barometric pressure changes in the mountains, due to storms and temperature variations, can be dramatic and can alter readings by hundreds of feet over the course of a day.

Summit Name	Elevation (ft)	Hike Number	Latitude	Longitude
Blanca Peak	14,345	59	37° 34' 38" N	105° 29' 07" W
Blizzardine Peak	12,005	3	37° 54' 10" N	105° 28' 42" W
Blueberry Peak	11,910	3	37° 54' 00" N	105° 28' 24" W
Broken Hand Peak	13,573	30, 49	37° 57' 24" N	105° 34' 00" W
Bushnell Peak	13,105	4, 5	38° 20' 28" N	105° 53' 20" W
California Peak	13,849	55	37° 36' 50" N	105° 29' 54" W
Carbonate Mountain	12,308	52	37° 41' 36" N	105° 28' 52" W
Challenger Point	14,080	48	37° 58' 49" N	105° 36' 24" W
Cleveland Peak	13,414	35	37° 54' 16" N	105° 32' 36" W
Colony Baldy	13,705	25	37° 59' 42" N	105° 33' 36" W
Comanche Peak	13,277	19, 20, 45	38° 02' 34" N	105° 36' 52" W
Cottonwood Peak	13,588	10, 38, 39	38° 13' 08" N	105° 45' 22" W
Crestone Needle	14,197	30, 49	37° 57' 52" N	105° 34' 36" W
Crestone Peak	14,294	31, 49	37° 58' 00" N	105° 35' 08" W
De Anza Peak	13,362	12, 13, 14, 41	38° 10' 00" N	105° 41' 12" W
Eagle Peak	13,205	10	38° 13' 46" N	105° 43' 20" W

Summit Name	Elevation (ft)	Hike Number	Latitude	Longitude
East Spanish Peak	12,683	62	37° 23' 36" N	104° 55' 11" W
Electric Peak	13,598	11, 12, 40, 41	38° 10' 54" N	105° 42' 30" W
Ellingwood Peak	14,042	59, 61	37° 34' 56" N	105° 29' 32" W
Eureka Mountain	13,507	16, 18, 19, 45	38° 04' 44" N	105° 38' 28" W
Fluted Peak	13,554	22, 23, 24, 45	38° 01' 26" N	105° 36' 04" W
Galena Peak	12,461	6	38° 18' 32" N	105° 52' 08" W
Gibbs Peak	13,553	12, 13, 14	38° 09' 48" N	105° 39' 58" W
Hermit Peak	13,350	16, 43	38° 05' 28" N	105° 39' 18" W
Horn Peak	13,450	22, 23	38° 02' 18" N	105° 35' 10" W
Humboldt Peak	14,064	28	37° 58' 34" N	105° 33' 18" W
Hunts Peak	13,071	2, 3	38° 22' 58" N	105° 56' 44" W
Iron Nipple	13,480	57	37° 35' 38" N	105° 27' 18" W
Kit Carson Mountain	14,165	29, 48	37° 58' 46" N	105° 36' 10" W
Lakes Peak	13,375	10, 11, 39,40	38° 11' 58" N	105° 43' 38" W
Little Baldy Mountain	12,982	24, 25	38° 00' 10" N	105° 35' 06" W
Little Bear Peak	14,037	60	37° 33' 58" N	105° 29' 50" W
Little Horn Peak	13,143	23, 24	38° 01' 30" N	105° 35' 02" W
Marble Mountain	13,266	32, 34	37° 57' 16" N	105° 31' 58" W
Milwaukee Peak	13,522	34, 49	37° 56' 52" N	105° 33' 04" W
Mount Adams	13,931	24, 45, 46, 47	38° 00' 26" N	105° 36' 16" W
Mount Lindsey	14,042	57	37° 35' 00" N	105° 26' 40" W
Mount Marcy	13,490	12, 13, 14, 41	38° 08' 46" N	105° 40' 36" W
Mount Niedhardt	12,844	11, 12, 40, 41	38° 10' 36" N	105° 43' 12" W
Mount Otto	12,865	5, 6	38° 19' 38" N	105° 52' 54" W
Mount Owen	13,340	42	38° 08' 20" N	105° 42' 48" W
Mount Seven	13,297	36	37° 50' 48" N	105° 29' 30" W
Mount Zwieschen	12,006	36, 52	37° 47' 28" N	105° 27' 19" W
Music Mountain	13,355	34	37° 56' 12" N	105° 32' 54" W
Nipple Mountain	12,199	7, 8, 9	38° 16' 00" N	105° 47' 48" W
Pico Asilado	13,611	34, 49	37° 56' 38" N	105° 33' 32" W
Red Mountain	12,994	2, 3, 4	38° 22' 04" N	105° 55' 12" W
Rito Alto Peak	13,794	15, 16, 43	38° 06' 10" N	105° 39' 40" W
Simmons Peak	12,050	2	38° 25' 14" N	105° 59' 02" W
Snowslide Mountain	11,664	3	37° 54' 54" N	105° 29' 28" W
Spread Eagle Peak	13,423	14, 15	38° 07' 30" N	105° 38' 36" W
Thirsty Peak	13,213	10, 11, 38, 39, 40	38° 12' 32" N	105° 44' 10" W
Tijeras Peak	13,604	34	37° 55' 28" N	105° 32' 24" W
Twin Peaks	13,580	61	37° 35' 22" N	105° 31' 08" W
Twin Sisters	13,012	2, 3, 4	38° 21' 06" N	105° 54' 04" W
Unnamed 12,401	12,401	2	38° 24' 36" N	105° 58' 12" W
Unnamed 13,524	13,524	14, 15	38° 07' 02" N	105° 39' 28" W
Unnamed 13,828	13,828	57	37° 30' 00" N	105° 26' 52" W
Venable Peak	13,334	19, 20, 45	38° 03' 18" N	105° 37' 46" W
West Spanish Peak	13,626	63	37° 22' 30" N	104° 59' 30" W

Trailhead List with GPS Coordinates

The following trailhead list gives approximate elevations and GPS coordinates for the trailheads listed in the text. Elevations have been obtained from USGS 7.5-minute quads by reading the nearest contour line, in intervals of either 20 or 40 feet. An attempt has been made to keep the names in this listing consistent with the text of the book and USGS standards. You might find forest service maps, proprietary maps, or trailhead signs that have slightly different designations.

These trailheads are all accessible by regular passenger cars or four-wheel-drive vehicles as described in the "Finding the trailhead" section of the hike chapter. The exception in the following list is that all entries designated as a "Trail" refer to side trails that intersect with the Rainbow Trail on the east side of the Sangre de Cristo. These trails are not points of access reachable by motorized vehicles.

Trailhead	Elevation (ft)	Latitude	Longitude
Balman Reservoir Road at the Rainbow Trail	9,000	38° 15' 50" N	105° 40' 50" W
Bear Creek	8,960	38° 26' 12" N	105° 57' 20" W
Black Canyon	8,920	38° 12' 40" N	105° 49' 22" W
Bushnell Lakes Trail	9,400	38° 21' 00" N	105° 51' 08" W
California Peak	10,200	37° 38' 18" N	105° 28' 16" W
Cloverdale Basin	11,280	38° 14' 08" N	105° 43' 54" W
Cordova Pass	11,248	37° 20' 54" N	105° 01' 28" W
Cotton Creek	8,600	38° 07' 52" N	105° 47' 16" W
Cottonwood Creek	7,280	38° 19' 00" N	105° 45' 20" W
Cottonwood Creek	8,400	37° 56' 02" N	105° 38' 42" W
Cottonwood Creek Trail	9,400	38° 04' 00" N	105° 33' 20" W
Dorsey Creek	10,120	38° 26' 14" N	106° 01' 42" W
Dry Creek Trail	9,240	38° 03' 10" N	105° 32' 28" W
Duckett Creek	8,740	38° 14' 44" N	105° 40' 06" W
Gibson Creek	9,120	38° 08' 16" N	105° 35' 56" W
Goodwin Creek Trail	9,600	38° 05' 18" N	105° 34' 46" W
Hayden Creek	7,720	38° 19' 46" N	105° 49' 25" W
Hayden Pass	10,700	38° 17' 36" N	105° 50' 00" W
Hermit Pass	13,000	38° 05' 40" N	105° 39' 18" W"
Hermit Road – at the Rainbow Trail heading north	9,640	38° 07' 06" N	105° 35' 57" W
Hermit Road – at the Rainbow Trail heading south	10,000	38° 06' 25" N	105° 36' 06" W
Holbrook Gulch Road, at the national forest boundary	8,800	37° 33' 02" N	105° 33' 38" W
Horn Creek	9,000	38° 03' 12" N	105° 32' 00" W
Horn Creek Trail	9,360	38° 02' 46" N	105° 32' 22" W
Horn Peak Trail	9,400	38° 03' 30" N	105° 32' 56" W
Hot Springs	8,600	38° 10' 46" N	105° 48' 42" W

Trailhead	Elevation (ft)	Latitude	Longitude
Hunts Lake Trail	9,120	38° 24' 20" N	105° 54' 00" W
Kerr Gulch	8,240	38° 22' 42" N	105° 50' 56" W
Lakes of the Clouds Trail	9,320	38° 08' 36" N	105° 36' 00" W
Lily Lake	10,680	37° 37' 16" N	105° 28' 20" W
Macey Creek Trail	10,200	38° 01' 28" N	105° 32' 18" W
Major Creek	8,640	38° 10' 06" N	105° 48' 26" W
Marble Mountain Trail	9,500	37° 57' 44" N	105° 29' 16" W
Medano Creek	8,080	37° 44' 20" N	105° 30' 58" W
Medano Lake	9,640	37° 51' 08" N	105° 26' 16" W
Medano Pass	9,960	37° 51' 22" N	105° 25' 58" W
Methodist Mountain	8,920	38° 28' 36" N	106° 00' 06" W
Mosca Creek	8,240	37° 44' 02" N	105° 30' 30" W
Mosca Pass	9,720	37° 43' 58" N	105° 27' 16" W
Music Pass, Lower	9,280	37° 55' 52" N	105° 27' 26" W
Music Pass, Upper	10,600	37° 55' 32" N	105° 29' 12" W
North Brush Creek	8,660	38° 14' 26" N	105° 39' 24" W
North Colony Creek Trail	9,720	38° 00' 40" N	105° 30' 48" W
North Crestone	8,440	38° 00' 56" N	105° 41' 22" W
North Decker Creek	9,800	38° 24' 00" N	105° 59' 38" W
North Rock Creek	9,680	38° 23' 22" N	105° 59' 18" W
North Taylor at the Rainbow Trail	9,440	38° 07' 26" N	105° 36' 04" W
Point of No Return	8,340	37° 45' 36" N	105° 30' 02" W
Rito Alto	8,340	38° 04' 34" N	105° 45' 46" W
San Isabel	8,240	38° 02' 00" N	105° 43' 02" W
Sand Creek (Great Sand Dunes)	8,460	37° 47' 46" N	105° 30' 16" W
South Brush Creek Trail	9,320	38° 11' 12" N	105° 37' 44" W
South Colony	11,040	37° 57' 48" N	105° 32' 48" W
South Colony at the Rainbow Trail	9,860	37° 58' 48" N	105° 29' 58" W
South Crestone	8,800	37° 59' 20" N	105° 39' 50" W
South Rock Creek	9,640	38° 22' 54" N	105° 59' 00" W
South Zapata	9,280	37° 37' 12" N	105° 33' 20" W
Texas Creek Trail	9,120	38° 09' 56" N	105° 36' 30" W
US 285	8,540	38° 26' 44" N	106° 06' 18" W
Venable Creek Trail	9,400	38° 04' 58" N	105° 34' 14" W
Venable-Comanche	9,080	38° 04' 46" N	105° 34' 00" W
Wahatoya	8,400	37° 25' 18" N	105° 58' 40" W
Wild Cherry	8,520	38° 06' 00" N	105° 46' 12" W

About the Author

Jason Moore grew up in Colorado near the town of Bailey on the Platte River. Being surrounded by mountains, water, rock, and snow had a profound and lasting impact on him. He has since developed his skills as an avid all-season backcountry hiker, climber, and backpacker. In 1990 Jason enrolled in the School of Engineering at Boulder's University of Colorado, and earned a Bachelor of Science degree in civil engineering. Jason continues to live in Boulder and spends as many days in the mountains as possible. As a part of the exploration of the Sangre de Cristo Wilderness, Jason has hiked and climbed all of the trails and summits described in this book, and has logged almost 1,000 miles of travel and 250,000 vertical feet of climbing. Jason has also climbed more than 100 summits over 12,000 feet, including many of Colorado's 14ers, and mountains in Wyoming, Washington, Oregon, and the Canadian Rockies.

Jason Moore at South Crestone Lake.